P9-CPW-942

Yale Publications in Religion, 7

David Horne, editor

Published under the direction of the Divinity School

THE QUAKERS IN

PURITAN ENGLAND

by Hugh Barbour

with a Foreword by Roland H. Bainton

New Haven and London, Yale University Press, 1964

Copyright © 1964 by Yale University.
Designed by John O. C. McCrillis,
set in Baskerville type,
and printed in the United States of America by
Vail-Ballou Press, Inc., Binghamton, N.Y.
All rights reserved. This book may not be
reproduced, in whole or in part, in any form
(except by reviewers for the public press),
without written permission from the publishers.

Library of Congress catalog card number: 63-13957

289.642
B23

TO SIRKKA

who has come to share in
the life of these Friends

22781

232481

Foreword

THE HISTORIAN of a new movement must neither exaggerate nor undervalue the element of newness. In his treatment of early Quakerism, Hugh Barbour has admirably steered the middle course with regard to ideas, attitudes, and social setting. Quakerism had its strength initially in the north of England, where the impoverished tenants had long objected to church tithes exacted by landlords who for the most part pocketed the money for themselves. The Quakers gave a religious sanction to an economic complaint. In the sphere of religion, they shared with the Puritans an intense excitement and a fervent hope for the establishment of a Holy Commonwealth in England. In these respects Quakerism was related to its time. But there were also differences. Quakerism emphasized a personal renewal through the power of the Spirit, which might speak apart from Scripture and prompt men to eccentricities but primarily would work in them a drastic moral transformation. From this would proceed the transformation of society rather than from constitutions and enactments. The refusal to take off the hat in the presence of the mighty and the practice of addressing them as "thee," as if they were inferiors, though meant as a rebuke to pride, served to advance social egalitarianism. (The Quaker peculiarity of using "thee" as a nominative comes from a north country dialect.) Responsiveness and readiness to follow all leadings of the Spirit engendered an acute social sensitivity which issued in opposition to slavery, war, and capital punishment. Changes in the Quaker outlook over the centuries are noted. As the fervent expectation waned of the Lord's coming to erect his kingdom, the Quakers came to think of themselves less as the heralds of a world transformation than as witnesses to a realizable hope. Without withdrawing from society, they have engaged persistently in what their forebears called "the Lamb's War." The concluding section wrestles with questions confronting contemporary Friends. This is an erudite work of history, objective and at the same time profoundly concerned with all of the problems of truth, right, and strategy with which the Society of Friends has been and still is agitated.

Roland H. Bainton

Preface

MODERN WORKS on Quaker history are impressive in number and quality, and the writing of yet another needs justification. The standard Rowntree Series, histories of the main periods of Quakerism by William C. Braithwaite and Rufus M. Jones, were written forty years ago, but the competent modern historians, Geoffrey F. Nuttall, Henry J. Cadbury, and Frederick B. Tolles, recognize their accuracy and are reissuing them with only minor editing.[1] The best recent books on Quakerism are more popular or are limited to individual men and issues, but omit few important facts or events.

Nevertheless, two main needs remain inadequately filled. The extensive study of puritan England during the last fifty years, by scholars from a wealth of social, political, and religious backgrounds, has developed new understanding of the meaning of Puritanism and thus of its relationship to Quakerism.[2] Secondly, since the narration of events and of the physical spread of Quakerism have preoccupied the authors of most older histories, few of them were able to grapple with the actual experiences of early Friends with a balanced theological insight. At the same time, the challenge of interpreting the relationship of the Quaker movement and its ethics to their inward life has too often been approached backwards—that is, from the final results—using modern social or humanitarian perspectives.

The student must make a leap of imagination to enter the historical setting in which Quakers first found themselves, and to appreciate their religious experience and how, consequently, they saw their world. Some of their concepts, such as those of the world and the Spirit, are no longer ours. Yet even the student must face

1. See Short Titles under Braithwaite and Jones.
2. See below, Bibliographical Note, p. 261.

the judgment of the early Quaker preachers themselves: they demanded that their hearers accept or reject the truth and the Light as they experienced it. The reader must finally decide what early Quaker experience means to him, and perhaps pass through several attitudes in his search. Thus the unreflective, earnest seeker, wanting to know God as directly as did early Friends, may make their experience into a model for his own faith. But this is hard for most moderns, to whom the actions and emotionalism of the first Quakers seem strange. The language used by seventeenth-century Friends has also become foreign to our daily use. In reaction, one may notice and study the social and psychological backgrounds that pressed upon pioneer Quakers and shaped their experience. This second approach is that of the alert observer, the historian of religion, avoiding theological assertions. But such a method may imply that God's power definitely was not at work in early Quaker experience. This in itself is a religious assertion. The effort to combine these two outlooks may lead to a third: the attempt to distinguish the purely human or cultural elements in early Quakerism from whatever is universal or divine. This, however, may lead one to identify the universal factors with experiences like one's own. But the experiences of men are not the same; and each man must confront God for himself and realize that God may come to other men in other ways. It is necessary, therefore, to assume that in every experience and situation both the action of God and the influence of cultural or psychological pressures may be involved. This book must risk the charge of incomplete faith in refusing to define the balance of divine and human causes in crucial cases. If the faith and experiences of early Friends can be allowed to speak in their own terms, they may bring real guidance to modern Quakerism as well as to the historian.

Quaker groups today need special caution against seeing early Friends in terms of modern religious experience. Early Quaker customs and Testimonies did not have the same meaning then that they have today, even where outward expression remains the same, for they arose within a different and more radical outlook on the world. Modern liberal Quakers, for example, make liberals of their ancestors. In their personal faith many Friends today are mystical or pantheistic. Though Quaker mysticism, as represented by Rufus Jones or Thomas Kelly, has tremendous power in its own right, early Friends were not basically mystics (with the exception of Isaac Pennington and a few others). The first Quakers passed through an experience more like that of Jonathan Edwards or of a modern penecostal convert than the way of the mystic. Early Friends expected to transform the world totally by a bitter struggle against human self-will and pride, whereas modern Quaker social action, based on respect for "that of God in every man," has a different root. Modern fundamentalist Quakers, on the other hand, are encouraged by finding that the first Friends used a vocabulary as biblical as their own and held meetings not unlike modern revivals. But such evangelical Quakers today seldom show the explosive transformation of individual and social life that early Quaker farmers and housewives demonstrated, or the continual searching and deepening of their inward lives. Truths of doctrine remain, but today the impact of God seems milder. Yet early Quaker experience is not so strange that we cannot partly understand it. Modern Christians of many groups may find in their own experience echoes of the lives of the Quaker pioneers. It is hoped that this book may open the way for deeper discussions between liberal and conservative Quakers, as well as between Friends and non-Friends.

The Quakers wrote about 2,750 tracts and books before 1715, and they collected over a thousand letters and at least as many other documents. During 1652–65, the years with which this book is most concerned, they produced at least 25,000 printed pages, and 3,000 survive in manuscript. Non-Quaker sources are commensurate. The quantity of quotation from such sources will make this book uneven reading. But illustrations help to reinforce some statements, and for others are essential. The original materials provide sharp flashes of narrative or statement showing the spirit of early Quakerism. They are only fragments, but no early Quaker tract, treatise, or journal has much merit as consecutive discourse. Fox's well-known writings have been less used here than works by other Quaker authors. Some of the works quoted, such as Nayler's "Lamb's War" and the journals of Banks and Burnyeat, deserve to be as widely read as those of Barclay, Ellwood, Penn, and Penington.

The framework of the book is topical. After the two opening chapters, which are mainly the history of the rise of puritanism and the Quaker movement, the main aspects of Quaker experience and life are discussed roughly in the order in which an individual Quaker experienced them. The crucial chapter, on the transforming inward experience of the early Friends, thus comes midway in the book.

The groundwork for the study was laid by a doctoral dissertation at Yale University,[3] under the guidance of Roland H. Bainton, whose skillful and human approach to the understanding of Christianity and its pioneers has been my model. Thanks are also due Earlham College, the Eli Lilly Foundation, and the Viittakivi Institute in Finland, who have in various ways made possible additional research and preparation. Hope Nagle, Henry Cadbury, Howard Brinton, Robert Agard, and David Horne in America, and Muriel Hicks, Harold Wilson, Edward Milligan, and, particularly, Geoffrey Nuttall in England have guided, supplemented, and improved many points in this study. Mildred Bultman prepared the index. My own family, especially my wife, has given both help and, most of all, patience. They will recognize the ways in which this book has grown.

Earlham College, Richmond, Indiana   H.B.
September 1963

3. "The Early Quaker Outlook upon 'the World' and Society, 1647–1662."

Contents

List of Illustrations

Short Titles

For discussion of many of these, see Bibliographical Note, pp. 258 ff., and Chapters 5 and 8.

ARBarc.
: A. R. Barclay Collection of early Quaker letters, now at Friends House, London. Excerpts from these letters have been published in *JFHS* from 1930 to date.

Banks
: Banks, John, *A Journal of the Life, Labours, Travels . . . ,* London, 1712.

Barclay, *Apology*
: Barclay, Robert, *An Apology for the True Christian Divinity as . . . Held Forth by the . . . Quakers* [London], 1678.

Bouch
: Bouch, C. M. Lowther, *Prelates and People of the Lake Counties,* Kendal, England, Titus Wilson, 1948.

Braithwaite, *Beginnings*
: Braithwaite, W. C., *The Beginnings of Quakerism,* London, Macmillan, 1912; 2d ed. Cambridge, Cambridge University Press, 1955.

Braithwaite, *Second Period*
: Braithwaite, W. C., *The Second Period of Quakerism,* London, Macmillan, 1919; 2d ed. Cambridge, Cambridge University Press, 1961.

Burnyeat
: *The Truth Exalted in the Writings of . . . John Burnyeat,* London, 1691.

Burrough, *Works*
: *The Memorable Works of a Son of Thunder and Consolation . . . Edward Burrough* London, 1672.

Camm and Audland, *Works*
: Camm, John and John Audland, *The Memory of the Righteous Revived . . .* London, 1689.

Cole, "Quakers and Politics"
: Cole, Alan, "The Quakers and Politics, 1652–1660," Cambridge University, 1955.

Dews.
: *Letters to William Dewsbury and Others,* ed.

Henry J. Cadbury, London, Friends Historical Society, 1948.

Edmondson

Edmondson, William, *A Journal of the Life* . . . 2d ed. London, 1774.

Ellwood, *Life*

The History of the Life of Thomas Ellwood . . . *Written by His Own Hand,* London, 1st ed., 1714.

EQL

Nuttall, Geoffrey F., *Early Quaker Letters from the Swarthmore MSS, to 1660,* London, Library of Friends House, 1952. A chronological numbering and summary of the letters in folios 1, 3, and 4 of Swarth. (see below), with exhaustive indexes and cross-references.

ESP

Extracts from State Papers Relating to Friends, 1654 to 1672, ed. Norman Penney, London, Friends Historical Society, 1913.

M. Fell

Fell, Margaret, *A Brief Collection of Remarkable Passages* . . . London, 1710.

Fisher, *Works*

Fisher, Samuel, *The Testimony of Truth Exalted* . . . *in the Works* . . . London, 1679.

Fox, *Doctrinals*

Fox, George, *Gospel-Truth Demonstrated in a Collection of Doctrinal Books by* . . . *George Fox,* London, 1706. The main collection of his tracts, also issued as Vols. 4, 5, and 6 of the collected *Works,* 8 vols. Philadelphia, 1831.

Fox, *Great Mistery*

Fox, George, *The Great Mistery of the Great Whore Unfolded* . . . London, 1659. Fox's main theological treatise, also issued as Vol. 3 of *Works,* Philadelphia, 1831.

Fox, *Journal,* 1694

Fox, George, *A Journal or Historical Account* . . . London, 1694. Edited after Fox' death by Thomas Ellwood, it includes the Testimony of Penn and many documents as first published.

Fox, *Journal,* Camb.

The Journal of George Fox, ed. Norman Penney, 2 vols. Cambridge, Cambridge University Press, 1911. Literatim from the Spence MS, as dictated by Fox to Thomas Lower in 1674–75.

Fox, *Journal,* Nickalls

The Journal of George Fox, ed. John L. Nickalls, Cambridge, Cambridge University Press, 1952. Combines texts of Spence MS, Short Journal, etc., with modern spelling and excellent notes.

FPT	*The First Publishers of Truth,* ed. Norman Penney, Friends Historical Society, London, 1907. See Bibliographical Note.
Haller, *Liberty*	Haller, William, *Liberty and Reformation in the Puritan Revolution,* New York, Columbia University Press, 1955. Treats the period 1640–49 only.
Haller, *Puritanism*	Haller, William, *The Rise of Puritanism,* New York, Columbia University Press, 1938.
Howgill, *Works*	Howgill, Francis, *The Dawnings of the Gospel-Day and Its Light* . . . n.p., 1676.
JFHS	*The Journal of the Friends Historical Society,* Friends House, London, since 1903.
Jones, *Colonies*	Jones, Rufus M., *The Quakers in the American Colonies,* London, Macmillan, 1923.
Jones, *Later Periods*	Jones, Rufus M., *The Later Periods of Quakerism,* 2 vols. London, Macmillan, 1921.
Kendal MS	Manuscripts in the strong room of Kendal Monthly Meeting, Westmorland, England.
Nayler, *Man of Sin*	Nayler, James, *A Discovery of the Man of Sin* . . . London, 1655.
Nayler, *Works*	*A Collection of Sundry Books, Epistles and Papers Written by James Nayler,* London, 1716. Omits controversial tracts.
Nuttall, *Holy Spirit*	Nuttall, Geoffrey F., *The Holy Spirit in Puritan Faith and Experience,* Oxford, Basil Blackwell, 1946.
Penn, *Witness*	*The Witness of William Penn,* ed. Frederick B. Tolles and E. Gordon Alderfer, New York, Macmillan, 1957. Annotated excerpts from his key works.
Penn, *Works*	*A Collection of the Works of William Penn,* 2 vols. London, 1726.
Swarth.	The Swarthmore Manuscripts (earlier often called the Devonshire House Collection). The basic collection of letters between early Quaker leaders, in 7 folios now at Friends House Library, London. My footnotes give in each case folio and letter number and number in Nuttall's sequence *(EQL).*

Tolles, *Atlantic Culture* — Tolles, Frederick B., *Quakers and the Atlantic Culture,* New York, Macmillan, 1960.

Tolles, *Meeting-House* — Tolles, Frederick B., *Meeting-House and Counting House,* Chapel Hill, University of North Carolina Press, 1948.

Watkins — Watkins, Owen C., "Spiritual Autobiography from 1649 to 1660," London, University of London, 1952.

White — White, Helen C., *Social Criticism in Popular Religious Literature of the Sixteenth Century,* New York, Macmillan, 1944.

Whitehead, *Two Seeds* — Whitehead, John, *The Enmitie between the Two Seeds,* London, 1655.

I

A Holy Nation: The Puritan Setting of Quakerism

THE early history of the Quakers has a special interest for both
scholars and religious laymen. The Quakers spoke of a religious experience more simple, sure, and direct than most men can claim.
They also changed society: they carried their ethical standards into
daily life with square-toed integrity and a sharp impact that created
an excitement in their history, as well as a religious challenge.

Early Quakerism was a movement of ordinary men. Quakers
have always been much admired from afar, and some in each period have deserved it; but in the first years almost every Quaker
man and woman shared with Luther and Wesley an intensity of
experience and a readiness for dramatic action. Each Friend himself came to know the same direct power which George Fox had
announced. Several hundred Friends shared fully in Fox's own
roles as preacher, tract-writer, and gatherer of Quaker Meetings.
Above all, Friends shared Fox's experience of the total world.
Their pattern of outward life was based not on a code of moral
teaching but on the implications of their own experience, which
was more unsettling and painful and in the end more joyful than
modern Quakerism. Early Friends spoke of "the Lamb's War," [1]
the struggle to conquer evil within and without, led by the Spirit
of Christ, who is the Lamb exalted to rule God's kingdom on earth.
The Quakers called all men to join this struggle and to surrender
their own wills to the constant judgment and guidance of the "in-

1. See Rev. 17:14. James Nayler used this phrase as the title for his most characteristic book, and it appears in the writings of almost every leading Quaker. For
fuller discussion of Quaker religious experience, see below, Chap. 4.

ward Light" of God or Christ. Most actual Quaker customs, from
the gray bonnet and the use of *thee* and *thou* to their stand against
war, must be understood as arising from this radical inward experience. That relationship is the central theme of this book.

Yet the Quakers were also puritans, living through the revo-
lutions of seventeenth-century England. Most of their insights in
ethics and worship were in fact the same as those of the puritans.
Even characteristically Quaker teachings were often puritan attitudes pushed to severe conclusions. Early Quakerism showed its
unique power in many areas, yet, in describing their faith, Friends
mainly used ideas and phrases which they shared with "spiritual
puritans" of the time. Their conflicts with puritan leaders had the
loving desperation of a family feud.[2]

Puritanism, though it was never drawn together into any single
platform or organization, has been the greatest religious movement
in English history. Puritans dominated morality, politics, and
church life for the entire century before Quakerism first arose in
1650. The heart of the movement was an experience of the sover-
eignty of God. As the newly converted puritan awoke to find that
his life was in God's hands, he pushed his own interests and worldly
values away. Such changes result from all great religious movements: daily activities are organized to serve a man's eternal des-
tiny. At the same time, the puritan, overwhelmed by the power and
glory of God in the ordering of the physical world and his wisdom
in ruling human history, could forget himself. He saw his own salvation as God's election and in no way under human control. The
doctrine of predestination was basically a description of the un-
expectedness and the power of God's love and mercy as it broke
into the lives of undeserving men. It left as a mystery the disquiet-
ing fact that many other men had not known this grace.

A daily life of good actions was thus the puritan's response to
God's mercy and not a self-purification that could earn his entrance into heaven. The puritan's desperate moral earnestness was
his protest against anything in the world that neglected or resisted
divine power and law as interpreted through the Bible and the
puritan conscience. The puritan—living in a world polarized into
positive and negative, good and evil, by the tension of God's pres-

2. See below, Chap. 5, and Ralph P. Bohn, "The Controversy between Puritans
and Quakers to 1660" (University of Edinburgh, 1955), pp. 3–4.

ence—found himself set apart from other men. He was a stranger and a pilgrim in a world mainly indifferent to his ideals, but his citizenship in the heavenly city did not make him otherworldly, for this world itself would be transformed into the New Jerusalem by God's power.

The puritan saw the work of God changing his own life, and therefore expected that any Christian would be converted and could recognize his conversion. Calvin himself had taught men to trust in God's ability to work in and through them if they were among the Elect. Those who responded to the gospel assumed that their willingness to do so had been God's gift, proving they were of the Elect. They could thus turn from worry about their own salvation to serve God's glory. But in the twilight world of half-puritanized England, men needed to reassure themselves that God's power had morally changed them. In careful spiritual diaries they tried to note the signs not of their heavenly bank-balance but of moments when God had demonstrably acted in their daily lives. Thus, for puritans, personal experience of conversion and sanctification became crucial as for no other Christian group: "To a poore soule, all such things as are in the soule are made known by *experiences*." [3] The double stress on conscious conversion and on "visible sainthood" became the special watchwords of Puritanism. These emphases still distinguish most English and American churches as offshoots of Puritanism from the original Calvinism preserved by the Scots, the Swiss, and the Reformed churches of Europe, who expect neither spectacular conversions nor sinless churchmen.

The puritan movement was at least a century older than Quakerism and much wider than Calvinist theology. Its history has many roots. A tradition of moral protest and austerity dates from Wycliffe and the Lollards in the 1370s. This nonconformist righteousness could be associated with the Roman Catholic creed, as Thomas More combined them. When the Church of England was cut away by Henry VIII from the control of the popes, its doctrines were at first not changed. The early lovers of Lutheranism in Britain, like William Tyndale and Thomas Bilney were banned and burned. Thereby the new Protestantism and the old tradition of moral protest came to be identified. King Henry died in 1547, and

3. John Rogers, *Ohel or Beth-Shemesh*, p. 355, quoted in Owen C. Watkins, "Spiritual Autobiography from 1649 to 1660" (University of London, 1952), p. 79.

under the boy Edward VI the Regents encouraged Protestantism. To this brief period belong Cranmer's great Book of Common Prayer and the tradition of fiery preaching begun by Bishop Hugh Latimer:

> Now what shal we say of these rich citizens of London: shal I cal them proude men of London, malicious men of London? . . . No, no, I may not say so, they wyl be offended with me than. . . . Therefore I say, repent O London, repent, repent. I think if Nebo had had the preachyng that Thou hast, they would haue conuerted. . . . What a do was there made in London, at a certain man, because he said . . . "Burgesses . . . nay butterflies." . . . And yet would God they wer no worse then butterflies. Butterflies do but theyr nature, the Butterfly is not couetous, is not greedy of other mens goodes, is not ful of enuye & hatred. . . . But London cannot abide to be rebuked.[4]

Though the great liturgy and sermons were remembered and later revived, little of Protestantism had been formally established in England before the young King's death in 1553. His sister, Mary Tudor, then tried to force England back to Rome; a more ruthless or longer-lived monarch might have succeeded. Instead, the burning of the great bishops and of some three hundred lesser Protestants merely aroused the fighting tradition which the puritans were to inherit. The ideal of the suffering church had been in most of Europe the self-image only of tiny persecuted sects, but in England it became Protestant orthodoxy. Foxe's *Booke of Martyrs* linked Mary with Nero, and her victims with Saint Stephen. So it became natural for later puritans and Quakers to identify kings as well as popes with Antichrist, with "the great beast" of the Book of Revelation. Rome remained "the scarlet woman, Babylon." Such a tradition of martyrdom taught all puritans to expect both suffering and triumph: without a cross there was no crown. Such a heritage Friends also shared, turning it against the puritans themselves when they persecuted Quakers: "O how dare you profess Reformation, when Cruelty and Tyranny Rules in the Land! O look back, and see, if ever there was the like, in all the Kings or Bishops time,

4. 27 *Sermons Preached by the Ryght Reuerende Father in God . . . Maister Hugh Latimer* (London, 1562), fol. 15, from "Fourth Sermon on the Plough."

since Queen *Mary's* Days, that slew the Martyrs, that so many Goals was furnish'd with Prisoners, only for Conscience sake." [5] Many English Protestants escaped to Europe from Mary Tudor's persecution. There they saw cities transformed by Protestantism: Geneva had become "the school of Christ." [6]

A second strand of the puritan tradition inherited by Quakerism was thus added: Calvin's dream of remaking each city and nation for the glory of God. The English refugees also learned Calvinist theology and Presbyterian models of church government in Geneva or along the Rhine. The Quakers took up the exiles' reforming passion for a godly nation, though they later rejected predestination and Presbyterianism.

From Geneva, John Knox slipped back to Scotland, and out of the chaos there he built an unshakable Presbyterianism. When Mary Tudor died in 1558, the exiles returning to England had the same eager hope, but Queen Elizabeth was satisfied with parish churches that were understaffed and uninspired and that lived by medieval customs and festivals. Most of Europe at this time was burning with religious wars. Except as loose federations, no nations with diverse churches had yet survived or been desired. To keep all England within a single national church was more important to Elizabeth than clear doctrines or prophetic zeal. Her revision of the Book of Common Prayer and the restoration of bishops was meant to be a policy supportable, however reluctantly, by both ex-Catholics and mild Protestants in England. Her compromises were imposed by fiat: warm devotion to Anglicanism grew only later. Even Richard Hooker's strongest argument for the new "Ecclesiastical Polity" was that God had endowed mankind with common sense.

The puritans also wanted a national church and led each new Parliament in projects for rebuilding the Church of England on a Calvinist pattern. The reformers were always firmly sent home but were in varying degrees still free to be parish ministers, elders, or lecturers at Cambridge. In 1603 the Scottish James Stuart became king, but he made it clear that he preferred ruling through bishops

5. Margaret Fell, *A Brief Collection of Remarkable Passages* (London, 1710), p. 42. In response to this letter in 1653 Colonel West released Fox from Lancaster
6. John Knox, quoted in Richard H. Tawney, *Religion and the Rise of Capitalism* (West Drayton, Middlesex, Penguin Books, 1948), p. 126. Cf. John Knox, *The Historie of the Reformation of . . . Scotland* (Edinburgh, 1732), pp. 92 ff.

to being ignored by presbyters. Puritan hopes produced little but
the King James Version of the Bible, though this carried its own
authority into every home.

Meanwhile, alongside the traditions of moral protest and rebuilding of the church and nation, other strains of the puritan
outlook grew up. For eighty years three generations of puritan
pastors changed the lives of their parishes while waiting for freedom to purify the Church of England. Freedom for the word of
God was at least secured through scripture and the pulpit, and this
freedom England never again overthrew. The Sunday sermon and
daily home prayers became basic elements in English life. Quartos
of printed sermons, devotional handbooks, and spiritual autobiographies of the puritan preachers were sold at county fairs and were
read by hungering men. The pastors were trained under great
leaders, especially at Cambridge University, to give their lives for
their people.

Puritan merchants and gentry were no less influential: pastors
and laymen were equal partners in building a godly life for families, for towns, but above all for congregations. This lay leadership, whatever its denominational label, became the typical pattern of churches in England and America, in contrast with dependence upon the Lord Bishop, the chaplain in the Manor House,
or the Lutheran Herr Pfarrer. The early Quakers inherited the
puritans' respect for the godly layman and their dislike of church
hierarchy. Moreover, the puritans themselves attacked the usual
type of English parish priests as "whole swarmes of idle, ignorant
and Ungodly Curates." [7] Many sharp biblical shafts aimed by
puritan pastors against the "idle shepherds" and "dumb dogs" who
did not preach were later turned by Quakers into ammunition
against all paid ministers. George Fox came close, in both words
and spirit, to reaffirming the ideal of the minister preached a century before by Bishop Latimer himself in a sermon, "To the
Clergy," assembled in national Convocation at Westminster:

> Ye have oft sat in consultacion, but what have ye done? Ye have
> had many thynges in deliberation, but what one is put forth,
> whereby Christe is more glorified, or els Christes people made

7. Laurence Chaderton, *Sermon . . . at St. Paul's Cross* (London, 1580) as quoted
in Helen C. White, *Social Criticism in Popular Religious Literature of the Sixteenth
Century* (New York, Macmillan, 1944), p. 184.

more holyer? I appele to your own conscience. . . . How came this thus: because there were no children of light . . . amonges you, which, setting the world at nought, would study to illustrate the glory of God? The Children of the world be lyke crafty hunters. . . . They go about to keepe other men in darkness. . . . Whereas the children of lyght . . . seke theyr adversaries health, welth and profite . . . and oft tymes with jeoperdy of their life: The children of the world . . . will sooner se them dead, that do them good, then systeyne any loss of temporal things.[8]

Puritan ideas about church buildings and rituals have given these earnest pastors a reputation as destroyers of beauty. They attacked all wasteful luxury, especially when they could point to "dead images . . . couered with golde . . . cladde with sylke garmentes, and . . . lade with precious gemmes . . . where as in the meane time, were Christes faithful and liuely ymages . . . an hugred, a thurst, a cold, and to lye in darknes, wrapped in al wretchednesse." But even more than waste, the puritans fought anything which seemed to them Roman Catholic superstition, especially saints' statues in any form, the lighting of candles, embroidered vestments of vicars, and the use of the ring in marriage. The puritans replaced the church altar by the communion table, around which pastor and laymen met, all dressed in sober black. Puritans kept a reverence for communion and for baptism, but they were afraid of any ritual wherein the priest might claim special power for his words. The puritans and, after them, the Quakers attacked all formal rituals as "wylworkes that come but of our own devotion . . . as though now man's inventions and fancies could please God better than God's preceptes." [9]

A puritan's life centered upon worship, requiring an hour of preaching twice each Sunday and once in midweek meeting. But the maker of sermons trusted the power of God's word and not human words. He hoped only that God could use his pulpit as an instrument of conversion, to assist the work of the Holy Spirit in men's hearts. To the unconverted, of course, the puritan pastor could "pronounce the word *Damne* with such an emphasis as left a

8. Latimer, 27 *Sermons,* "Ad Clerum," fol. 8.
9. Ibid., fol. 4.

dolefull Echo in his auditours ears a good while after," [10] but he also turned men to the love of God and the grace He had given them. The aim of puritan preaching was no different from that of the early Quakers, who were no less sternly against sin and just as anxious to identify their word with God's. Even the spontaneity of Quaker worship evolved by stages from the puritan Bible-study sessions or "prophesyings," which were weekday meetings of groups of pastors and laymen to expound and discuss scripture passages impromptu.

But the puritan lived to glorify God and purify the world, not simply for worship. "If I can be the Instrument of advancing His Glory in the world," wrote Cotton Mather, "and bringing others to acknowledge it, I am raptured with inexpressible Consolation." [11] Such a sense of being a divine instrument gave the puritan, as it gave the early Moslem and the modern communist, a certainty of being on the side of right and of victory. Human effort was strengthened: despite all sufferings, each event and object in nature could be met in the confidence that it was ruled by God's providence.

The trust in providence led puritans to search for hidden meanings in inward and outward events that seemed to other men mere chance occurrences. In history and psychology the puritans taught later generations to ignore nothing and record everything. Physical nature, moreover, was for them God's instrument and was ruled by divine order as fully as the inward world. The puritan was free to look for uniform laws in science without excluding God's purposes from anything. Miracles were possible but seldom necessary, since God ruled all events. Spirit and matter were not independent worlds. Though the great puritan preachers had little time for science, later leaders like Winthrop and Penn corresponded with the Royal Society as eagerly as any Cavalier scientist.

The theocratic spirit was carried by puritans into all their relations with the physical world: "All the world are our servants, that we may be the servants of God. . . . How many thousand plants

10. Thomas Fuller, as quoted in Louis B. Wright, "William Perkins: Elizabethan Apostle of Practical Divinity," in *Huntington Library Quarterly*, *3* (1940), 173. Cf. William Perkins, *A Golden Chaine* (London, 1597), for a practical guidebook for conscientious pastors.

11. Cotton Mather, *Diary*, 7, 515–16, quoted in Ralph Barton Perry, *Puritanism and Democracy* (New York, Random House, 1944), p. 322.

and flowers and fruits and birds and beasts do all attend us! The
sea, with its inhabitants, the air, the wind, the frost and snow, the
heat and fire, the clouds and rain, all wait upon us while we do our
work." [12] The puritan faced every job not merely as a situation
where God could be loved and served but as a positive means for
remaking the world for His glory. If this was too clearly impossible, the puritan changed jobs—that is, he was alert to God's call
in a new direction. Puritanism thus at first led more to social mo-
bility than to individualism. Until 1650, most puritans expected
divine support only if they humbly obeyed God's plan for the
whole nation. Many puritans in seemingly interim jobs, and finally
even those who attained power in the government, were forced by
frustrations to postpone working as a unified people of God. Their
own successes were no longer part of the total work of the body of
the Elect. Each man's personal call was sufficient; obedience to it
now led to individualism. This problem was still being fought
when Quakerism arose to present it in sharper focus.

The economic life of puritans was energetic and austere but not
lawless. The merchants wanted freedom from control by the King,
but they had not broken away from the medieval tradition that
business ethics were ruled by the church. Puritan pastors were evidently besieged in their libraries by anxious tradesmen wanting
guidance. They turned to the enormous case-books of William
Ames and William Perkins, and two generations later to Richard
Baxter's *Christian Directory*, which tried to answer every moral
dilemma likely to arise. (When may a merchant profit by a rising
market? When he holds no monopoly and it is not a time of need.
Must one keep a verbal agreement? Yes, even if it was made in ignorance, unless the other party grants release from it. Must one
point out the faults of one's wares? Only if they are not obvious.) In
general, the Christian was meant to manage his business so as to
"avoid sin rather than loss." [13] But more and more, even the guide-
books had to turn the merchant back to the prompting of his individual conscience.

Up to the time of Cromwell and the rise of Quakerism, the com-

---

12. Richard Baxter, quoted in J. W. Allen, *English Political Thought, 1603–1660*
(London, Methuen, 1938), p. 293.
13. Richard Baxter, *Christian Directory*, quoted in Tawney, *Religion*, p. 223;
cf. pp. 215–16.

mon goal of remaking England set a compass bearing for a puritan's conscience and gave purpose and group support to his renunciations of worldly life:

> The Christian convent and monastery are within, where the soul is encloistered from sin; and this religious house the true followers of Christ carry about with them, who exempt not themselves from the conversation of the world, though they keep themselves from the evil of the world in their conversation. . . . True godliness don't turn men out of the world, but enables them to live better in it and excites their endeavors to mend it.[14]

Later scholars and social idealists, such as Max Weber and R. H. Tawney, have been fascinated by this paradox of "diligence in worldly businesses and yet deadnesse to the world." [15] It was at first the self-discipline of the athlete or the soldier, with just as clear a goal. But the fading of their common ideal left the puritans in the end seriously adrift. Then the puritan conscience became an intense but aimless conscientiousness, like the popular image of the "puritanical" New Englander or the English "Nonconformist," who is horrified at the fact that other men "eat, drink, play, game and sport away their health, estates, and above all, their irrevocable precious time, which should be dedicated to the Lord." [16]

The monkish austerity of the puritans, and their bourgeois tastes in beauty, made them for a time devastating to English music, art, and drama, all of which were rooted in the Middle Ages and spiced with Renaissance libertinism. Puritan discipline nevertheless made sense while it served the dream of purifying and simplifying national life. The simplicity of life within early Quakerism came from this same wholeheartedness. Even the puritan's inner warfare against temptation was part of a world struggle.[17] The greatest harm always sprang from turning this pruning spirit to serve personal righteousness alone. If the puritan vision of the world

14. William Penn, *The Witness of William Penn*, ed. Frederick B. Tolles and E. Gordon Alderfer (New York, Macmillan, 1957), p. 48.

15. John Cotton, *Christ the Fountaine of Life*, p. 110, quoted by Karl Herbert Hertz, "Bible Commonwealth and Holy Experiment" (University of Chicago, 1948), p. 91.

16. Penn, *Witness*, p. 59.

17. This attitude lends itself to parody:
> "I sing my *Self*, my *Civil Warrs* within,
> The *Victories* I howrely lose and win;

ruled by God's word had prevailed, it might have produced a new art and a new music. In Milton it did evoke new poetry, which gave style to English hymn-writing and solemnity to Victorian poets. In New England, Puritanism led similarly to a clean craftsmanship in houses, furniture, and metalware.

Puritans expected God to rule both church and state through His Elect. They felt that since Christ reigned in the commonwealth as well as in the church, it was "this Theocratical Policy or Divine Commonwealth which is the unquestionable reign of Christ on earth, which all Christians are agreed may be justly sought." [18] But, believing that God controls all things, the Saints were free to use whatever form of government was most effective. In Massachusetts, John Cotton's proposal for a law code based on "Moses his Judicialls" in the Book of Deuteronomy was set aside in favor of a code based on common law.[19] In England under Cromwell, the Levellers and radicals were religious in motive but fought for a democratic republic. Democracy could achieve theocracy so long as elections chose from the Elect, since "in one and the same action, God, by the peoples suffrages, makes such an one Governour or Magistrate, and not another." [20] Magistrate and minister were to protect each other: if both were equally Saints, neither needed to

---

> The dayly *Duel*, the continuall strife,
> The *War*, that ends not till I end my life;
> And yet, not Mine alone, not onely Mine,
> But every-One's that, under th' honor'd Signe
> Of CHRIST his standard, shal his Name enroule
> With holy Vowes of Body and of Soule."

The poem by George Goodwin from which this comes survives only in Josuah Sylvester's translation (London, 1607) as *Automachia*, and is included in Sylvester's *Works*, ed. Alexander B. Grosart (2 vols. Edinburgh, 1880); and in 1621, 1633 and 1641 editions of Sylvester's translations of Guillaume Saluste du Bartas' *Devine Weekes, Judith*, etc. As George Goodwin is otherwise known only as a "Christian Satyrist," however (*Melissa religionis pontificae*, 1620, was translated as *Babels Balm or the Honey-combe of Rome's Religion*), doubts arise whether he was entirely serious here. In 1644 John Goodwin published a Civil War sermon entitled *Theomachia*.

18. Richard Baxter, *Holy Commonwealth* (1659), p. 221, quoted in Perry, *Puritanism and Democracy*, p. 115.

19. See Judith Welles, "John Cotton, 1584–1652, Churchman and Theologian" (University of Edinburgh, 1948), p. 269. The code actually used was Nathaniel Ward's "Breviate of Liberties."

20. John Davenport, "A Sermon Preached at the Election of the Governour, at Boston . . . 1669," quoted in Hertz, "Bible Commonwealth," p. 99. See also Willem A. Visser 't Hooft, *The Background of the Social Gospel in American Protestantism* (Haarlem, 1928).

dominate. Both England and America inherit this tradition of religious idealism within a government independent of church control. Now, however, all our citizens are considered potentially God's Elect.

Puritan rulers expected to rewrite and to change laws. This made them, among other things, the spoilers of Sunday. Yet all medieval thought had assumed that rulers would be Christians, enforcing both Christian and natural law. The prince would be a loyal member of the church or even the pope's own vassal. But the Middle Ages, and Luther too, saw society as a static pyramid. Justice was a fixed barrier against human ambition and cruelty. The ideal ruler shown in tapestry or stained glass was not the lawmaker Charlemagne, still less Justinian; he was Roland or King Arthur or David of Israel, the heroic defender of established laws to protect the oppressed. By contrast, Calvinist and puritan ideals were dynamic, based on God's limitless power to change the world. The ruler could transform the customs of society, and justice could overthrow the power of established evil; thus the puritans began to write constitutions, even though in the process nonpuritan ideals broke through.

Puritan church government has seemed to modern laymen even more stern and barren than their statecraft. Earnest fights for a biblical church-pattern produced, indeed, no agreement on what that would be. Much of their eighty-year struggle against Elizabeth and the Stuart kings was a protest against rule by bishops, yet out of puritanism many and varied forms of church polity arose. Basic always, however, remained the insistence that the church must be God's instrument; the variety of forms were all ways of making the church serve God and not men.

The puritans assumed that God had planned to give His saving grace to the Elect mainly through the church (though not, as Catholics maintained, that salvation depended on the Church). The means of grace, which for the puritan was above all the preached or written Word, thus became central in church life. By preaching and teaching, even the reprobate might be brought to an outwardly sober and godly life. Therefore, the Calvinist churches, like the Catholic, meant to include everyone, within the pew if not at the communion table. Early puritans accepted the universal baptism of the children of Christians: every child should be raised under the church's influence if possible. The outreach was to be as wide as the nation. In this way puritans kept the ancient tradition of the national church.

Puritans also felt an opposite pressure—that of limiting church membership rolls to the Elect. This was not snobbery, for God's direct election of the Saint to salvation made official church membership less important to him. But the church in its mission to remake the nation and the world had to act as a clear-cut force through its fully committed members. Logic and the Bible pressed the puritans to put church government and discipline into the hands of the Elect and to take control away from appointed bishops and hereditary church wardens. Ideally, "in the matter of their Churches, they would have none allowed but visible Saints. In the exercise of Church-censure, they leave that power to the Elders and Brethren of the same Church whereof the delinquent is a member." [21] The true Saints were identified as far as possible by their conversion experiences and their ethical conduct. The local congregation was formed on members' voluntary agreement or church covenant. This was sometimes a written document but corresponded to God's own covenant in simultaneously choosing the Saints and promising to transform their own lives and the world through them. A "testimony" describing the time and background of his conversion was expected of each new applicant for membership.

The patterns of resulting church government represented shades within the limited spectrum this outlook allowed. They were not clearly marked, though their names were crystallized much later into denominations. Most puritans favored in practice a presbyterian form of federated churches, which would balance the need of national unity against the Saints' need of freedom in their work. A united national presbyterian church could stand against monarchs as well as popes. But where isolation or lack of opposition made a centralized church authority unnecessary, as in New England, a congregational system resulted, with covenanted congregations loosely interlinked. In England its advocates were called Independents. Before 1640, these names meant little, since all but a few puritans remained members of the Church of England, where the actual authority still lay with the bishops.

The separatists were the first to break the formal ties. In the long

21. John Cotton, *The Way of the Congregational Churches Cleared* (London, 1644), p. 27.

years of waiting under Queen Elizabeth and James I, some half-dozen puritan congregations decided upon "Reformation without Tarying for Anie." [22] Their leaders—Browne, Barrowe, Robinson, and Smyth—had mostly begun as Cambridge-trained parish pastors; the members were mostly workingmen. They followed puritan ideals in purging all use of altars, uniform prayers, hymns, and the colored vestments and white surplices of parsons. In worship they would

> begynne with a prayer, after reade some one or tow chapters of the Bible, gyve the sence thereof, and conferr upon the same; that done, we lay aside oure bookes, and after a solemne prayer made by the .1. speaker, he propoundeth some text owt of the Scripture and prophecieth owt of the same, by the space of one hower. After him standeth up a .2. speaker and prophecieth owt of the said text the like tyme and space. . . . After him the .3. the .4. the .5. &c, as the tyme will give leave; then the .1. speaker concludeth with prayer.[23]

This sounds like puritan "prophesying," but what stands out—apart from their fortitude in listening to five hours of preaching on the same text—is the lack of distinction between laymen and ministers. "It was agreed that anie might protest, appeal, complaine, exhort, dispute, reprove, etc. as he had occasion." [24]

The separatists also remained puritan in hoping to see all England remade according to their own biblical pattern. Wherever the established churches seemed to be doing this, as in Massachusetts, the separatists greeted them as brothers. Yet the separatists in England found themselves under sentence of death, and their leaders executed. Several congregations had to escape to Holland, whence the "Pilgrim fathers" later went on to Plymouth. Both the orthodox puritans and the Anglicans condemned the separatists for breaking the unity of their nation and undercutting its laws. Now English separatists were not simply a sect, self-righteously ignoring

22. This was the title of Robert Browne's most famous tract (1582). See Champlin Burrage, *The Early English Dissenters* (2 vols. Cambridge, Cambridge University Press, 1912), and William Haller, *The Rise of Puritanism* (New York, Columbia University Press, 1938), Chap. 7.

23. Harleian Miscellanies, quoted in Burrage, *Dissenters, 1,* 236.

24. The Brownists' *True and Short Declaration,* pp. 19–20, quoted in Burrage, *Dissenters, 1,* 99.

the mass of mankind. Fearful Englishmen unfairly compared them with the bloody revolution and polygamy of the sect of Anabaptists who had taken over Münster in 1535. But any church that rejects in principle the ultimate authority under which the rest of the nation lives is potentially subversive.

A few separatists, like Roger Williams, did conclude that true Christians would always be a persecuted minority, a "garden in the wilderness." So said also the milder Anabaptists and the Mennonites of Europe, forerunners of the American Amish. These withdrew from social contacts with men at large, wherever religious issues might arise. They refused to baptize anyone not fully converted and committed, and often rebaptized those who were. Williams took separatism to its logical limit, by withdrawing even from the congregation he had formed. Few separatists went so far. The Quakers seemed to their opponents the ultimate separatists, in rejecting the validity of all churches but their own and in disobeying all "ungodly" laws; [25] but even the Friends expected to transform the whole nation and convince or reach all men in the world.

The separatists in fact presented an upsetting challenge to all puritans. They withdrew from the Church of England and its worship because their first concern was to "utterlie flee and avoide such like disorders & wickednes." [26] Yet all puritans held a similar doctrine about Catholicism, even when it was the national faith: "it is unlawful to be present at Masse or any idolatrous service . . . worshipping the beast . . . the Church of Rome, now no better than an hereticall and apostaticall Synagogue." [27] The separatists extended this condemnation to the Anglican liturgy and to those puritans who accepted it. Puritans were also inconsistent in hoping that a church membership purely of Saints could be simultaneously an inclusive national church, for it involved persuading the ungodly to accept permanent second-class status. Adult baptism and enrollment in churches limited to fully converted Christians

25. See Johannes Kühn, *Toleranz und Offenbarung* (Leipzig, 1923); W. K. Jordan, *The Development of Religious Toleration* (4 vols. London, Allen and Unwin, 1932–40); and Michael Freund, *Die Idee der Toleranz im England der Grossen Revolution* (Halle/Saale, 1927).

26. From the Covenant of Robert Browne's congregation at Norwich, 1580, as quoted in Burrage, *Dissenters, 1,* 98.

27. Perkins, *Golden Chaine,* pp. 59–61.

had for 1,300 years been considered not only self-righteous and exclusive but heretical. More and more puritans now became attracted to the idea, though before 1640 distinct Baptist groups were rare: there were five English Baptist congregations in 1626 and only eight in 1641.[28]

By 1624, the year of George Fox's birth, the puritans thus faced a crisis. They were the most powerful religious movement in Europe now that the Lutherans, the Huguenots, and revived Catholicism had begun to exhaust one another by decades of war. Like those other movements, Puritanism had long been fertile in many quiet ways: puritans had been writing or translating thousands of books for laymen, founding schools and colleges, developing catechisms and prayers for the home, and teaching ordinary men to think and write and speak. The puritans included most of the active ministers and laymen in England; yet for two generations the price had been frustration and unhappy compromise with the bishops and their prayer books. In 1624 they faced complete defeat: the coming of Charles I as king led to Bishop Laud's power over the Church of England and consequently to conformity, rigidly enforced. The puritans faced the choice of giving up their basic pattern of church life or disavowing their nation, church, and king, and all hope of reforming these. As final blows, new royal taxes were required, and a depression developed in the cloth-weaving towns northeast of London.

Massachusetts was the way out, and puritan merchants gained a charter for administering a trading post in America. By migrating there together and carrying their charter with them, they engineered their own self-government. Ten thousand leading puritans joined together, including many of the best pastors, though they still considered themselves part of England. They had not rejected the King or the national church, even if their bishops could not reach them. Their church rules and the elected government of their commonwealth were the same they hoped to see in England. The smaller colonies that were satellites of Boston, such as Hartford and New Hampshire, and the new settlements planted directly from England, such as New Haven, formed together the

28. These figures are based on A. C. Underwood, *A History of the English Baptists* (London, 1947) and W. A. Whitley, *A History of British Baptists* (London, Charles Griffin, 1923).

puritan community of New England, continuing the brotherhood that began at Cambridge University. In the 1640s many New Englanders eagerly sailed home again to join the puritan revolution in England.

The separatist problem was not fully solved by the New England migration. Even in Boston a few individualists like Ann Hutchinson and Roger Williams stood against the biblical Commonwealth; but they had wilderness enough into which to withdraw. Massachusetts represented for most puritans a great ideal and a providential achievement. The tiny and still unchartered Rhode Island settlements and the smaller group of old separatists at Plymouth were regarded by the Boston puritans with suspicion but little fear. In England, however, the puritans who remained were harried by Laud and increasingly doubted their ability to enforce presbyterianism on the nation. Some, the Independents, were willing to accept autonomy for each congregation within the national church. Separatist spirit also grew, and a few new separatist churches gathered. Tracts began to appear urging outright religious liberty, but the decade after the settlement of Boston in 1630 was relatively fruitless for puritans in England.

In 1640 the chance finally came: the puritan fight against bishops and liturgies allied itself with the fight of Parliament against the King's power and the resistance of the merchants to his taxes. Charles' foolish attempt to impose the English church and bureaucracy upon his Scottish subjects led to his humiliating retreat. The Scottish leaders came to Westminster to protect their Kirk by an alliance with Parliament and the English puritans, whose perspective was still centered on freedom to preach and opposition to episcopacy "with all its dependencies, rootes and branches." [29]

Both King Charles and his various opponents found compromise hard, and they were more or less deadlocked throughout 1641. Parliament tried and executed Charles' chief minister, Strafford; imprisoned Archbishop Laud; and drove the other bishops out of the House of Lords. The King in reprisal tried to arrest five parliamentary leaders. At this point new revolts in Ireland and Scotland forced both sides in England to compete for the right to recruit and

29. *The First and Large Petition of the Citie of London* (London, 1641), quoted in William Haller, *Liberty and Reformation in the Puritan Revolution* (New York, Columbia University Press, 1955), p. 20.

control the English militia, which led to civil war in the summer of 1642. Neither side had men or money enough to force a victory. Parliament was meanwhile able to rule at least the south and east of England and was persuaded by the Scots and the puritans to call together the leading ministers of both kingdoms in the Westminster Assembly to draw up a new pattern for the English church. To the joy of the impatient Scots they brought out, after more than a year of debate, the Westminster Confession and the Westminster Catechisms, which have been standards for Presbyterians ever since. The Assembly also set down an essentially presbyterian constitution for the Church of England, which Parliament in due course enacted by law. By the time it had been approved, however, it had become doubtful whether this constitution could be enforced, and the Presbyterian party was on the defensive.

The Civil War had brought the Independents into prominence. After a victory of the Scots and Parliamentarians at Marston Moor in 1644 had been offset by the surrender of Essex' army in Cornwall, the decisive military force in 1645 was the "New Model Army." These regiments were raised by the Independent squire Oliver Cromwell, on a basis of individual commitment to the puritan cause: "Not every recruit, at the time he enlisted or was pressed into the New Model, was a Puritan saint, but the men Cromwell favored for . . . leadership generally had the root of the matter in them, and the others knew what saints might be expected to feel." [30] His regiments formed themselves into "gathered" churches for worship, with only dubious authority from the national church, following chaplains who were for the most part more radical than the great Presbyterians who had blessed the earlier campaigns.

The confusion and partisanship of the war had meanwhile also set free the separatist impulses among puritans. In many towns Independent, separatist, and Baptist churches were springing up. The control of book printing by the king and bishops was gone; the parliamentary commission and the Stationers' Company, which claimed authority, could no longer enforce censorship. In 1644, as part of a great outburst of all opinions into print, came three of the greatest of the toleration tracts: Milton's *Areopagitica*, Roger Williams' *Bloudy Tenant of Persecution*, and John Goodwin's *Theomachia*, urging freedom even "for the most Paganish, Jewish,

30. Haller, *Liberty*, p. 192.

Turkish or Antichristian consciences and worships." [31] In the midst of this national confusion George Fox, a shoemaker's apprentice from Leicestershire, wandered to the puritan centers of Northampton and London looking for answers to his own religious confusion.

By 1646 Cromwell's army had captured the King and broken down the remaining royalist castles. The army found itself dominated by Independents and the champion of religious toleration for separatists and Baptists. They were aligned with the minority of Independents in Parliament and with a strong residue of anticlerical skeptics and secularists, in opposition to the Presbyterian majority in Parliament and the Westminster Assembly, who were ready to impose their newly drafted church pattern upon England. But the immediate need was to get the King's agreement to any stable constitution of government in church and state. The Presbyterians and the army separatists found themselves also divided over how far compromise with the King was justified. Charles, though defeated, wanted in fact no constitutional monarchy. He escaped to the Isle of Wight and, without accepting any formal charter other than the Scottish "Solemn League and Covenant," convinced the Scots and the Presbyterians that he would cooperate with them.

War broke out again. Cromwell, by a brilliant march across the north of England, defeated the Scots at Preston before either the English Presbyterians or the Royalists could join them. He now faced hard decisions. The "Second Civil War" seemed to him to have proved the Independents right and the Presbyterian party unrealistic about both the King and the church. With no authority other than the backing of the citizen army, Cromwell's party shut out the Presbyterian majority from Parliament and used the Rump, or remnant of members who were left, to stage the trial and execution of King Charles I for treason in January 1649. Europe felt the shock of this news, and the puritan revolution could not thereafter turn back.

For three more years Cromwell campaigned against the remain-

31. Roger Williams, *The Bloudy Tenant*, quoted in Haller, *Liberty*, p. 129. On Williams cf. Freund, *Idee der Toleranz*, and Kühn, *Toleranz und Offenbarung*. The same year also saw the publication of toleration tracts by Walwyn, Robinson, Overton, and Milton himself. Over control of the militia, and later over the King's execution, the orthodox puritans also appealed to natural law but did not contrast it with inward divine law, as did the separatists.

ing resistance, centering upon the King's son (later to rule as Charles II). He found himself drawn into the permanent military occupation of Scotland and Ireland, and so devastated the latter that the hatred and division between the Irish and the newly planted English settlements have survived until the present time. Many dedicated puritans remained on garrison duty for as long as a decade, and the spirit of Cromwell's movement gradually became more and more military and professional. Law and order were at no time a matter of course during the adulthood of George Fox and most of the early Quakers.

But Cromwell himself and his army saw the spectacular victories of Preston, Dunbar, and Worcester as the hand of God, and the failure of both King and Presbyterians as God's providence, for "wherever anything in this world . . . exalts itself, God will pull it down." When Cromwell saw the enemy "draw up and march in gallant order toward us, and we a company of poor ignorant men . . . I could not but smile out to God in praises, in assurance of victory . . . God would, by things that are not, bring to nought things that are." [32] In 1652, though many Englishmen and even some puritans hesitated, it seemed to the radical Saints who had hoped and fought together that the chance had finally come to build Jerusalem in England's green and pleasant land.[33]

In 1653 Cromwell replaced the Rump of the Long Parliament that had met since 1640 with a newly chosen "Parliament of Saints," representing not the old landowning voters of the boroughs and counties of England but the puritan congregations. This "nominated Parliament" met in deep religious earnestness and dedicated itself to reforming and simplifying the laws of England, improving the prisons, extending the franchise, and improving public morals. They tried to restore adequate poor relief and to limit the enclosure of common fields; they intended to modify the tithe laws. Meanwhile, Cromwell appointed "Tryers and Ejectors," who attempted to weed out from the parish churches lazy ministers and Anglican ritualists and to recruit puritan pastors instead. As the puritans saw it, these commissioners

32. *Writings and Speeches of Oliver Cromwell*, ed. W. C. Abbott (4 vols. Cambridge, Mass., Harvard University Press, 1937), *1*, 365, 638, quoted in Haller, *Liberty*, pp. 214, 330.

33. William Blake's hymn shows the persistence of the puritan dream in England for the next century. Its popularity continues today.

saved many a Congregation from ignorant, ungodly drunken Teachers, that sort of men that . . . say a sermon as Readers say their Common Prayers . . . and the rest of the week go . . . to the Alehouse . . . those that used the ministry but as a Common Trade to live by, and were never likely to convert a soul; all these they usually rejected, and in their stead, admitted of any that were serious preachers, and lived a godly Life, of what tollerable Opinion soever they were. So that, though they were many of them somewhat partial for the Independents, Separatists, Fifth-Monarch-men and Anabaptists. . . . many thousands of souls blessed God for the faithful Ministers whom they let in.[34]

Toleration, however, was a problem which even the Parliament of Saints could not solve. They went home with their work incomplete, and later in the year Cromwell drew up an "Instrument of Government" by which the Commonwealth was for the time being administered by a council of state. Cromwell had taken for himself the title of Protector, which had been used by the reforming regents during the reign of young Edward VI. Yet his consolidation did not kill the great hopes, which had clearly taken on more radical and creative forms since the beginning of the Civil War.

Two important themes had now emerged in Puritanism: social justice and spiritual inspiration. These produced a radical puritan movement that diverged from Presbyterian orthodoxy in ethics as well as theology. Both new themes reflected the working-class nature of many of Cromwell's supporters. Cromwell himself was at ease with men of all ranks. Though "very ordinarily apparelled, with a plain cloth-sute, which seemed to have been made by an ill country-taylor," [35] he was well schooled and a gentleman. But depositions of Francis Johnson's separatist congregation in London, when they were arrested in 1593, show that they included six shipwrights, five tailors, four servants, three ministers, three weavers or clothworkers, three carpenters, three clerks, and scriveners, two fishmongers, two haberdashers, two shoemakers, two

---

34. *Reliquiae Baxterianae,* quoted in B. Nightingale, *The Ejected of 1662 in Cumberland and Westmorland* (2 vols. Manchester, Manchester University Press, 1911), *1,* 6–7.

35. W. N. Weech, *A History of the World* (2d ed. London, Odham Press, 1951), p. 634, quoted without source.

pursemakers, a glover, a capmaker, a goldsmith, a "scholler," a broadweaver, an apothecary, a coppersmith, and two schoolmasters. Most were men under thirty-five years old.[36] When the Civil War let separatists and Baptists gather freely, the new groups were mostly made up of "the laborious Husbandman, the Handicraftsman and all kinds of honest Tradesmen." [37] By 1660 there were 297 Baptist congregations.

Baptist preachers and elders were also workingmen, but men who felt they had a direct call from God. Despite lack of training, they preached sermons closer to their hearers' lives than did university-bred pastors. The Presbyterians had stressed Election, but were shocked at the result: "Instead of Orthodoxe Divines, they set up all kinde of Mechanicks, [such] as Shooe-Makers . . . Boxe-Makers, Coach-men and Felt-makers and Bottle-Ale sellers." [38] In reply, Bunyan, the Baptist tinker, pointed to Jesus the carpenter and his unlearned apostles. As the Presbyterians parodied one Baptist preacher:

> Gainst Schooles and learning, he exclaim'd amain,
> Tongues, Science, Logick, Rhetorick, all are vain,
> And wisdom much unfitting for a Preacher,
> Because the Spirit is the only Teacher.
> For Christ chose not the Rabines of the Jewes,
> No Doctors, Scribes or Pharisees did chuse,
> The poore unlearned simple Fisherman . . .[39]

The praise of workingmen as ministers linked itself easily to the radical message of social justice for all men: "God uses the common people and the multitude to proclaim that the Lord . . . reigneth." Gerrard Winstanley above all others preached that "the rich doth lock up the treasures of the earth. . . . The poor are those in

36. Figures based on indictment record reproduced in Burrage, *Dissenters, 1,* 146–48.

37. *Proposals in Behalfe of the Poor of this Nation,* quoted in W. Schenk, *The Concern for Social Justice in the Puritan Revolution* (London, Longmans, Green, 1948), p. 67.

38. *The Schismatick Stigmatized,* quoted in Haller, *Puritanism,* p. 263.

39. John Tayler, *A Swarme of Sectaries,* quoted in William York Tindall, *John Bunyan, Mechanick Preacher* (New York, Columbia University Press, 1934), pp. 72–73. Tindall writes more to bury Bunyan than to praise him: "the remains of John Bunyan were interred . . . in Tindall's Burying Ground, better known as Bunhill Fields" (ibid., p. 214).

whom the blessing lies, for they first receive the gospel." [40] The concern for social justice in England stemmed from the Middle Ages, from the sermons of Franciscan friars at the "market crosses," from the social protest in the poem of *Piers Plowman,* and from the "spontaneous doctrineless communism of the open-field village." [41] In early Tudor times had come the last great peasant revolts in England, giving rise to more poems and sermons in the *Piers Plowman* tradition. Landowners had enclosed the farmland and common meadow-land of their tenants, and often drove them out homeless. About 1548 Bishop Latimer and the "Commonwealthsmen" around him formed a Royal Commission in a vain effort to halt this, but the enclosures continued until 1846.

The Tudor tenants still protested bitterly in God's name:

> You thoughte that I would not requyre
> The blodde of all such at your hands,
> But be you sure, eternall fyre
> Is ready for eche hell fyrebrande.
> Both for the housynge and lande
> That you have taken from the pore,
> Ye shall in hell dwell evermore.[42]

Yet the theoretical doctrine that "Christen mens goodes should be comen unto everi mans nede" [43] was rarely preached. Of course, the orthodox puritan merchants and parsons thought of Christian life as doing one's duty within one's calling and as "contentation" with the social status God had given. But the most radical puritans seldom turned their "prophet motive" toward economic communism but rather toward mutual responsibility of rich and poor:

> Diggers & Dikers, Drudgers, Carters Swaines,
> Sheepheards, & Cowards, friend thee at thy neede,
> The poorest persons worke the richest gaines

40. Anon., *A Glimpse of Sion's Glory* (1641), and G. Winstanley, *The New Law of Righteousness,* both quoted in *The Works of Gerrard Winstanley,* ed. George H. Sabine (Ithaca, Cornell University Press, 1941), pp. 24, 181.

41. Richard H. Tawney, *The Agrarian Problem in the Sixteenth Century* (London, Longmans, Green, 1912), p. 338.

42. Robert Crowley, *Select Works,* quoted in Tawney, *Religion and Capitalism,* p. 151. On Crowley see White, pp. 110–16, 146–50.

43. Thomas Lever, *A Fruitfull Sermon Made in Poules Church,* quoted in White, p. 126.

> Thy Dropsie with Commodities to feede.
> Coblers & Carriers, Tinkers, Tanners, all
> Support thy state, else would thy fortresse fall.[44]

The single exception to this was the "Digger" movement of Gerrard Winstanley, a former Baptist tract-writer of Lancashire and London. In 1649 he led a handful of men in an attempt to set up a farm settlement on the common land at Kingston Hill and Cobham: "God . . . gave the earth to be a common treasurie to whole mankind"; [45] They were chased away by the local authorities. Some of his ideas have been claimed by modern Marxists as a foreshadowing of socialism, but his own motives, though hazy, were warmly and pantheistically religious:

> The gentrye are all round,—stand up now, stand up now . . .
> The gentrye are all round, on each side they are found,
> Theire wisdom's so profound, to cheat us of our ground . . .
> The clergy they come in—stand up now, stand up now . . .
> The clergy they come in, and say it is a sin
> That we should now begin, our freedom for to win.
> Stand up now, Diggers all.
> To conquer them by love, come in now, come in now . . .
> To conquer them by love, as it does you behove,
> For He is King above; no power is like to love;
> Glory here, Diggers all.[46]

The political expression of puritan radicalism was the Leveller movement. When the Saints were "mechanick" Baptists, the rule of the Saints was likely to have drastic results. William Walwyn, a very independent silk merchant of London, worked out the political implications of the ideas that all the Elect were equal before God and that God's love and free grace were offered to all men universally. The resulting tenets—workingmens' suffrage, annual parliaments, religious toleration, and the abolition of tithes and merchant monopolies—were made into a popular platform by John Lilburne. A London apprentice from Durham, Lilburne had

44. Arthur Warren, *The Poore Man's Passions,* quoted in White, p. 280.
45. Winstanley, *Watchword to the City of London,* quoted in *Works,* p. 332.
46. Quoted in George M. Trevelyan, *England under the Stuarts* (London, Methuen, 1904), pp. 282–83 n. The last verse is not given in the version in Winstanley, *Works,* pp. 663–64.

found his inner vocation fulfilled as a politician. He was able to identify his personal fight against authority with Christian liberty and the national struggle for the ancient rights of the freeborn Englishman. His skill in spreading his program throughout Cromwell's army led to the debates within the Army Council at Putney in 1647 between the Leveller representatives and the more conservative officers. Cromwell reimposed his own authority, but at the cost of a minor mutiny; Lilburne's manifesto, "The Agreement of the People," reached Parliament, though it died there.

Early Quakers, often accused of being Levellers, had no part in Lilburne's agitation. Both groups combined political and religious ideals: Lilburne too asserted "the incommunicable Prerogative of Jesus Christ alone to be King of his Saints, and Law-giver to his Church and people, and to reigne in the soules and consciences of his chosen ones." [47] Most Leveller leaders were ardent Baptists, and Lilburne himself became a Quaker after he concluded that the root of evil lay not in institutions but in men.

The second new emphasis in Cromwellian Puritanism (which was often combined with the emphasis on social equality) was upon the Holy Spirit. The orthodox puritans all believed that the Spirit pierced the heart with the message of God through scripture, and in this or other ways caused conversion itself. They looked for the Spirit's work in all events of their lives and especially in spiritual growth. The radical puritans pushed the link of conversion and the Spirit much further, stressing the emotional fruits of the Spirit in conscious experience. To the Elect, "the holy Ghost will not barely say it but perswadeth such that they are the children of God." [48]

In their urgency for a pure church made up of visible saints, these men naturally demanded a converted ministry. The uncommitted minister has always been a center of conflict in every struggle between a new religious awakening and a lukewarm church, especially in the American revivals and in Wesley's England. The "mechanick" preachers knew themselves converted and were on

47. John Lilburne, *A Copie of a Letter . . . to Mr. William Prinne,* quoted in Haller, *Liberty,* p. 260. Other Leveller leaders also later became Quakers: cf. *JFHS, 33* (1936), 70; and see below, Chap. 7.

48. Perkins, *Golden Chaine,* p. 210. For important comment on these problems see Geoffrey F. Nuttall, *The Holy Spirit in Puritan Faith and Experience* (Oxford, Basil Blackwell, 1946).

fire to preach. Without the Spirit, they said, the ministers would
not be able to preach the Word powerfully enough. "It warms the
hearts of none, it inflames the spirit of none, but leaves men still
frozen in their sins." [49] Generically, the worship of unrepressed
working-people seems to be more emotional than coldly sober
upper-class worship. Whenever respectability has closed too many
hearts, even wellborn and educated Christians may attach themselves to new church groups which seem to possess spiritual power.
Thus Oliver Cromwell, Sir Harry Vane, and many puritan pastors
or army chaplains turned to the separatist and Baptist groups. In
the same spirit William Penn and the Peningtons later joined
Quakerism.[50]

The radical puritans linked the Spirit with direct "leadings"—
that is, specific impulses to act or speak—just as did the Quakers.
The Spirit had been partly identified with reason by the gentle
Cambridge Platonists, with nature by Winstanley and Overton,
and with providence in history by Cromwell. Among radical puritans the Spirit was far more often seen as the cause of a sudden
insight or with the "opening" of a suddenly remembered Bible
verse, such as happened constantly to John Bunyan.

In separatist or Baptist worship, dependence upon the Spirit
required freedom from fixed forms, since it meant the "Sufficiencie
of the Spirits Teaching without Human Learning." In the "Primitive Churches, the ministers were not so tyed to any fourme of
prayers invented by men; but as the spirit moved them, so they
poured forth harty supplications to the Lord." [51] The basis of
Quaker worship was already laid in radical Puritanism. The Spirit
was also directly linked to social justice. The medieval Piers Plowman was mainly a symbol of Christ rather than of the proletarian.
The actual Tudor plowmen were more class-conscious, but they
too claimed "the secret motyon of the holy goost" as the source of

49. William Dell, *The Select Works* (London, 1773), p. 30. For similar reactions
among other groups see Tindall, *Bunyan,* and Edwin Scott Gaustad, *The Great
Awakening in New England* (New York, Harper, 1957).

50. The defection of the intellectuals occurs more fully and obviously in a
political or social revolution: cf. C. Crane Brinton, *The Anatomy of Revolution*
(New York, 1938).

51. John Penry, *Answer to 15 Slanderous Articles,* quoted in Burrage, *Dissenters,*
2, 76–77. Bunyan described his Bible "openings" in *Grace Abounding,* ed. Roger
Sharrock (Oxford, Clarendon Press, 1962), e.g. pp. 22–23, 25, 30, 36

their protests.[52] Gerrard Winstanley and even, on occasion, Lilburne felt the uplift or guidance of the Spirit in their campaigning.

The central work of the Spirit as viewed by both orthodox and radical puritans was to cause ethical change in the Elect. Historical events, even within the Bible, could be treated as allegorical symbols of the Pilgrim's inner progress or the battle for Man-Soul. The inwardness of combat between the Spirit and evil was used by both puritans and Quakers to argue against physical coercion in religion. But the Spirit was no part of man's own spirit; "natural" men would by human depravity inevitably oppose the Spirit. The spiritual man must suffer. Like the early Friends, however, these radical puritans thought of the "World," the mass of unredeemed humanity, not as a hopeless mass of evil but as an active enemy which the Spirit must conquer: "the whole world in general is offended at Christ." [53]

Among the radical puritans a major group can be called "spiritual puritans," because of their total dependence upon the Spirit in worship and conduct. Direct followers of the mystics and spiritual reformers of Germany and Holland were few. Many men were called Behmenists or Familists because their ideas were like those of Jakob Boehme or Henry Niclaes, though they had not studied the teachings of either. A few knew manuscripts which had circulated quietly among friends. John Everard and one or two others knew European mysticism well, though they were also active puritans.[54] But Cromwell's chaplains included many who stressed the Spirit as a practical guide. John Saltmarsh, William Dell, Peter Sterry, and Walter Cradock attacked all worship that came from human gifts and warned against having "the form of godliness, when men are godly without God . . . Without this power of the Holy Spirit . . . the least touch of evil causes them to pull in their horns." [55] William Dell and John Owen preached constantly

52. *A Godly Dyalogue . . . betwene Pyers Plowman and a Popysh Preest*, quoted in White, p. 33.

53. Dell, *Select Works*, p. 333. Cf. Winstanley, *Works*, pp. 112–13, 334.

54. See Theodor Sippell, *Werdendes Quäkertum* (Stuttgart, 1937), a careful study with many original documents that serves to correct overemphasis in Rufus Jones, *Spiritual Reformers in the Sixteenth and Seventeenth Centuries* (London, 1914). See also Stephen Hobhouse, "Jacob Boehme's Influence in England," *JFHS*, 33 (1936), 52–54.

55. Dell, *Select Works*, pp. 4, 33.

on "The trial of Spirits," "Christ's Spirit the Christian's Strength," "The truly Christian and Spiritual Church," and similar topics. Both men were university graduates who rejected the necessity of scholarly training as preparation for the ministry and were appointed by Cromwell to be, respectively, Master of Caius College and Chancellor of Oxford. Hugh Peters returned from a pastorate at Salem, Massachusetts, to be a chaplain in the New Model army and Cromwell's agent to Parliament. In 1660 he lost his life for his part in the trial of Charles I. Francis Rous and Sir Harry Vane at various times led Parliament in their own right. Vane had been governor in Boston—a brilliant, sensitive, unstable man who tried to take over Cromwell's role after his death.

The writings of all these men spread widely, were especially popular in the army, and must have been thoroughly discussed in every town, as the regiments marched about the country and books reached outlying churches and prayer groups. Some little sects arose which especially emphasized the direct guidance or inspiration of the Spirit. These were noted with horror by orthodox puritans: Etheringtonians, Grindletonians, Muggletonians, Manifestarians, and the followers of Mrs. Hutchinson and Mrs. Attaway, as well as the Diggers, the Ranters, the Seekers, and the Quakers. Many of these sects had ideas much like the Friends, and several have been suggested by people of their own time and by modern historians as the root from which Quakerism sprang.[56] But the climate of ideas of spiritual Puritanism was too pervasive to allow us to trace such simple links. The same ideas were everywhere. The Friends themselves, of course, were slow to admit such forefathers: newness of experience hid the familiarity of the phrases they used and made each finder a new prophet. Hundreds besides the Quakers felt at this time that they had discovered spiritual religion for themselves; but thousands came into the Quaker movement with their ideas already largely shaped by spiritual puritan books and preachers.

56. See Richard Baxter, *The Quakers Catechism* (London, 1655); Thomas Underhill, *Hell Broke Loose, or an History of the Quakers* (London, 1660); Richard Blome, *The Fanatick History* (London, 1660). In recent years, Rufus Jones has linked Friends to the Familists and mystics, and Winthrop Hudson has ascribed to them the possible influence of Winstanley. Nuttall has shown connections between early Quakers and Roger Brerely's "Grindletonians": see appendix to Nuttall, *The Holy Spirit*.

Puritan leaders such as Cromwell accepted kinship with all these groups. They were dubious about the wilder sects, rejected the claims of any to uniqueness, and entirely disowned the Ranters' antinomian indifference to right and wrong. But they protected all groups in their freedom except where political issues forced restraint of Catholics and prelatists. They even welcomed the mushrooming of little churches as one further sign of the power of God at work:

> Where Christ sends the ministration of the Spirit there many young people are brought into Christ, as being most free from the forms of the former age, and from the doctrines and traditions of men . . . whereas many old professors, who are wholly in the form, prove the greatest enemies of the power of godliness . . . Now this great and sudden increase of the faithful is that which doth so exceedingly trouble the world.[57]

The puritan movement, despite its setbacks and divisions, remained a great wave of idealism, which the war had intensified. The overthrow of evil rulers, the outpouring of the Spirit, the conversion of new men, and the setting up of new churches were for all radical puritans divine signs pointing toward a climax.

The Commonwealth, being the fruit of Cromwell's victories, was a period of both political and religious hope. Some 30,000 tracts were published, most with religious overtones and immediate demands. In all puritan groups there was a strong apocalyptic hope: the fulfillment of biblical prophecies made men turn to the books of Daniel and Revelation. It had been easy to identify the king and popery with Antichrist. Accordingly, the puritans' victory was seen as the final one, when Christ's own kingdom would be set up: "Christ is the only right Heir of the Crown of England . . . and he is now come to take possession of his Kingdom, making England first in that blessed work of setting up the Kingdom of the Lord Jesus." [58] So wrote the sober John Eliot, missionary to the Indians in Massachusetts. Hopes for the reign of Christ, whether inward or outward, were widespread enough to prevent Cromwell himself from taking the throne.

These intense hopes strengthened Cromwell's government in its

57. Dell, *Select Works,* p. 75.
58. John Eliot, quoted in Whitley, *British Baptists,* p. 84.

reforms. But the political realities were confusing as he faced them at the height of his power in 1653. There was, in fact, no party or policy backed by a clear majority in the nation. The defeated Anglicans and Royalists had tried in vain to force the whole country into their own pattern. The Presbyterians had meant to do the same; so, for that matter, had the few English Catholics. But the Independents and Baptists were also a minority in wanting toleration. Cromwell thus found that despite their high ideals, neither the old Presbyterian Long Parliament nor the new Parliament of Saints in 1653 could hope for majority support. His mediating policy of religious toleration had to be maintained by his own authority and by force, not only in Scotland but even in England. He did his best to respect both orthodox and separatist puritans and to protect them from each other, but he satisfied neither. He found himself protecting the freedom and progress achieved to date, no longer building Christ's kingdom but defending the new status quo.

Many radical puritans were still impatient to push on and hoped for the renewal of the program of the Parliament of Saints. The "Fifth Monarchy Men" (viewing their time as the fifth and final era foretold in Daniel 7) were mostly Baptists and army officers, sober and peaceful in their methods. But a few became violent: "A glorious Evangelical inquisition shall be set up in due time, and the ministers of the Gospel shall be Gospel-inquisitors." The ungodly must be rooted out: "The Saints sitting in Counsel shall bring those Beasts to a judiciall Triall." [59] Cromwell loved no inquisitors, Spanish or English. The radicals felt that Cromwell had betrayed the revolution and plotted new revolts, and he had to imprison their leaders in 1654 and 1657. He kept his army busy in Ireland and the West Indies, restored the old pattern for electing Parliaments, and tried to legitimize his government. The great drive toward the remaking of England petered out.

As both Parliament and army failed, the eagerness and joy faded from "the good old cause." Victories over satanic rulers were replaced by constabulary duties; the idealists' lot was not a happy one. Men who left the army wandered across England looking for work and religious certainty. Many ex-soldiers turned from outward to inward reform and joined purely religious groups—Bap-

59. Christopher Feake, *The Oppressed Close Prisoner,* and William Aspinwall, *An Explication of Daniel 7,* both quoted in Tindall, *Bunyan,* p. 160.

tist, Congregational, or sectarian. Many more new congregations arose after 1653 than before. Cromwell's loosely organized network of puritan parish churches in places made use of the classis or presbytery system, supposedly set up in each county by the Westminster Assembly. But variety of doctrine and worship was encouraged even within these tithe-supported pulpits, and freedom to gather was also given to Baptist and separatist congregations. As yet there was nothing in any way similar to the later organization of denominations. Baptist churches tried to keep in touch with one another by informal assemblies and general messengers. Some congregations separated further into factions and were shattered. The smaller sectarian groups were usually followers of a single inspired leader.

Many men were spiritual orphans, going "from one forme of religion unto another . . . wandering up and downe among the drie hils and mountaines." [60] Some were simply restless spirits, like the "nomad" of whom Presbyterian Richard Vines made fun, because he would not "endure to sit at the feet of a constant godly ministry," but "wanders away the Sabbath by peeping in at Church-doors, and taking essay of a sentence or two, and then, if there be no scratch for his itch, *lambit et fugit,* he is gone." [61] Others were men like Fox, who were basically at odds with all the churches they knew. Some called themselves "Seekers."

The Seeker group has been credited in Quaker histories as the seedbed of Quakerism. The name is misleading: the Seekers were not a sect and had no distinct literature. Strictly speaking, the name "Seeker" belonged to those Separatists who denied the existence of any true ministry, church, or sacraments, hence "whose Custom was when met Together, neither To preach nor pray vocally, butt to Read the Scriptures & Discourse of Religion, Expecting a farther Manifestation" [62] of God's will for true worship. Some were already using the ways of worship that Quakers made permanent and "sat down sometimes in silence, and as any found a Concern upon their Spirits . . . they Kneeled down, and sought the Lord; so that

60. Edmond Jessop, quoted in Burrage, *Dissenters, 1,* 266.

61. Richard Vines, *Impostures of Seducing Teachers Discovered,* quoted in Haller, *Liberty,* pp. 165–66.

62. *First Publishers of Truth,* ed. Norman Penney (London, Headley Brothers, 1907), p. 18; cf. pp. 54–55. See Bibliographical Note for details on this collection of early Quaker historical reports.

sometimes, before the day ended, there might be Twenty of us might pray, Men and Women and sometimes Children." [63] Evidently these Seekers ranged from convinced and powerful "spiritual puritans" to men like Isaac Penington, who were in weariness and darkness of spirit until they became Quakers. Socially, spiritually, and geographically, all the separatist groups tended to be on the fringes of the great puritan movement. Early Quakerism arose in this setting and only gradually came to develop a character of its own.

63. Christopher Marshall, *Sion's Travellers Comforted,* quoted in Nuttall, *Holy Spirit,* p. 68.

2

"The Lamb's War": The Quaker Awakening

A chronological framework, here, of the rise and spread of Quakerism will give more meaning to succeeding topical chapters, which interpret outlooks and experiences characteristic of the movement. The reader already familar with the events of early Quakerism may prefer to turn to the later chapters at once.[1]

That George Fox's *Journal* is almost the only source for the obscure beginnings of the Quaker movement gives greater prominence his work and personality than even his leadership warrants. He was brought up in the English Midlands by a father who was a weaver and a mother "good, honest, virtuous, and right-natured," and evidently a firm puritan. Fox records his father's nickname of "Righteous Christer"; and he tells of an occasion, as George was debating against their own parish "priest" (a strong puritan well trained in the Bible), when his "father in the flesh thwacked his cane on the ground and said: 'Well . . . I see that he that will but stand to the truth, it will carry him out,'—though he was a hearer and follower of the priests." [2] George Fox retained all his life an intense awareness of being judged, which may have been cultivated in him by either or both of his parents. He seems to have developed acute inner tensions over obedience, love, and rebellion. These probably underlay his later attitudes toward all

---

1. For more detailed narrative the reader is referred to the Rowntree Series histories by W. C. Braithwaite and R. M. Jones.

2. *The Journal of George Fox,* ed. John L. Nickalls (Cambridge, Cambridge University Press, 1952), p. 190.

authorities, his indifference to marriage, and his terse but intense description of leaving home in Leicestershire at the age of nineteen in darkness of spirit. His rebellious restraint in meeting fellow townsfolk on later visits home—"afraid if I did not go, they would say I was disobedient to my parents"—is curious.[3] He seems always to have avoided situations where he would be dependent or morally humbled. Some years afterward, he refused his family's offer to bail him out of prison at Derby. Fox again went through three months of darkness similar to this period in his youth when in 1659 he faced a difficult decision in which both paths meant inescapable guilt.

On first leaving home, he supported himself as an apprentice cobbler and shepherd, and stayed some months with a Baptist uncle in London, visited other puritan towns, but "was fearful and returned home." He talked with any pastor in the area "who was accounted an experienced man," and "reasoned with him about the ground of despair and temptation," [4] but he rejected as too shallow all counsel he was offered.

Fox's terrible anxiousness and separatism were, however, united with a basic integrity both in self-support and in speaking truly; with awe and openness of spirit he gave himself totally to what he felt to be God's will. He began to have experiences in which he found truth or comfort from within himself. These affirmed the inadequacy of university-taught ministers and of ordinary Christian "professors" who professed conversion:

> I was afraid of all company, for I saw them perfectly where they were, through the love of God which let me see myself. I had not fellowship with any people, priests, or professors, nor any sort of separated people, but with Christ, who hath the key . . . And I was afraid of all carnal talk and talkers . . . lest, being a tender young man, I should be hurt . . . Yet I was under great temptations sometimes, and my inward sufferings were heavy. . . . The natures of dogs, swine, vipers, of Sodom and Egypt . . . these I saw within. . . . And I cried to the Lord, saying "Why should I be thus, seeing I was never addicted to commit those evils?" And the Lord answered

3. Ibid., p. 189, cf. pp. 3, 4, 50, 60; also Anton T. Boisen, *Religion in Crisis and Custom* (New York, 1955).

4. *Journal*, Nickalls, pp. 4, 5, 6.

that it was needful I should have a sense of all conditions, how else should I speak to all conditions. . . . I saw also that there was an ocean of darkness and death, but an infinite ocean of light and love, which flowed over the ocean of darkness. And in that also I saw the infinite love of God; and I had great openings.[5]

Fox was able to identify as divine the power he increasingly felt at work within him: "I found that there were two thirsts in me, the one after the creatures, to have gotten help and strength there, and the other after the Lord the creator. . . . The Lord did stay my desires on himself." The inner guide and power were the Light and Spirit of Christ, for "there is one, even Jesus Christ, that can speak to thy condition." [6] To other men Fox sometimes seemed un-gracious and infuriatingly self-righteous, but his identification with the spirit of God involved obedience and self-giving. Fiery emotions and imagination dominated his life; yet his sensitivity usually let him respond intensely but appropriately to the real situation of men and events, and it was for this that his friends loved him. His genius for self-dramatization was focused on the work of God rather than on his human individuality. In this way he was like Bunyan, Milton, Lilburne, and Winstanley, the great puritan dramatists. But Fox, in his responsiveness to the direct guidance and power of God in the actual world, outreached them all. On a few occasions his mystical experience seems to have been more intense: "Now was I come up in spirit through the flaming sword into the paradise of God. All things were new, and all the creation gave another smell unto me than before, beyond what words can utter." [7] Even at these times, however, he lived awake to the moment and "in unity with the creation," not withdrawn into union with God's infinity.

Fox's growing discovery of strength from within came about four years after he first left home in 1643. By this time he was set-tled at Mansfield in Nottinghamshire,[8] probably working as a

5. Ibid., pp. 10, 12, 19. This narrative should be a key passage for study of the psychology of separatism.

6. Ibid., pp. 11, 12.

7. Ibid., p. 27. Cf. Arthur O. Roberts, *Through Flaming Sword* (Portland, Ore., 1959), p. 20.

8. See maps below, pp. 42–43.

cobbler but spending much time with little groups of Baptists and separatists throughout the Midlands. He found them kindred spirits and perhaps learned from them more than he records. He casually uses the name "Friends" for some of these groups in and around Nottingham, in Clawson, Leicestershire, and in Eaton, Derbyshire, where already by 1646–48 "meetings of Friends . . . were gathered to God's teaching." He said explicitly that it was in these groups that "the Truth sprang up first to us so as to be a people to the Lord," [9] and evidently there had already broken out among them group experiences of trembling, contrition, and rapture, which he called the "breaking forth of the power of God." It was these which gave rise to the nickname "Quaker," as Fisher and Barclay later readily admitted, though Fox did so more reluctantly. In Quaker Meetings, Barclay wrote, "there will be such a painfull travel found in the soul, that it will even work upon the outward man, so that . . . the body will be greatly shaken, and many groans sighs and tears. . . . Sometimes the Power of God will break forth into a whole meeting, . . . and thereby trembling . . . will be upon most . . . which as the power of truth prevailes, will from pangs and groans end with the sweet sound of thanksgiving and praise." [10] Apparently such emotional outbursts first appeared among the separatists of Mansfield and Nottinghamshire when Fox himself came back to speak at great meetings there. He may also have introduced there the custom of going into parish "steeplehouses" to challenge the divine calling of the paid min-

9. Fox, *Journal*, Nickalls, pp. 27, 709. Cf. pp. 22, 26, 28. Fox's summary of Quaker origins, quoted from a fragment of manuscript (ibid., p. 709), makes tantalizing references to many events before 1650 about which it seems impossible to recover a clear picture: "The Truth sprang up first to us so as to be a people of the Lord, in Leicestershire in 1644, in Warwickshire in 1645, in Nottinghamshire in 1646, in Derbyshire in 1647, and in the adjacent counties in 1648, 1649, and 1650; and in Yorkshire in 1651, and in Lancashire and Westmorland in 1652, and in Cumberland, Bishoprick and Northumberland in 1653, in London and most parts of the nation and Scotland and Ireland in 1654."

10. Robert Barclay, *An Apology for the True Christian Divinity as . . . Held Forth by the . . . Quakers* (London, 1678), Proposition 11, §8; the sections and texts, though not the pagination, of all the subsequent editions of this theological classic are the same. Cf. Samuel Fisher, *The Testimony of Truth Exalted . . . in the Works . . .* (London, 1679), pp. 16, 211; James Nailor [sic], *An Answer to . . . the Quaker's Catechism by Richard Baxter* (London, 1655); "Thomas Camm's Testimony," in John Camm and John Audland, *Works, The Memory of the Righteous Revived* (London, 1689).

isters; he and others had certainly done this in Leicester and Derbyshire.

Fox was by now traveling widely and taking each new step in
response to what he felt were inward directions from God, yet he
seems at this stage simply one among many active spirits in a kind
of unorganized revival movement spreading through the separatist
groups in the Midlands. He reported a time of wider commission,
about 1648, when the Lord commanded him to "go abroad into the
world." The immediate result, however, seems merely to have
been one more trip down into Leicestershire and back, interrupted
by two long imprisonments at Nottingham and Derby which ended
late in 1651. In the latter case at least, his original arrest for chal-
lenging a minister was overlaid with charges of blasphemy arising
from his claims to the indwelling of Christ.[11] The magistrates' ex-
asperation over his debates with visitors in prison, letters of prophetic warning to all and sundry in Derby, and his intense preaching in the markets and streets, when he was allowed times of liberty, probably prolonged his sentence. We hear of few new Friends
whom Fox himself "convinced" during these years, except for a
small group around Elizabeth Hooton near Mansfield. In general,
though Fox and other colleagues revisited the Midland areas pe-
riodically, little is known of these Friends and Meetings in Nottinghamshire, Derbyshire, and Leicestershire in the following decades.
Some of the Friends, like Rice Jones of Nottingham, evidently rejected Fox, but their own groups often fell apart.

In the winter of 1651 Fox left Derby and visited, perhaps as a
result of previous contacts, two groups of separatists in southern
Yorkshire. They already shared ideas much like his own and similar
inner experiences. These became Fox's key allies, whose leaders
were his fellow preachers and co-workers in journeys from then on.
The letters of most early Friends to Fox were written in the tone of
a son to a beloved father, but these Yorkshire leaders usually addressed him as a brother. In the villages of Warmsworth, Balby, and
Tickhill, near Doncaster, Fox met and won the friendship of four
men especially: Richard Farnworth, the most tireless traveler and
organizer of Quaker preachers in the north; Thomas Aldam,

11. Fox, *Journal*, Nickalls, pp. 25–26, 33, 51–52. On the problem raised by the
claim of indwelling by Christ, see below, Chap. 5.

briefly a leader equal to Fox until he was shut up, for two and a half of the movement's most crucial years, in York Castle dungeon; and Aldam's brothers-in-law, the Killams. Near Wakefield some miles northwestward, Fox found Thomas Goodaire and the two most effective preachers after Fox himself, William Dewsbury and James Nayler. Most of these men were yeomen about thirty years old, and had already been through years of Cromwellian wars and spiritual development before Fox came. Nayler's sensitive spirit made him the best writer on theology among early Friends. Dewsbury, less sophisticated, was likewise regarded with a love and respect almost equal to that given Fox. As a preacher, "his Testimony was Peirceing: many faces did gather Paleness, and the Stout hearted were made to Bow." Fox seems to have gained Dewsbury as a fellow preacher during a moonlight walk after a home prayer meeting. Many seemed to have remembered such personal talks with him as high moments. Four years after this,

> G:F: went from Worcester, & with him went Edw: Bourne part of the way towards Tewxbury, to whom G:F: speake of many Heavenly things in discourse, wch were delightfull & pleasant to E:B: . . . and after Edward Bourne and G:F: parted, G:F: Reigned his Horse about to speake to him, & put of[f] His Hatt, saying "The Lord Jesus Christ goe along wth thee", by wch E:B: was greatly Comforted & refreshed . . . & went away rejoiceing.[12]

Even the mature and sober farmer Francis Howgill was to use words to Fox he would hardly have used to his own father: "Glory for evermor, I am melted, I amelted with thy love It is not lawfull to uter, pray for me thy deare son." [13] It was natural for all members to share excited language in the first days as they went out together to proclaim the Day of the Lord. As is often true with religious movements, the leader stirred up such emotions and words in less-balanced followers that he himself was troubled. Barbara Blaugdone wrote: "have seene i haue seene i haue seene thy beautie

---

12. *FPT*, pp. 276, 294. Throughout the *FPT* and Swarth., the Quaker leaders are usually indicated by initials.

13. A. R. Barclay Collection of early Quaker letters, No. 117.

and tasted a little of thy power praisis glory eternal prayses be to our god and our King for ever more I should have come to thee long since When thou bid me come i shall." [14] Fox did not summon her; she remained in Bristol, and later went on a mission to Ireland.

More will be said in later chapters about the ideas or message of Quakerism. The meaning of the Friends' doctrines was rooted in the experience they had been through, and this must be understood first. Fox presents a useful summary of his main teachings early in his *Journal:*

> Now, when the Lord God and his son, Jesus Christ, did send me forth into the world, to preach his everlasting gospel and kingdom, I was . . . commanded to turn people to that inward light, spirit and grace . . . even that divine Spirit which would lead them into all Truth. . . . I was to bring people off from all their own ways to Christ . . . and from their churches, which men had made and gathered, to the Church in God . . . And I was to bring people off . . . from men's inventions . . . with their schools and colleges for making ministers of Christ . . . and from all their images and crosses, and sprinkling of infants, with all their holy days (so called). . . . I was moved to declare against them all.
>
> Moreover, when the Lord sent me forth into the world, he forbade me to put off my hat to any, high or low; and I was required to "thee" and "thou" all men and women, without any respect to rich or poor, great or small. And as I travelled up and down, I was not to bid people "good morrow" or "good evening". . . . About this time, I was . . . exercised in going to their courts to cry for justice, and in speaking and writing to judges and justices . . . and in testifying against their wakes or feasts, their May-games, sports, plays and shows. . . . In fairs also, and in markets, I was made to declare against their cheating and cozening, warning all to deal justly, to speak the truth, to let their "yea" be "yea" and their "nay" be "nay"

14. Swarth. 1/155 (undatable). On styles of address to Fox, contrast ARBarc./117 from Howgill with the much less deferential ARBarc./122 from Aldam. Aldam's early leadership even from prison shows what he might have achieved if given freedom. Whitehead wrote ARBarc./129 to Fox or Aldam.

. . . and forewarning all of the great and terrible day of the Lord which would come upon them all.[15]

This digest of teachings, however, does not carry the impact of early Quaker preaching. Fox and his friends felt there was a stark contrast between the world's ways and the way of Christ, but they called men to share in a world struggle and not to withdraw. They named their campaign "the Lamb's War": "The Lamb . . . hath called us to make War in righteousnes for his name's sake, against Hell and death, and all the powers of darkness. . . . And they that follow the Lamb shall overcome, and get the victory over the beast, and over the Dragon, and over the gates of Hell." [16] The Lamb in the Book of Revelation is the conquering Christ who destroys the Antichrist, Rome, and Satan and sets up his world dominion for the millennium. The sweep of the Quaker mission through Europe caught up the symbolism of the Saints in Cromwell's armies as they swept the Royalists from England. Friends also expected direct political and social results from the world conquest of the Spirit, but the confidence of victory was not based or bounded in specific blueprints: "Put on your Armour, and gird on your Sword . . . and prepare your selves to battel, for the Nations doth defie our God. . . . Arise, arise, and sound forth the everlasting word of war and judgment in the ears of all Nations. . . . Wound the Lofty, and tread under foot the Honourable of the earth . . . And the Lamb shall get the victory." [17]

The Lamb's War, however, was in essence not an outward struggle but an inward one. Its main weapon was the preaching of repentance and the Light of Christ within men. The most direct effects of such preaching were inward battles against pride and self-will:

> *The Lamb's War* YOU must know, before you can witness his kingdom. . . . The *Lamb wars* . . . in whomsoever he ap-

15. Fox, *Journal*, Nickalls, pp. 34–38. This passage is in Ellwood's edition (London, 1694) but not in the Spence or Short Journal manuscripts. Whether this summary of Quaker teaching is by Ellwood, Penn, or Fox himself, it reflects the sober retrospect of the years after persecution.

16. Edward Burrough, in his Epistle to the Reader, introducing George Fox, *The Great Mistery of the Great Whore Unfolded* . . . (London, 1659).

17. Edward Burrough and Francis Howgill, *To the Camp of the Lord in England* (London, 1655), p. 9. Cf. Edward Burrough, *The Memorable Works of a Son of Thunder and Consolation* . . . (London, 1672), p. 67.

pears, and calls them to joyn with him herein . . . with all their Might . . . that he may form a new Man, a new Heart, new Thoughts, and a new Obedience . . . and *there is his Kingdom*. . . . Do you deny your selves of your pleasures, profits, ease and liberty, that you may hold forth a chaste . . . life of gentleness, faithfulness and truth. . . . Is this your War, and these your Weapons? [18]

The preachers had themselves been through the same struggle and judgment to which they called others, and had afterward found the sweetness of face and spirit and the strength in outward hardship for which Friends were later known. The struggle itself was their greatest bond in their first work.

Fox and his co-workers turned in the winter of 1651 toward the North of England, the crucial region of early Quakerism. As a striking contrast, Puritanism was least strong in this region. Yorkshire, northern Lancashire, Westmorland, and Cumberland became the areas where Quakerism was strongest. With Durham, Cheshire, and Northumberland, these seven northern counties held only one-seventh of the population of Cromwellian England. Yet from them came 160 of the 250 most active Friends during the 1650s, and at least 90 of the 192 Quaker leaders of the whole first generation.[19] By contrast, one representative list of 149 leading Presbyterian and Independent ministers during the century before 1650 includes only 24 who held pastorates in the North, and 18 were within the puritan stronghold of southern Lancashire. Puritan pastors who did preach in the North concentrated around the commercial towns of Liverpool, Manchester, Sheffield, Leeds, and Hull.[20] These areas, with the sharp exception of some villages

18. James Nayler, *Works, A Collection of Sundry Books, Epistles and Papers* . . . (London, 1716), pp. 385, 391–92, from "The Lamb's War."

19. The first figure represents Friends active in 1652–60 whose names were encountered in the A. R. Barclay and Swarthmore MSS. The second list, of Quaker leaders only, is more representative of wider periods and areas; it was drawn up for my dissertation, "Early Quaker Outlooks," and may be found in detail there. A brief digest of both these lists and of the puritan leaders by areas will be found below, p. 257. See also Tawney, *Religion*, pp. 202–03.

20. For detailed data on puritans in Yorkshire (summarized in Map 2, p. 43, though not in the Table, p. 257) see John A. Newton, "Puritanism in the Diocese of York" (University of London, 1955). For Westmorland and Cumberland see C. M. Lowther Bouch, *Prelates and People of the Lake Counties* (Kendal, England, Titus Wilson, 1948). For Lancashire see Robert Halley, *Lancashire: Its Puritanism*

around Doncaster and Wakefield, produced few Quakers. The areas
which the Civil War demonstrated to be the real heartland of Puritanism were even more cold to Quaker preachers: Norfolk, Suffolk,
Essex, Cambridge, and, except for London, the rest of the South-
east. The firmly organized Baptist congregations were located in
the same southern areas. Fox himself, despite his boyhood connections with the Baptists, describes only five contacts among them
in the northern counties, as against eight in the Midlands and over
a dozen in the London area after he returned to preach there. The
Baptists were also strong, of course, in Cromwell's garrisons in
Ireland and Scotland. The Independents centered in the south as
well. Of 171 Congregational ministers disestablished in 1662, fifty
were in the counties of Norfolk and Suffolk, in London, or in
Gloucestershire and Bristol.[21] These were, in Fox's time, the places
where churches were vital, where prayer, Bible study, and sermons
were life-and-death issues.

Though Quakerism was strongest in the North and Puritanism
of all degrees flourished in the South, London and Bristol became
Quaker as well as puritan strongholds; it will be shown that local
Quaker groups often began from informal separatist groups on the
fringes of strong puritan areas. Yet clearly Quakerism was not a
mere reaction against Puritanism but much more a movement into
untouched territory. In the North the frontier character made this
an "awakening" among the unchurched not unlike the Great
Awakening under Jonathan Edwards or the Kentucky camp meetings of the American Second Awakening. The similarity of early
Quakerism in the North to John Wesley's mission among the English factory workers and miners has been noted.[22]

and *Nonconformity* (Manchester, 1872); B. Nightingale, *Early Stages of the Quaker
Movement in Lancashire* (London, 1921); and *The Victoria History of the County
of Lancaster*, ed. W. Farrar and J. Broomhall (7 vols. London, 1906–12). For Durham see Geoffrey F. Nuttall, "George Fox and the Rise of Quakerism in the
Bishoprick," *Durham University Journal*, *36* (1944), 94–97.

21. On Independent ministers see Geoffrey F. Nuttall, *Visible Saints: The Con
gregational Way, 1640–1660* (Oxford, Basil Blackwell, 1957), p. 23. There were
nevertheless eight Independents in Cumberland. On Quaker-Baptist contacts see
index of Fox, *Journal*, Nickalls, and indexes in *Early Quaker Letters*, ed. Geoffrey
F. Nuttall (London, Library of Friends House, 1952), pp. 408–09. There it is shown
that Friends met Baptists mainly away from the Quaker centers, in southern England (33 times), in Northumberland (3 times), in the Irish (6) and Scottish (3)
garrisons, and 5 times in the Midlands.

22. Henry Hodgkin's comment in *FPT*, p. xiv, was picked up by Frederick B.
Tolles in "Quietism vs. Enthusiasm: the Philadelphia Quakers and the Great

ENGLAND IN 1660
WITH PARTS OF SCOTLAND
AND IRELAND

Centers of Puritan
Strength – 1600-60
in CAPITALS

Centers of Quaker
Strength – 1650-60
underlined

Aberdeen

Dundee
Perth

Dunbar

Glasgow
Edinburgh
Berwick

LONDONDERRY

Newcastle

BELFAST
Lurgan

Carlisle
Durham

Pardshaw

Cavan

Isle of
Man

Kendal
Sedbergh
Richmond

Ulverston
(Swarthmoor
Hall)

Malton

Drogheda

Settle
YORK

Skipton

Preston
Wakefield
HULL

DUBLIN

BOLTON
MANCHESTER
Doncaster
(Balby)

LIVERPOOL
WARRINGTON
SHEFFIELD
Lincoln

Chester
Mansfield

WREXHAM
Derby
BOSTON

Swannington
Nottingham

terford
Wexford

Shrewsbury
Litchfield

LYNN

Leicester
(Birmingham)
PETERBOROUGH
NORWICH

HUNTINGDON
ELY

KIDDERMINSTER
NORTHAMPTON
CAMBRIDGE
IPSWICH

Worcester
BEDFORD

Ross
Evesham
COLCHESTER

GLOUCESTER
HERTFORD

Oxford
CHELMSFORD

Pembroke
Cardiff
Nailsworth
ST. ALBANS

LONDON

BRISTOL
ROCHESTER
CHATHAM

READING
KINGSTON
Canterbury

Winchester
DOVER

EXETER
Bridport
Poole

Launceston
St. Austell
Plymouth

Land's End

0   50   100 MILES

Figure 1

Figure 2

The North of England is roughly oval and is subdivided by the T-shaped hills of the Pennine chain into four main regions. The lowland of Yorkshire in the east is mostly rich farm and pasture land. Royalist nobles and gentry clustered there, but seaports and weaving or metal-working centers like Leeds and Sheffield had produced wealthy merchants. In these towns Puritanism took hold and separatists flourished in some nearby villages. The northeast corner of this lowland, however, was a poor and isolated area of chalk and moorland called Cleveland and Holderness, between the rich lands and the sea. The Lancashire Lowlands west of the ridge were like those around York: the gentry were bitterly royalist, and some were famous papists. But in southeastern Lancashire around Manchester a cluster of puritan weaving-towns had sprung up. The Tyne valley, which also shipped coal from Newcastle, separates a third region, the Scottish Border, from the rest of the North. Here the old Roman wall ran from Newcastle to Carlisle, both still fortress towns in early Quaker times. Northumberland north of the Tyne was moorland, famous for its fierce raiders, and for centuries a law unto itself. The fourth section is the center of the North Country, a T-shaped hill area; it also is moorland, crags, and sheep pasture, with deep valleys or dales and men proud of their individuality. The central Pennine ridge itself runs north from "the Peak" in Derbyshire, and mostly lies in western Yorkshire. In the northeast the hills slope down to the sea past Durham, whose bishops still ruled as medieval princes the county which Fox knew as "Bishoprick." Westward, in Cumberland and Westmorland, the moors slope up from the Pennines to the steep fells of the Lake District, the highest hills in England. All this central upland became important for early Quakerism.

The first area of mission was northeastern Yorkshire. Fox himself, in the early weeks of 1652, traveled up and down through the area beyond York, preaching repentance and the Day of the Lord. In the peninsula of Holderness he was made welcome by individual puritan pastors, squires, and home gatherings, though not without public stir and opposition. In the Cleveland moors around Malton and Staithes he was more warmly received by several separatist groups; in some villages pulpits were opened to him and church

Awakening," *Pennsylvania Magazine of History and Biography* (1945), pp. 27–49, in contrasting the similarity of origins with the hostility between eighteenth–century Quakers and emotional revivalists.

bells announced his coming. This area had "tasted of the power of God" in some previous revival that burned itself out into the moral indifference of the Ranters, and that may have consisted of sheer emotionalism. Fox circled northward, "turned to Malton again, and very great meetings were there." He does not give dates for this visit, but thereafter the movement of repentance was evidently kept alive by Roger Hebden and other local separatist leaders. Perhaps as early as July, Richard Farnworth came back from working with Fox in western Yorkshire to preach at Malton. In the same summer of 1652 Aldam reported that Jane Holmes was there with them, and "the Power" broke out as she preached. She took part in a dramatic episode in this "mighty work" when "some shopekeepers was caused to burne a great deal of riboning of silkes and braveries and such things." The meetings and excitement continued throughout the year, supported by a preaching tour of William Dewsbury in October and a further visit by Farnworth and Dewsbury about Christmas, when nearly two hundred Friends met for many nights. At Staithes, "towards the seaside, the worke of the Lord and his poures doth mightyly breake forth," [23] and the whole region responded. Less is heard of such mass gatherings in later years, but solid little Quaker groups were drawn together throughout the area.

The leaders had begun for themselves a life of almost continuous travel, preaching, and danger. In a campaign around Wakefield and Doncaster during the Malton revival, Fox was three times stoned and beaten up, mostly as a result of his preaching in steeple houses during services. Farnworth had faced stones that "flew as fast as bullets in a battle," and Aldam was arrested and imprisoned at York, where he remained in the Castle until 1655 despite several petitions to Cromwell; Mary Fisher and at least three other Yorkshire Friends joined him there in the next four months.[24] Fox and

23. See Swarth. *1*/373 *Early Quaker Letters*, No. 4), Thos. Aldam from York [July 1652]; *4*/229 (*EQL* 6), Richard Farnworth to Fox [Aug.–Sept. 1652]; *4*/83 (*EQL* 20), Farnworth to M. Fell (Jan. 7 [1652/53]). Cf. also *JFHS, 33* (1936), 28–31, on the revival at Malton.

24. Jane Holmes, arrested in August, became more and more unrestrained while imprisoned in York Castle. Marmaduke Lambert and Christopher Gilburne were put there more briefly in November. Besides Aldam, Roger Hebden, Benjamin Nicholson, and others were probably also already there in 1652 (See *FPT*, p. 319; ARBarc./15). Dorothy Benson gave birth there to a child in February 1653/54. Other women there were Elizabeth Hooton and Agnes Wilkinson. This York frustration may have driven Friends' expansion westward.

Farnworth headed northwestward, visiting some separatist groups, and late in May they continued up the dales from Halifax into the heart of the central hills. There Fox was moved to climb Pendle Hill: from the top he saw the sea to the west and "sounded the day of the Lord." On the summit, and again in the valley at an inn that night, he had visions of "a great people to be gathered" [25] by his preaching.

The immediate sequel was unfortunately the complete rejection of Fox by a congregation of Independents he visited in Dentdale, while Farnworth was returning across Yorkshire alone. Fox, however, was wholeheartedly accepted the next week end by a separatist group at Judge Gervase Benson's home in Sedbergh, which was part of a loose federation of kindred groups extending eastward down Swaledale and Wensleydale and westward to Preston Patrick and Yealand. He went on to speak at a fair that week at Sedbergh, to a gathering at Draw-Well Farm, at an open-air assembly on Firbank Fell, and to the Seekers' monthly meeting at Preston Patrick chapel. The cluster of separatist groups came over to follow Fox in a body, and from this event 1652 is often reckoned the birth year of Quakerism. The squires in whose homes the nearer congregations met, Justice Benson and Richard Robinson of Briggflatts, responded at once. So also did the farmers who led their worship, Francis Howgill, John Camm, and their younger colleague John Audland. Fox also later met and won Thomas Taylor, the man who had previously been pastor of the separatist gatherings and had already given up his parish ministry and its tithes. Most of the active members of these Seeker groups, including the women, became key Quaker leaders and preached throughout England.[26] In these groups Fox found little argument or opposition, and public meetings of a thousand people gathered to hear him.

Even here, however, the newcomers did not enter the Quaker life easily or instantly, for many who were intellectually convinced at once told afterward of months of inward struggle. Fox frequently returned to visit and guide these separatists through the summer

25. Fox, *Journal*, Nickalls, pp. 103–04. Cf. W. C. Braithwaite, *The Beginnings of Quakerism* (2d ed. Cambridge, Cambridge University Press, 1955), pp. 78–79.

26. Ann Audland and Mary Howgill as well as Ann Blaykling, Elizabeth Fletcher, Elizabeth Leavens (Holme), and Jane and Dorothy Waugh all later became preachers: see Swarth., passim; also Isabel Ross, *Margaret Fell, Mother of Quakerism* (London, 1949).

and autumn of 1652, and eventually the meetings were firmly established in a way of life based on silent worship and the inward Light.

Fox next journeyed to Kendal, Westmorland, the market town for the area and a weaving center. Here and in the village of Underbarrow beyond he held meetings which probably followed links already formed by his separatist friends. A series of household meetings continued in Kendal throughout the following year, on week nights as well as Sundays and often in three or four homes at one time, to the scandal of both puritan and cavalier neighbors. Some Quakers were swept away from sane behavior by emotionalism and became the target for later puritan tracts. But in the end the Quaker Meetings around Kendal became the central resource for later workers. The roster is impressive: Edward Burrough, a thundering young preacher and the best tract-writer among early Friends; sober George Taylor and Thomas Willan, who later administered the Quaker funds; Thomas Holme, eager and immature; Miles Halhead, Miles Bateman, and Miles and Stephen Hubbersty, who covered great distances as Quaker militants; also Robert Widder and Richard Hubberthorne from Yealand and Kellet to the south, two slow-spoken yeomen who later traveled widely and began many meetings.

For most of the months that Fox circulated in the Kendal area, he used as his base Swarthmore Hall, a little manor house near Ulverston in Furness, the western fragment of Lancashire beyond Kendal. Judge Thomas Fell, to whom Swarthmore belonged, was a puritan in a royalist area and thus constantly busy in Cromwell's service. Margaret Fell kept open house for traveling preachers, and soon her home became the center for all Quaker missions and publications. She heard Fox confront the puritan pastor at Ulverston; two weeks later she herself was caught up by the power, and on her patient husband's return managed to win his toleration for the strange men of the new sect. Margaret Fell's seven daughters and her retainers—Thomas Salthouse, Will Caton, Leonard Fell, and the Cleatons—made a major addition to the list of Quakers who went out preaching as the "first publishers of Truth." [27]

27. It would seem from Swarth. *1*/373 (*EQL* 4) and ARBarc./16 that two of Margaret Fell's daughters, already in the first week of July, traveled across the mountains to York to deliver a letter from Fox to Aldam. Their long talks with the

In Furness especially, and at Ulverston, Fox was mobbed, stoned, and beaten with a ferocity even he had rarely encountered; he was stoned when he tried to land on Walney Island, and upon his return,

> After G.F. was put over the water . . . hee walkt to a towne called Cocken & theire the barborus people came out of the houses with there fleales & staves & hedge staikes & Fell upon G.F. . . . And, all bloody as hee was, hee was taken . . . to Tho. Huttons house, haveing pitty of him: & there Tho. Huttons wiffe washed his sorses & dresst & bound up his wounds: & shee was convinced & reacht by the power of God.[28]

Such violent positive and negative reactions were more than back-country yokels' traditional response to a stranger, for when Fox had first come to Swarthmore three months before, he had been received merely by small boys with stones, calling "a fox, a fox." Evidently he had meanwhile become well known: Nayler, who now joined him for the first of their few preaching trips together, was not molested. Deep religious and social hatreds resulting from the puritan wars underlay the situation and were demonstrated when the puritan justices Fell and West rescued Fox and Nayler from the hostile cavalier judges who arraigned them for blasphemy at Lancaster assizes. Nayler was soon rearrested and spent the winter in Appleby jail; Fox apparently lay low at Swarthmore until May 1653.[29]

In the summer of 1653 Fox traveled in Cumberland and spent two months in Carlisle jail, where he was saved from a possible hanging (for a second conviction for blasphemy) by the intervention of the Parliament of Saints. During this high tide of radical Puritanism, however, relatively few Quaker preachers were arrested. Nayler, Dewsbury, Howgill, and some dozen of the recently won Westmorland Friends worked intensively up and down

Quaker prisoners in York Castle helped to convince both girls. They were brave spirits: Fox again ran into them in Derbyshire late in 1654 (*Journal*, Nickalls, p. 181). See also M. Fell, *A Collection*, pp. 2–3. To what extent the Cleatons, Salthouse, etc. were members of the Fell household is not clear: see *FPT* Supplement in *JFHS, 31* (1934), 7.

28. *FPT* Supplement, *JFHS, 31* (1934), 11.

29. Fox and Nayler further answered the challenges, raised at the Lancaster Assizes, in Fox, *Saul's Errand to Damascus* (London, 1653). There seems to be little evidence on what Fox did during the winter months of 1652–53 and 1653–54.

through Cumberland. They began with the Independents around Cockermouth and the little separatist groups at Wigton and Bolton. Meetings first gathered in homes, but were often forced out of doors because of large crowds. On Pardshaw crag near Cockermouth and on hills above Isell, Bolton, and (later) Kirklinton, regular outdoor meetings were established, some of which divided again into house meetings during the winters. An opponent's description suggests the eagerness with which Friends met:

> sometimes thirty, sometimes forty or sixty, sometimes a hundred or two hundred in a swarm. The places of their Meetings are for the most part such private houses as are most solitary and remote from their Neighbours, scituated in Dales and by-places. Sometimes the open fields, sometimes the top of an Hill . . . Their speakers, and others that have nothing else to do but follow them, wander from one Parish . . . to another, sometimes . . . a whole Troop of them together: and by their Agents and Letters, which they send beforehand, gather people together. . . . Theire Speaker . . . standing . . . with his hat on, his countenance severe, his face downward, his eyes mostly fixed towards the Earth, his hands & fingers expanded, continually striking gently on his breast. . . . If . . . theire chiefe Speakers be . . . absent, any of them speak that will pretend a revelation; sometimes girles are vocall. . . . Sometimes . . . there is not a whisper among them for an houre or two together.[30]

A description by a Friend gives much the same impression: in 1653 Francis Howgill and Thomas Stubbs came together at the house of William Bond, a carpenter in Scotby, and held a meeting. It was "attended with a Rabble that some thought they should have pulled down the house, yet there was but little of Contraversie that appeared, for the Lords power prevailed, & several were convinced that day." [31]

Both Friends and their opponents spoke of a moral revival throughout the county. Quakers boasted about the Earl of Carlisle having said that they had accomplished more in the suppression

---

30. Francis Higginson, *A Brief Relation of the Irreligion of the Northern Quakers* (London, 1653), pp. 11–14, written by a puritan eyewitness.
31. *FPT*, p. 68.

of lawlessness along the border than all of his troopers, and they were known generally as "persons of most exemplar regular course of life, fre from all debauchery." [32] Two earnest clergymen, Thomas Lawson of Furness and John Wilkinson of Brigham, joined the Quakers: the ministers of Cockermouth angrily reported that their congregations were splintered or their buildings empty. Parish surveys imply that about a tenth of the population of Westmorland and Cumberland was reached by this awakening, though only one in forty became a Quaker permanently.

Quakerism was nevertheless a slow leaven, both in individuals and in the community, though the work continued. Dewsbury preached in Cartmel market two years after Fox began the Meeting there; Quakerism did not effectively reach Dent, Hawkshead, and Carlisle until 1655; and Cockermouth itself did not have a meeting house before 1688.

During the winter of 1653–54 a group of Quaker preachers turned southward toward Cheshire, encountering more opposition. At Colne behind Pendle Hill, "Willi: Dewsbury being moved to goe to Colne on the 21th day of the 10th mon 1653 & Coming to the Market Cross declared the Word of the Lord to the people untill one James Foster of Colne came behind him & fell upon him & so smote him downe, & so they hworyed him out of the Towne." [33] Hubberthorne and John Lawson spoke before Morgan Llwyd's revivalistic church in Wrexham and a separatist group at Malpas in Cheshire, before both were thrown into Chester prison. Thomas Holme was also sent there early in 1654 for the first of several times during his enthusiastic campaigning on the Welsh border. Elizabeth Leavens joined him there, which led to their imprudent marriage and to an unintended child two years later.

Three or four Meetings in Cheshire had begun solidly, however, and their members met at a great rally the following autumn. In February and March 1654 there began a much more intensive and systematic mission into Durham and Northumberland by at least sixteen Quaker preachers, who were reinforced by Nayler two months later. Eight Friends tackled the churches of a single town on one day, though this saturation attack did not leave as perma-

---

32. *FPT*, p. 63; Lord Langdale, in *Extracts from State Papers*, ed. Norman Penney (London, 1913), p. 124.
33. *FPT* Supplement in *JFHS*, *31* (1934), 18; cf. Swarth. 3/1.

nent results as it had done in other places. Headquarters for the Durham work was the manor of Anthony Pearson, who was at this time prominent in parliamentary politics, though he later dropped away from Quakerism. Camm, Burrough, and Atkinson went on to Berwick, and in Northumberland found themselves among the wildest people they had yet preached to. They saw "no appearance of anything of God but only a little about this town, and deep in the earth it lies." [34] In the Newcastle area, however, some active Quaker groups sprang up.

Meanwhile, Isabel Buttery had gone to London with a letter of Fox's for publication, Benjamin Nicholson had already made important contacts there, and Camm and Howgill came south to see Cromwell himself in March. One Quaker, Amor Stoddard, had already settled in London. The connection between these events and the sudden spreading of Quaker missionaries throughout southern England is not clear. In any case, between the summer of 1654 and the summer following, over sixty northern Quakers came south, traveling on foot and in pairs like Christ's own Apostles, carrying only a Bible and an inkhorn. "He hath appeared as the Son of God in the North Region of the World," they announced, "and hath made the Mountains melt before him. . . . O nations . . . under the whole face of Heaven . . . none shall stop his way. . . . He . . . is bringing a Handful out of the North Country who have been Eye-witnesses of his power. . . . They shall be his Witnesses to the Ends of the World." [35] Burrough wrote a call "to the Camp of the Lord in England," rousing the men of the North to take their part in the Lamb's War.

Probably there was no central plan for this mission. "General Meetings" were still only local assemblies for worship, and the first Quaker Monthly Meetings, which began at this time, were organized for poor relief. The flood of letters to Swarthmore from traveling preachers had hardly begun. Fox, Killam, Nayler, Dewsbury, Farnworth, young Thomas Holme, and the imprisoned Aldam wrote often among themselves, but these leaders all remained in the North or the Midlands throughout 1654. In any

34. Swarth. 4/170 (*EQL* 62), Burrough to Nayler, April 25, 1654.
35. Francis Howgill, *Works, The Dawnings of the Gospel-Day* (London, 1676), pp. 101–02. On the beginnings of the mission to the South see Braithwaite, *Beginnings,* Chap. 8; ARBarc./20, 39, 127; and Swarth. 3/93 (*EQL* 69).

case, each Friend traveled as he was led by the inward Spirit. Nayler, whose itinerary that year took him to Scotland, down to Nottingham, and all over Yorkshire, was "maid free to wander any way the lord shall move me soe that I may doe his will." [36] They all covered wide territory: the Killams spread from Mansfield to Coventry; Dewsbury, in one month between imprisonments at York and Derby, covered Lincolnshire, Nottingham, Wellingborough, and Leicester. Soon after his second release he concluded the year 1654 in jail in Northampton. In July, Fox was speaking before 2,500 people at Cinder Hill near Sheffield.[37]

To the lesser preachers who came south certain places such as the university cities naturally presented themselves as key targets. At Oxford and Cambridge four young Quaker women cried for repentance through the streets and were whipped by the authorities and doused and stripped by the students. Yet the appeal of virgin territory remained strong and probably accounts for the spreading of Quaker preachers throughout the entire country, including several expeditions to Land's End in Cornwall. Ayrey and Audland spent some days in Plymouth, although the Meeting was not gathered until Salthouse and Halhead came the following year.

As Friends from the northwest preached throughout southern England, their routes often crisscrossed, but the sharing of a sense of concern for special needs usually made up for the lack of discipline and plan. In general, the most mature and able preachers were needed in London and Bristol: Burrough and Howgill, Camm and Audland, and later Fox and Nayler. These men also made circuits through rural counties wherever new Meetings were started by the work of minor leaders. As in the North, newly convinced Friends often became ready within a few weeks or months to carry on the work in the smaller villages of their own areas; from Somerset they spread into Cornwall, from London into Essex.

In a new town the missionaries might feel a call to sound a warning through the market square or in the Sunday worship at the church, but usually they began, if possible, with the groups most nearly ready for their message, as Saint Paul had done 1,600 years

---

36. Swarth. 3/60 (*EQL* 29), Nayler to Fox [July 1653]. Cf. Swarth. 4/133 (*EQL* 74), 4/140 (*EQL* 80), 1/3 (*EQL* 98), 1/374 (*EQL* 129), on Dewsbury and the Killams.

37. For a vigorous itinerary, see Alexander Parker's, mostly in Yorkshire, Cheshire, and Shropshire, in Swarth. 1/164 (*EQL* 260). Also Farnworth's circuit in Sept.–Dec. 1652, in Swarth. 4/229 (*EQL* 6), 3/58 (*EQL* 12), and 3/50–53 (*EQL* 34–36).

before. In the South the people most open to appeal were usually
the Baptists: "In the year 1655, George Fox was at Pool[e, in
Dorset,] . . . accompanied by Edward Pyott of Bristoll. At Pool,
they came to an Inn, & on enquirey for a Baptist Teacher was directed to the house of Walter Spurrier, a taylor. G.ff, willing to
have a Meeting with them that Evening, desired he would give notice to his Brethren, which was accordingly Effected . . . Severall
being Convinced of the blessed Truth at that Meeting, of whome
was . . . William Baily, another of their Teachers" (and a ship-
master who later went on a Quaker mission to America).[38] Often
a single home was open to receive the wanderers, even if no congregation was willing to hear them. In some cases the host had
already discovered Quakerism on a visit to the North, as had Edward Edwards of Denbighshire. A few new converts, such as William Edmondson in Ireland, began at once to draw together Meetings as soon as they moved or returned to other parts of the country. Evidently the preachers in the South, if no other home was
open, hunted out any North-Countryman who had settled there.
Two such men, John Crook and Brian Wilkinson, had emerged
from the civil wars with substantial estates in Bedfordshire, which
thus became gathering places for Quaker ministers.[39]

The day of a Quaker minister was seldom dull, at least. One
Sunday in 1655 James Parnell, who was still in his teens, was in
Colchester and "preached the Gospell first at his Lodgings, then
in a steeple House after their Worship was over, and next in a
Large Meeting appointed on purpose. . . . In John ffurlys yard,
he speaking out of a hay Chamber window, where Its thought were
about a Thousand people; and after that, the same day, he had
a dispute In one of John ffurlys Chambers, lett to a french Schoolmaster" with the town church's ordained lecturer and a seventh-
day baptist preacher.[40]

The Quaker preachers did not always stay long enough to gather
a Meeting, but this was of course the ultimate aim of their work.
After a number of meetings for "threshing upon the mountains"
had been held in a town in as public a manner as possible, a few
responsive hearers from each were drawn together into a group

38. *FPT*, p. 80.
39. Cf. *FPT*, pp. 6, 16, 60 n., 235, 323 n.
40. *FPT*, pp. 91, 96.

to give each other mutual help in entering the new life. A typical report is from John Whitehead in Newport Pagnell, Buckinghamshire: "A small remnant is there confirmed and came to gether when I was with them at 3 meetings. The wittnesse was raised and they [were] parsuaded to meete in silence." [41] Thereafter, a deep responsibility lay upon all Quaker ministers in the area to visit the new Meeting frequently. When a group was started, if visiting Friends were "not staying with them, they comeinge to silent meetings, many is famished for want of words, & soe they not being willinge to wayt in the silence are turned back." [42] Moreover, those who were "slack in coming to meetings" [43] were likely, after the first mass excitement had passed, to find the long struggle toward inward obedience and purification too hard for them. Consequently, a gradual but inevitable transition occurred from pioneer preaching to pastoral care. More and more, the "First Publishers" found inner leadings to visit little groups of Friends at a distance, when they heard that help was needed.

Along with unannounced messages to priests and congregations, the early Quakers loved public debates. On the most famous occasion, Richard Farnworth and Thomas Goodaire met an Independent pastor and a parish minister in Worcestershire early in 1655. They hoped to draw Richard Baxter, the most significant puritan minister in the West, into the debate, and they even spoke aloud in his Kidderminster Church. But Baxter, though he later met Edward Bourne and other Friends at leisure face to face, preferred to carry on his argument with Quakers in writing, where he could be sure he was not misquoted.[44] Distance or dignity led most ministers to write tracts against Quakerism rather than enter a debate, and a major portion of the thousands of Quaker pamphlets written at this time were in answer to such attacks. Out of 150 authors who wrote against Quakerism between 1653 and 1660, only six went without an answer. The issues raised in these arguments are taken up later in this book. Some Quaker tracts were also written as direct appeals to the reading public, and some

41. *Letters to William Dewsbury and Others*, ed. Henry J. Cadbury (London, Friends Historical Society, 1948), Letter 20, John Whitehead to Dewsbury (Feb. 12, 1655/6). See also Swarth. 3/39 (*EQL* 43), Aldam to Fox, York, Dec. 1653.
42. ARBarc./57, Richard Waller to M. Fell, Waterford, August 10, 1657.
43. Swarth. 3/97 (*EQL* 185), Richard Weaver to M. Fell (Brotherton).
44. See *FPT*, p. 285; Baxter, *Quaker's Catechism*.

Friends boldly read them aloud in churchyards and in the markets. The dramatic Quaker methods were so effective as publicity that word of the preachers' coming usually went ahead of them, and in each town some hearers were stirred up to receive their challenge.

Public response varied greatly according to both the place and the occasion, however. When Ann Audland was tried for blasphemy at Banbury in 1655, the jury refused to convict her; but just as often the crowds were hostile. In Henley-on-Thames, "Joseph Coale, a very young man . . . got sum meetings att the house of Wm Waters . . . at one of the playtims called Easter. . . . There was gathered together in the street (in order to go to play) severall men & boys. . . . One of the men said, 'Yonder coms a Quaker, throw stones at him,' wch was accordingly don, but he passed gently on his way, and took noe notice of our abusing him." Even in Kendal hostile public reaction was evidently the cause for the arrest of several Quakers.[45]

Naturally, the strongest opposition came from local parsons and magistrates, who tried many kinds of violent methods to keep preachers away. As vagrants, John Stubbs and Will Caton were stripped and put in the stocks in Kent, and two Quaker women spent a grim night upside down in the stocks at Evesham. Interrupting parish church worship and preaching judgment in marketplaces not only were illegal but usually aroused strong anger. Especially disturbing was the Quaker custom of "going naked for a sign" to symbolize the spiritual nakedness of a smug city. Most of the First Publishers of Truth spent weeks or months each year in various prisons. James Parnell was arrested only days after his great meeting at Colchester and died in the castle there following eight months of imprisonment, cold, exposure, and a ten-foot fall from the "Little, low Hole Called the Oven" cut into the dungeon wall, which was his cell. At Pontymoile in Wales a Quaker group shared a night's sleep as prisoners in a steeplehouse.[46]

Cromwell's government was not mainly involved in these perse-

45. *FPT*, p. 218; note by the change of pronoun that one of the boys became a Friend. On Kendal see *FPT*, p. 257; on Ann Audland see Swarth. 1/391 (*EQL* 183), John Audland to M. Fell, October 1, 1655.

46. *FPT*, p. 93; On Parnell see also the opening testimonies in *A Collection of the Several Writings of James Parnell* (London, 1675). See also Swarth. 4/252 (*EQL* 518), Thomas Holme to Fox [1660].

cutions, but in the summer and again in the winter of 1654, during the "Fifth Monarchy" mutiny and the conservative reaction against the Parliament of Saints, the Council of State ordered the breaking up of Quaker meetings in Derbyshire and Leicestershire.[47]

Friends, however, could turn even arrest and imprisonment into missionary opportunities. When Fox and some companions were being escorted to Leicester jail in 1662, they passed people harvesting in the fields, and "with our open Bibles in our handes, declared howe wee were the prisoners of the Lord Jesus Christ for his name & truth sake, & the people was mightily affected." [48] Quakers in prison not only wrote letters and tracts freely, sending them out through visitors, but held meetings for worship in which fellow prisoners were often won over. Thomas Aldam apparently preached four times in York Minster during hours of liberty from his cell in the castle, though this may have prolonged his incarceration. He was summoned for jury duty, though also fined for attending.[49]

This general period of expanding ministry in 1654 and 1655 included several major campaigns which must be described individually. The work in London, which had begun casually, soon became a major mission. As a result of the interest—and even a few conversions—which had been stimulated by the earlier visits of Isabel Buttery, Gervase Benson, Camm, and Howgill, the last two men returned to London in July 1654. Burrough went with them, and Hubberthorne and Audland joined them there in August from Oxford and Plymouth. Small meetings were held regularly in four or five homes around the city. Those of Simon and Robert Dring and Gerrard Roberts also came to be used as hostels for traveling Friends and forwarding places for correspondence. The Quaker preachers visited London churches, Baptist meetings, and sectarian groups of all kinds, and as the "Report spread About the City that there was A sort of People Come there that went by the name of Plaine north Cuntry Plow men," [50] many inquirers showed interest in seeing them. By midwinter a public hall had to be rented at the Bull and Mouth Tavern, and Friends continued

47. *ESP*, pp. 1–6.
48. *The Journal of George Fox,* ed. Norman Penney (2 vols. Cambridge, Cambridge University Press, 1911), 2, 15.
49. ARBarc./113.
50. *FPT*, p. 163.

to meet there for ten years. When this was first used early in 1655, however, it allowed Howgill and Burrough to preach to the large crowds without overwhelming the struggling little meetings of those who declared themselves convinced. The hall held a thousand standing listeners:

> The room . . . hath been filled with people many of whom have been in uproars, contending one with another, some . . . against the Quakers, accusing . . . them with heresy blasphemy, sedition and what not . . . [and] others endeavouring to vindicate them . . . in the midst of all which noise and contention [Edward Burrough] hath stood upon a bench, with his Bible in his hand . . . speaking to the people with great authority. . . . The whole multitude were overcome thereby, and became exceeding calm and attentive, and departed peaceably and with seeming satisfaction.[51]

By spring 1655, with two such "threshing-floors" and five or six weekly Meetings for convinced Friends, Fox himself had joined them, having been sent up to London under arrest from Leicester and later set free after a fascinating meeting with Cromwell. Fox traveled through all the surrounding counties, but Nayler, who came up in June, worked mainly in the city and built there an impressive reputation which later contributed to his undoing.

Meanwhile, an even more spectacular program was carried on in Bristol. By mutual agreement with Burrough and Howgill, Camm and Audland left London and

> came to the City of *Bristol* in the 5th month, 1654, and first they came among a seeking people, who kept one day in the week in fasting and praying . . . and amongst us they spoke the powerful Word of Life, . . . and we were seized on and smitten even to the Heart. . . . Some [further] meetings we had before the general gathering in . . . On a first day . . . *John Audland* said: "Is there any one that has any interest

51. William Crouch, *Posthuma Christiana*, quoted in Braithwaite, *Beginnings*, pp. 182–83. Cf. also Swarth. 3/34 (*EQL* 70), 4/35 (*EQL* 76), 1/89 (*EQL* 81), 4/210 (*EQL* 128) about the London mission. Camm and Howgill had already visited several groups of interested individuals while waiting to see the Protector in March 1654, and together with Stoddard, Benson, and Isabel Buttery appealed to other Friends for help. Benjamin Nicholson had come south after his release from York Castle. See Fig. 3 and p. 100, Swarth. 3/52 (*EQL* 36); ARBarc/15.

in any Field?" An ancient man said: I have, in a Field pretty near. . . . The people in the house . . . came forth; and as we went along, people in the Streets went also to the Field called Earls-mead.

John Camm began to speak tenderly, and in great zeal, directing [men] to the heavenly grace of God, and testifying against Sin . . . fervently. . . . John Audland, who very much trembled, after . . . stood up, full of dread and shining brightness in his countenance, lifted up his Voice as a Trumpet, and said: "I proclaim spiritual War with the Inhabitants of the Earth, who are in the Fall and Separation from God" . . . and so went on in the mighty Power of God. . . . But ah, the seizings of souls, and prickings at heart, which attended. . . . Some fell on the ground, others crying out, under the sence of opening of their [inward] States. . . .

At this Meeting many were effectually convinced, and from Darkness to Light turned, after which our Meetings grew larger and larger. . . . Oh, the strippings of all needless Apparel, and the forsaking of superfluities in Meats [and] Drinks; and in the plain self-denying Path we walked, having the fear and dread of God on our Souls, that we were afraid of offending in word or deed: our Words were few and savory . . . our Countenances Grave and Deportment Weighty. . . . Indeed we were a plain broken-hearted, contrite spirited, self-denying people . . .

Our Meetings were so large that we were forced to meet out of doors, and that in Frost and Snow. . . . In the fulness of . . . time . . . we were right glad, although when the Lord discovered our states, he laid Judgment to the Line . . . and gave to us the Cup of trembling.[52]

These "Great Meetings at the orchard" were long remembered, and continued for months. In July 1655 Audland reported that the Meetings were still enormous.[53]

---

52. "Christopher Marshall's Testimony," in Camm and Audland, *Works*. Audland and Ayrey had been in Bristol briefly in July 1654 to look over the field (cf. *FPT*, p. 226) en route to their unsuccessful mission in Plymouth from which Ayrey retreated home to Kendal, only to find himself reproached by other Friends.

53. ARBarc./58, John Audland to Howgill and Burrough (Bristol, July 2, 1655). This letter has been wrongly attributed to Parnell.

As in London, those who were convinced were gathered into two or three small Meetings; others were gathered in villages in Gloucester and Somerset, which could be visited from Bristol, especially at Nailsworth among the weavers. This area became eventually the third great region of Quaker strength after London and the North Country.

Another major mission was attempted at the same time in the eastern counties, but with strikingly smaller success. The orthodox puritan judges and sheriffs were hostile: Hubberthorne was imprisoned at Cambridge and a month later at Norwich, where George Whitehead, Christopher Atkinson, and James Lancaster were also locked up in rapid succession. Dewsbury spent more than a year in prison in the puritan stronghold of Northampton, and the others spent more time in prison than out. Official hostility did not prevent the gathering of active little Meetings at Norwich,[54] Colchester, and especially Coggleshall in Essex, where Parnell preached and Fox drew 2,000 to a meeting in 1655. But most of the puritan centers were cold to the Quaker message.

Just after Christmas of 1654, Fox, who was still on his way southward and was holding large but seemingly fruitless meetings in and around Leicestershire, called together all the Quaker leaders for a general meeting at Swannington. The Bristol and London teams came, and about two hundred others. More careful planning was evident in some Quaker campaigns thereafter, and frequent letters and reports were thenceforth received by Margaret Fell at Swarthmore Hall, not only from the key leaders and her own friends, but from many minor Quaker ministers who had never met her.[55] A few months before, Friends in the North had begun to send money to a fund at Kendal to help those Quakers facing expensive journeys and imprisonments. Margaret Fell's appeals had combined depth with tact:

> Now, that every particular Member of the Body may be sensible of the Hardship and Sufferings of others . . . Our Friends in *Westmoreland* have been sent forth into the Lord's Service . . . and . . . our Friends at *Kendal* . . . have been very serviceable . . . to them that have suffer'd Imprisonment, and

54. See Swarth. 1/29 (*EQL* 154), Richard Cleaton to M. Fell, May 23, 1655.

55. Nuttall in *EQL* records 57 Swarthmore letters for 1654, but 108 for 1655 and 133 for 1656; the ARBarclay letters are proportional.

for dispersing Books. . . . All and every Member . . . ought to be serviceable in their places. . . . So you may come to be one with them in their Sufferings, in their Tryals, Travels, Troubles, Buffetings . . . Prisonings . . . who are sent as Lambs among Wolves. . . . For he shall have the Victory, who is King of Kings.[56]

The meeting at Swannington was the first General Meeting of the ministers, and they returned to work encouraged: "The lord hath made our way plaine, and the shoute of a king is with us; and plainely may we say there is noe enchantment against Jacob, for the lord hath appeared for us." [57]

The year 1655 saw, besides the intensified work in London and Bristol, a thorough penetration of all the south-coast counties from Kent to Devonshire and a sudden concentration of seven of the most powerful Quaker speakers upon Bedfordshire in March. Wales, which had so far seen mostly the work (between four imprisonments) of Thomas Holme in the North, was attacked from the south by Farnworth and in the center by two Welsh converts, John ap John and Edward Edwards. At Wrexham, a visit by Hubberthorne and Thomas Lawson in October 1653 had already split a congregation gathered there by Walter Cradock. In January 1656 Holme returned to South Wales and went through to Pembrokeshire, that "little England beyond Wales." But despite some recruits from broken Baptist groups in central Wales, the movement there remained small.[58] From this point onward, in fact, it is impossible in a short book even to take account of all the main centers of Quaker work. Hardly a county or city in England was overlooked, and episodes from Dorset, Cumberland, and Worcestershire have already been described.

The bravest new efforts, however, were made toward reaching the settlers in the West Indies and the American colonies, and the

56. M. Fell, pp. 58, 97.

57. Swarth. 1/7 (*EQL* 114), Audland to M. Fell, Swannington, January 3, 1654/55.

58. On Bedfordshire see Swarth. 1/161 (*EQL* 140), Parker and Howgill to M. Fell, April 3, 1655. This was probably also a meeting to plan strategy: cf. Braithwaite, *Beginnings*, p. 185. On Wales see Swarth. 1/204 (*EQL* 281), Holme to M. Fell; also 4/247 (*EQL* 239), 3/55 (*EQL* 146), and Evelyn S. Whiting, "The Yearly Meeting for Wales," *JFHS*, 47 (1955), 57–70, and especially Geoffrey F. Nuttall: *The Welsh Saints, 1640–1660* (Cardiff, 1957), chap. 4, showing the relationships of Friends to other religious movements in Wales.

peoples of Holland, Scotland, and Ireland. The American wor
began with a trip to Barbados by Mary Fisher and Ann Austin i
1655 and 1656, and Elizabeth Harris' winter trip to Virginia. Late
episodes can be found in the chapters on persecution and its after
math. Altogether, forty-three Quakers sailed for the American col
nies between 1655 and 1660; most stayed for at least a year, althoug
Hester Biddle in Newfoundland and John Bowron in Surinam soo
moved to more responsive places and more temperate climates.⁵
The new Quaker groups were in most cases formed where ther
were "orphaned" separatists or puritans, as in Rhode Island, Ply
mouth colony, or the pastorless English settlements on Long Islan
and in Barbados and Maryland. The disciplined puritan colonie
of Massachusetts and Connecticut were hostile.

The best work in Holland was done by Will Caton and Joh
Stubbs, who arrived in 1655, following some brief and impetuou
visits to France and Holland the year before by Caton, Atkinson
and several women.⁶⁰ Sectarian groups had freedom in Holland
and Caton and Stubbs found some response among the Mennonite
and Collegianten of Amsterdam and Rotterdam. By continue
visits and with the help of Ames and Furly, eight Dutch Quake
Meetings had been set up by 1670. The strongest was the Meetin
near Amsterdam, attended by the future historian of Quakerisn
Willem Sewel.⁶¹ There Will Caton learned Dutch and came i
contact with the active Jewish community in Holland, includin
their greatest rabbi, Manasseh-ben-Israel, and perhaps the phi
losopher Spinoza. Ames also traveled into Germany, and betwee
1659 and 1671 six rather weak Meetings were set up in as man
German cities, again mostly among the sectarians.⁶²

In Ireland and Scotland it was the Cromwellian garrisons tha

---

59. Frederick B. Tolles, *Quakers and the Atlantic Culture* (New York, Macmillan
1960), pp. 23, 138–39.

60. Cf. Swarth. 1/89 (*EQL* 81) and Braithwaite, *Beginnings*, pp. 406, 576.

61. ARBarc./55, George Rofe to Fox (Amsterdam, June 23, 1659). Cf. Henr
J. Cadbury, "The First Settlement of Meetings in Europe," *JFHS*, 44 (1952), 11–12
William I. Hull, *The Rise of Quakerism in Amsterdam*, Swarthmore College Mono
graphs on Quaker History, 4 (Swarthmore, Penn., 1938), and Hull's *Benjamin Furl
and Quakerism in Rotterdam*, Swarthmore College Monographs on Quaker History
5 (Swarthmore, Penn., 1941).

62. Cf. Swarth. 4/28 (*EQL* 384); *EQL* p. 228 n.; Braithwaite, *Beginnings*, pr
409–11; M. Fell, pp. 101 ff. On Germany see Henry J. Cadbury, "Quakerism i
Friedrichstadt," *JFHS*, 43 (1951), 17–21; and *JFHS*, 44 (1952), 11–12.

stened most willingly to the Quakers. The Irish mission began
with a sense of divine calling as dramatic as that of St. Paul to
Macedonia; Burrough and Howgill wrote out careful descriptions
of how the Lord had moved each independently. William Edmondson had settled and quietly worked for Quakerism in Ulster, but
1 June 1655 the landing of Burrough and Howgill in Dublin began an intensive campaign which Richard Waller, Richard Roper,
and others followed up. They divided, and while Burrough worked
steadily in Dublin and then in Waterford, Howgill went through
southern Ireland to Kinsale and Cork. The officers of Cromwell's
garrisons were mainly Baptists, many of them friendly to Quakerism, but the council of the Governor, Henry Cromwell, interfered
and forced Burrough's deportation. For this young Cromwell received a biblically worded rebuke from Barbara Blaugdone of
Bristol, who providentially landed that day. Several dozen little
Meetings were eventually formed in Ireland, consisting almost entirely of English folk, despite official disapproval.[63]

In Scotland, Presbyterianism was so solidly established that repeated Quaker visits made little headway. Most converts were members or associates of Cromwell's garrisons, except for two small
Congregational churches, which Fox was glad to find. Quakers seldom got beyond the Lowlands, and some visits there in 1654–56
were merely side trips from preaching work in northern England.
Dewsbury went through the mountains to Inverness, and John Hall
patiently tackled Edinburgh. Alexander Parker's reaction was po-
etic: "Thou knowst . . . the treasure lies deep in this land, the
mountaines are high, and the rocks are hard. . . . Here is a thick
mist come over the high mountains, out of which a dark cloud is
risen, and a great storm, that tries the building." [64] Three notable
Scots were won over, however: Lady Margaret Hamilton and, a
little later, Robert Barclay and George Keith, students at Aberdeen.

63. Cf. John M. Douglas, "Early Quakerism in Ireland," *JFHS, 48* (1956); William
Edmondson, *A Journal of the Life* . . . (2d ed. London, 1774); Swarth. 1/27 (*EQL*
25), Richard Cleaton to M. Fell; Swarth. 4/75 (*EQL* 355), Thomas Morford to
M. Fell; Swarth. 3/133 (*EQL* 253), Richard Waller to M. Fell; comments by Nuttall,
EQL, pp. 215–16.

64. Swarth. 3/140 (*EQL* 425), Alex. Parker to Fox, Leith, January 13, 1657/58.
Cf. Fox, *Journal*, Nickalls, pp. 315–30; Swarth. 4/140 (*EQL* 457), 4/64 (*EQL* 365),
4/65 (*EQL* 376), 1/301 (*EQL* 408), 4/214 (*EQL* 463).

In January 1656, after a trip to Scotland, Fox was in the strongly royalist region of Cornwall with Edward Pyott and William Salt. They gathered a symbolic little Meeting at Land's End and a more prominent one in the home of Loveday Hambly near St. Austell's. Returning eastward, Fox's party preached in defiance of warnings and were arrested and thrown into the "Doomsdale" dungeon at Launceston Castle.[65] All the Quaker preachers who could do so began at once to converge upon Launceston. The early Friends' compulsion to "march toward the sound of the battle"[66] was the source of their victory in many campaigns. The multitude of visitors and meetings at Fox's dungeon impressed even the Government in London, which eventually arranged for his release after a brutal eight months underground. Meanwhile, however, Salthouse, Halhead, and four women were jailed at Exeter, and by July there were twenty-three Quakers in that prison alone, which led Alexander Parker to report that "there is not a friende in the Ministry within 3 or 4 score miles that is att liberty."[67] Parker had traveled from Manchester to Launceston to see Fox and had failed to get through, because there were watches all through the county to capture Friends traveling to Launceston. When Fox was released, the efficiency of the Quaker communication system showed itself: the news was brought to Gloucestershire by Walter Clement, his fellow prisoner, on the same day Fox was freed. As an ironic afternote, the freeing of the Friends dissipated the sense of urgency, and those freed soon left the area, so that Salthouse reported in November 1656 that there were none left but Alexander Parker and himself. A similar report asking for help the following year may have brought Dewsbury down to Land's End.[68]

During this period the sense of crisis at Launceston and the jailing of the preachers had led to a tragedy which centered on James Nayler. In the days of his acclaim in London, Nayler had

65. *FPT*, pp. 20 ff. Cf. L. Violet Hodgkin (Holdsworth), *A Quaker Saint of Cornwall: Loveday Hambly and Her Guests* (London, 1927).

66. Early German victories in the Franco-Prussian War of 1870 were attributed to the speed with which junior officers threw their units into battle without waiting for orders.

67. Swarth. 1/166 (*EQL* 304), Parker to M. Fell, St. Austell, August 19, 1656. Cf. *ESP*, pp. 3–6.

68. See Swarth. 1/81 (*EQL* 300), Henry Fell to M. Fell; 3/158 (*EQL* 311) and 3/162 (*EQL* 333), Salthouse to M. Fell; also 1/38 (*EQL* 394), 4/145 (*EQL* 416).

attracted a group of intensely emotional women who claimed to be led by the Holy Spirit in their Messianic praises of Nayler and their rejection of any criticism. Nayler would not condemn them; his own pride perhaps confused his judgment as to whether the Spirit was really at work in the women. This was a deep and frequent problem in early Quakerism. Fox also refrained from judging most Quakers' "leadings," such as to "go naked for a sign" or to act in other strange ways.[69] When Nayler set out from London for Launceston, the women went along. The Bristol Quaker preachers were troubled and "went with n.J. . . . aboute 15 mille. Hee said little to us, but he did one whilles weepe exceedingly, soe wee returned & they rode on."[70] Nayler's party were turned back from Launceston and jailed at Exeter. Visitors there found him fasting and weak: "still much a like as to the frame of spirit . . . but the life which I have once known to breath forth I find not."[71] Nayler was trying to be humble and open to God. His gentle spirit impressed other Friends, but it was a symptom of his mental exhaustion. He showed this again in his inability to react decisively to the still clinging women and in his confused response to the evidently stern attitude of Fox, who visited him when released from Launceston. Probably unrealized jealousy between the two men (who stood then almost equal as Quaker pillars) made each doubt the Spirit in the other, and weakened them both in a time of need; but the prevailing judgment of both Fox and Hubberthorne at this time went against the women.[72]

Though he carried a warning from Fox in his pocket, Nayler allowed his group of friends to lead him into Bristol in a re-enactment of Jesus' entry into Jerusalem on Palm Sunday. It was in-

69. See below, p. 121.

70. ARBarc./114, Howgill and Audland to Burrough, Bristol, August 2, 1656.

71. John Bolton's report passed on to Margaret Fell by Audland in Swarth. 1/12 (*EQL* 303), Olveston, August 18, 1656.

72. Nayler's refusal at Exeter to uncover his head during Fox's prayer and Fox's rebuff there of Nayler's "kiss of peace," seem to mean that they doubted each other's leadings from the Spirit. Richard Hubberthorne found Nayler "low and tender" and blamed Martha Simmonds (Swarth. 3/153, *EQL* 315, Sept. 16, 1656). Rawlinson also approved Nayler's mood (3/12, *EQL* 307, Aug. 23, 1656), but on the same day John Braithwaite felt Nayler needed "carefulness" (3/86, *EQL* 306). On Nayler's fall, see Geoffrey Nuttall, *James Nayler, a Fresh Approach* (London, 1954); Nuttall, *Studies in Christian Enthusiasm, Illustrated from Early Quakerism and Its Allies* (Wallingford, Penn., Pendle Hill, 1946); Jordan, *Religious Toleration, 3,* 218–46; also Swarth. 3/131 (*EQL* 324).

tended to symbolize the coming of the inward Christ into ever
heart, but the women sang "Holy, holy, holy" before Nayler.]
rained all day; and the procession concluded at the White Har
"a bad inn." [73] Local Friends ignored the episode, but the report o
some bystanders who considered Nayler blasphemous came to Lor
don at a time of political crisis. Cromwell's persistent effort t
maintain a balance between the conservative and the radical pur
tans was turning both sides against him: to strengthen himself h
had arranged a parliamentary election, but the Presbyterians se
cured a majority. The Nayler case seemed to the Presbyterians
perfect issue over which to upset Cromwell's policy of toleratio
for all sects. Parliament called Nayler to London, and tried an
convicted him with no legal authority, invoking the laws of Deu
teronomy against blasphemy and the customs of the defunct Hous
of Lords. Cromwell reminded them of their illegality but appar
ently did not dare to override the sentence. Nayler was whippe
through the city with 310 lashes and, despite wide protestation, wa
branded with a hot iron and pierced through the tongue. Afte
a public humiliation in Bristol, he was imprisoned for an indefinit
period.[74]

The outcome was destructive to all groups involved. Cromwel
had lost his role as champion of freedom, and his prestige anc
authority sank for the remaining two years of his life. Parliamen
had gained no glory, nor even a precedent they dared use agair
(Cromwell soon sent them home in the vain hope that another elec
tion would produce a more constructive group.) The Friend
themselves for the first time lost their confidence and the habit o
victory. Letters expressing their confusion came to Margaret Fel
from Friends all over the world. In Plymouth, "this bisines abou
J. N. hath made a great tumult in the minds of many weal
friends"; [75] in Holland, "strang Reports concerning J.N. is gone
over"; [76] and in Barbados many strangers "blaspheme the name o

73. Swarth. 1/188 (*EQL* 326), George Bishop to M. Fell, Bristol, Oct. 27, 1656
Cf. 3/195 (*EQL* 317). It is uncertain whether the inn's owner was a Quaker, he
whose orchard had been used for the "great meetings" throughout the previous
year. Cf. Nuttall's notes in *EQL*, p. 205; Braithwaite, *Beginnings*, p. 566.
74. Cf. *ESP*, pp. 21–27.
75. Swarth. 3/185 (*EQL* 357), from Tho. Salthouse, January 30, 1656/57.
76. Swarth. 1/314 (*EQL* 356), from Will Caton, January 19, 1656/57.

ur God, because of reports which come out of England concerning
. N." [77] George Fox and some others disowned Nayler. Certain
riends were more sensitive and sympathized with him in his
ifferings. Nayler himself wanted reconciliation with Fox, but
as slow to condemn outright the act for which he had suffered
disproportionately. William Dewsbury eventually felt that "the
ord layed it on me that deare G ff: and J N. might meet together.
. . The lord Cloathed my deare Brethren, G ff: EB: ff H: with a
retious Wisdome. A healinge spirit did abound within them." [78]
The reactions of Friends to Nayler were linked with their need
look again at the meaning of Quakerism. The early days of the
amb's War had seemed to them to be the beginning of a conquest
f the world. All persecution and outside criticism could be there-
ore shrugged off as the inevitable result of wounded pride or the
levil's rage; hostility only made the Quaker preacher more strong
announce judgment. But the martyr outlook, even when com-
ined with the personal humility of Nayler, had produced actions
vhich some Friends now felt the world was right to condemn. Dur-
ng and after Nayler's trial, moreover, some Quaker women were
lriven by the crisis to much more intense and provocative signs
nd actions than before. These were aimed also at even the mod-
rate Friends who had disowned Nayler's ride. Women sang and
houted in Quaker Meetings, and in London, Mildred Crouch
ried a "filibuster" against Richard Hubberthorne:

> Yesterday . . . wee had A meeting at the bull & mouth &
> mildred was there in all Impudence. . . . She was tormented
> & shee resolved soe to speake as that I should not speake any
> more to them. . . . In the livinge power of the lord I was cept
> & was moved to stay. . . . wee stayed almost untill midnight
> . . . untill All her naturall parts was spent, and her senses
> distracted, that she was even realy mad; the truth reaigned in
> pure dominion. But the next meetings she did not come at all
> for shee . . . is soe horse that shee cannot speake at present,
> and it is like gods judgments.[79]

77. Swarth. 1/69 (*EQL* 381), from H. Fell, April 14, 1657. Cf. 1/293 (*EQL* 344).
78. Swarth. 4/134 (*EQL* 517), Dewsbury to M. Fell (March 1660). Cf. 4/24 (*EQL*
54), John Stubbs; 4/12 (*EQL* 435), R. Hubberthorne.
79. Swarth. 4/12 (*EQL* 435), Farnworth to Fox, March 20, 1656/57 (?). Cf. Braith-
vaite, *Beginnings*, pp. 269–70, 567.

The trial of Nayler directed and perhaps speeded the growth of a popular reaction that was coming, in any case, against the mass enthusiasm Quakers had aroused in 1654 and 1655. It was rather like the negative reaction in New England after the Great Awakening. The number of Swarthmore letters dropped off sharply, though more were coming now from overseas. Fewer and fewer Friends reported gathering great crowds or forming new Meetings in England. Dewsbury was still successful, and in Northamptonshire had addressed a gathering in a field that a captain tried in vain to break up with a trumpeter and six cavalrymen.[80] A surprising number of Dorsetshire Meetings began in 1657, and these were the years of the greatest headway in Wales, Ireland, and Scotland, but the number of Quakers in English prisons rose steadily.

The basic strength of Quakerism, and of George Fox himself, is demonstrated by their reactions to this confusing situation. They produced no books of self-analysis, as did Jonathan Edwards, yet Fox and other leaders responded by concentrating on helping established Meetings and on work in Scotland. General Meetings for an entire region were gathered fairly often, and from 1658 to 1661 a series of these at Skipton and Balby and at John Crook's in Bedfordshire were intended to be yearly Meetings for the whole country. Formal Monthly Meetings for planning the business in local areas were set up, as well as separate Men's and Women's Meetings.

From this time onward, much less is heard of Quakers openly violating English law and sentiment by going naked for a sign or interrupting pastors' sermons. Instead, they concentrated their attacks on the one law they still hoped Cromwell would change, that concerning the payment of tithes. Perhaps because tithes were collected more forcibly during this period of conservatism, issues over the tithes became the main source of persecution and imprisonment for the next two or three years.[81]

This period also saw a greater flood of controversial tracts and

---

80. Swarth. 4/143 (*EQL* 275), Dewsbury to M. Fell, June 1, 1656, before Nayler's fall. According to Nuttall's datings, there is a drop from 133 Swarthmore letters for 1656 to 71 in 1657 (12 being from overseas), 43 in 1658, and 37 in 1659. Of course, this fall-off was matched by a drop in Margaret Fell's own writing: it was the time of her husband's death. Yet the shift to letters written overseas is striking, though Henry Fell alone wrote 12 in 1656–58, mainly from Barbados.

81. See below, p. 796. Out of 119 Quaker prisoners in 1658, 60 were for tithes.

books in which Friends attacked Presbyterian and Baptist doctrines and defended their own. George Fox and Samuel Fisher each set down 750 folio pages in one volume, intending to demolish all opponents at once.[82]

It seems clear that the Quakers had not let the Lamb's War become defensive, and this is particularly evident in the missions overseas. In the period between 1656 and 1660, when preaching in England was shrinking, Friends went to "Germany, America and many other islands and places, such as Florence, Mantua, Palatine, Tuscany, Italy, Rome, Turkey, Jerusalem, France, Geneva, Norway, Barbados, Antigua, Jamaica, Surinam, Newfoundland," [83] with a fine carelessness about geography or about language difficulties. Some stayed a year or more in the new land, learned the language and customs, and began new Quaker groups, as had been done in Holland. In other cases the traveler delivered the single message which he had felt laid upon him when he set out from England, and then started his journey home. These were not the first of such distant missions, but they make evident the two special lines of emphasis now emerging: the universal vision and the fighting spirit.

Characteristically, the more restless spirits expressed their sense of the meaning of Quakerism after Nayler's trial by setting out to reach the Pope, the Sultan, the kings of France and Spain, and all nations upon earth. Each of these expeditions makes an adventure story in itself. William Ames eventually reached Danzig and Copenhagen; John Harwood and George Bayly were imprisoned in Paris, where Bayly died and Harwood learned French from a Bible he was given in the Bastille.[84] Thomas Hayman and George Robinson set out for Jerusalem; there Robinson escaped from the friars (who were responsible for keeping pilgrims out of trouble with the Moslems) only to be arrested by the Pasha. But this gave him the chance to deliver his message and freed him to go home. During the same winter of 1657–58 William Salt and John Browne were also in France, George Nayles was in Venice, and six other Friends were setting out for Turkey. Two of these, John Perrot and John

---

82. Fox, *Great Mistery;* Fisher, "Rusticus ad Academicos," the main section of his *Works* (1676) and apparently not printed earlier.

83. Fox, as quoted in Braithwaite, *Beginnings,* p. 337.

84. Swarth. 3/96 (*EQL* 446), John Harwood to Luke Howard, Paris, 1657; Swarth. 1/301 (*EQL* 408), George Taylor to M. Fell September 12, 1657.

Luffe, after they were turned back in the Adriatic, felt called upon
to convert the Pope. They were not successful: Perrot was im
prisoned by the Inquisition and Luffe was killed. Meanwhile, Mar
Fisher (who had already preached in New England) and Beatric
Beckly succeeded in reaching the Sultan of Turkey, who heard ther
courteously and asked what the Friends thought of Mohammec
"she said that they might judge of him to be true or false accordin
to the words and prophecies which he spoke. . . . The Turks cor
fessed this to be true." [85] A letter from George Fox to the Emperc
of China demonstrates the same universalist spirit. It was carrie
by John Stubbs, Henry Fell, Richard Scosthrop, and Daniel Bake
They did not reach China, and Scosthrop died en route, but Stubl
and Fell reached Alexandria, and Baker made a gallant attempt t
free Katharine Evans and Sarah Chevers from the Inquisition a
Malta. Fox's letter begins:

> For the Emperor of China and his Subordinate Kings an
> Princes, From the People of God in England, in Englis
> called Quakers: Friends, There is a Power above all Power
> and this Power is making itself manifest: And this is God . .
> the Creator, and Former, and Maker of all things in Heave
> and Earth . . . in whose Hands is the Breath and Life of a
> Mankind, who . . . would have all to know him, and to wo
> ship him . . . in the Light. . . . Now this is the Light whic
> Jesus Christ hath enlightened you withal, that doth let yo
> see your evil thoughts, and the naughty words, and the . .
> evil ways you run into. . . . And so all ye Kings and Powe
> of the Earth, God is come to Rule . . . whose Power is goin
> over all Nations of men.[86]

The Emperor K'ang Hsi, Confucian scholar and friend of Jesu
scientists, would no doubt have received the letter with courtes
and approval, but the only actual Quaker bridges made to nor
Christian people at this time were to unshakeable Moslems, to I

---

85. Willem Sewel, *History of the Rise, Increase, and Progress of the . . . Qua
ers* (2 vols. 5th ed. London, 1811), *1*, 433–35. Cf. Braithwaite, *Beginnings*, pp. 418–2
Swarth. 3/124 (*EQL* 413), Thomas Hayman to Fox and Burrough. On other journe
in Europe, see Swarth. 4/12 (*EQL* 435), Hubberthorne, 3/7 (*EQL* 442), Thomas Har
86. George Fox, *Gospel-Truth Demonstrated in a Collection of Doctrin
Books . . .* (London, 1706), pp. 207–08.

ians in Maryland and northward, and to a few negroes in Bar-
ados.

In America, on the other hand, the note of combat is dominant
1 this early period, except for Barbados and the newly acquired
nglish colonies of Jamaica and Bermuda.[87] Since the New Eng-
.nd puritans tried to keep the Quakers out, Massachusetts held the
.me fascination for Friends in 1658 and 1659 that Launceston had
.eld two years before. Five times, Quaker teams went directly to
Iassachusetts to challenge the restrictions, and four Quakers were
.anged in Boston before English authorities finally intervened in
661.[88]

At best, a Quaker mission in those days was dangerous: Peter
:owsnocke and two Warwick Friends, trying to join the attack
pon New England, were lost at sea in 1658. Henry Fell disposed of
.is horse and property more or less as a bequest before setting out
.r Barbados, and later spent eleven weeks at sea between New
ngland and Barbados. During this voyage most passengers fell seri-
.usly ill and twenty-five died, including several Friends. Quakers
.ere frequently refused passage in ships and driven to roundabout
.utes for their voyages. Some would hide their identity, and
vindicated the quackers att a distance, and so they knew us not
ll we cam over." [89] It no doubt added to the tension when Quak-
.s prayed and preached on board, and when any day might bring
.em an inward leading to turn aside for ministry at some un-
:heduled port. Travel on land was more free but often slower and
.ore dangerous than by sea. Thurston, Josiah Coale, and Chapman
escribed how they set out northward from Virginia in 1658.

> After about 11 Miles travell wee Cam amongst the Indians
> who Courtiously Received us and . . . severall of them acom-

87. See ARBarc./62, 63, from George Rofe and Josiah Coale in 1661 on the
Vest Indies.

88. See below, pp. 217–18.

89. ARBarc./118, from Howgill, with Burrough and Eliz. Fletcher, Dublin,
eptember 3, 1655. On Cowsnocke cf. Swarth. 4/212 (*EQL* 397); 4/107 (*EQL* 520);
nd Nuttall's notes in *EQL* 57, 71, 72. On Henry Fell, see especially his letters
warth. 1/142 (*EQL* 305) and 1/70 (*EQL* 410). On difficulties of shipping see 3/132
EQL 431), to the Isle of Man; 4/218 (*EQL* 508), to Barbados; 4/75 (*EQL* 355),
• Ireland; 1/79 (*EQL* 387), on sailing from Scotland when English ports refused
uakers.

panied us about 200 miles farther through ye wildernes or
woods. . . . Whielst T. Thurston was sick the Indians would
goe forth some houres in to the Woods to seek for Wild
Turkeyes to make broth for him. When wee Cam amongst
the dutch [in New Amsterdam, shortly to become New York]
they presently put us in prison. . . . Thes dutch sayd they
Marvelled how wee Cam through amongst them, for If they
should goe but a Litl way from theyr plantations, the Indians
would kill them. [Later, in New England, Coale came near
Plymouth to the] Indian Sagamores hous, which is theyre
king, who sayd that the English men did not Love quakers,
but this is noe English mans sea or land, and quakers shall
Com here and welcom.[90]

After 1658, the chronological story of Quakerism in England is
closely tied up with political events, and so, from here onward,
it must be taken up mainly in later chapters. The death of Oliver
Cromwell led to two years of chaos during which the radical puritans and Quakers re-examined their hopes of a rule by the Saints.
In 1660 the Presbyterians and General Monk recalled Charles II
as king in the effort to assure stability and their own control. But
the Anglicans and the Cavalier squires returned to power and to
Parliament along with the King. The "Clarendon Code" system-
atically crushed all congregations except the restored Episcopal
Church of England. From 1662 on, the prisons were filled with
Quakers and Nonconformists, and the puritan movement's first
fight was for survival. Most of the younger Quaker leaders died
in prison; 450 Friends died altogether. Fifteen thousand were
jailed, and 243 were sentenced to penal colonies overseas, though
only a few dozen were actually transported.[91] Heavy fines and con-
fiscations left many bankrupt. Some new members, however, were
attracted by the brave stand of the Quakers, and new preaching
was done in the colonies. But the expectation of indefinite expansion was gone, and the hope of conquering the world had faded.

Friends now appealed to kings and parliaments for toleration
rather than for repentance. The once fire-eating Quaker was now
known as "a Man for Peace, and an Enemy to Strife and Dissen-

90. ARBarc./13.
91. W. C. Braithwaite, *The Second Period of Quakerism* (2d ed. Cambridge,
Cambridge University Press, 1961), pp. 46–54, 114–15, 655.

sion . . . a Man of publick Spirit, [who] laboured for the . . . good of all, but especially for those he was in Fellowship with." [92] Individual new members were won both during and after the persecutions. The spirit of worship had steadily deepened and mellowed during all the years of pressure, but the Friends had become a sect. Membership became hereditary. They did not withdraw from the world, the nation, or business life, but their sense of responsibility for reforming these areas was kept at arms length from the inward life of Quaker Meetings. After a period of adjustment, the Quakers in England from about 1720, and in America from about 1760, entered a century of quietism: group activity centered on silent worship and only as individuals did they reach into national life. When Quakers began to emerge from this cocoon stage in the middle of the nineteenth century, it was in new directions of evangelicalism, liberalism, mysticism, and political action. But in all later periods the Friends remained unique in the intensity of their involvement with the outward world, a fact that has always set them apart from other sects. This spirit is rooted in the puritan tradition and in the Lamb's War of early Quakerism. Therefore, for an understanding of both modern and original Quakerism, it is important to examine intensively the backgrounds and inward experiences of the early Friends.

92. "Testimony of Patrick Livingston" to Robert Barclay, as quoted in J. Philip Wragge, *The Faith of Robert Barclay* (London, Friends Home Service Committee, 1948), p. 8.

3

The Quaker Galilee:
Regional and Personal Backgrounds

O thou North of England who are accounted as desolat
and barren, and reckoned the least of the Nations, yet out c
thee did the branch spring, and the Star arise which gives ligh
unto all the Regions round about . . . and out of thee th
terror of the *Lord* proceeded, which makes the earth to trem
ble and be removed; out of thee Kings, Princes and Prophet
did come forth in the name and power of the most High.[1]

LIKE other regions of England before modern industry and trave
the North Country, the Quaker Galilee, had a strong character c
its own. The pioneer Quaker preachers were mostly farmers, an
this rural and regional background shaped their religious outloo
as strongly as the national background of puritan England. Othe
regions and issues also were important, but the special characte
of the North played a primary role in shaping the Quaker awaken
ing, and any attempt to trace the experience of a typical earl
Quaker should begin with his home life in the North.

The North as a whole was "the Border" between England an
Scotland. The great earls had for centuries made raids back an
forth, the Scots burning cities as far south as Preston, Richmond
and Ulverston. "The Percy" from England and "the Douglas"
from Scotland were celebrated in ballads, but their main contribu
tion to farm life was the burning of cottages and seizing of cattle

1. Edward Burrough, "To the Camp of the Lord in England" (1655), in *Work*
p. 66.

he English Lord Dacre wrote happily home from beyond the
cottish border: "I have . . . caused to be burnt and distroyed sex
ymes moo townys and howsys within the West and Middill
Iarches of Scotland in the same season then is done to us." [2] De-
:nse of the Border was left mainly to the Border nobles and their
:nants. The King's direct appointees, such as the Captain of Car-
sle, were the butt of local humor, like revenue men in the Ken-
ucky hills.

After the great battles of Flodden and Pinkie in Henry VIII's
me, there was nominal peace on the Border until the Civil War,
ut this only increased the isolation of the North, and fierce raids
y "moss-troopers" continued until 1595. Small fishing, trading,
nd mining towns grew up in all areas of England, though in the
Jorth their success varied widely. The crucial factor was ease of
ccess, for trade was carried on mostly by sea. As late as 1770 over-
und transportation, even to the market towns, was by pack horse;
ridges were few until the eighteenth century, and many were only
f horse width. Lord Howard of Naworth entered in his account
ook: "March 22, 1626: Hewing the way for the coach beyond the
elt Bridge, 2s. 3d." [3]

Feudalism remained longest and strongest in the North. A few
owerful families owned most of the manors in the six northern
ounties: the Cliffords, Nevilles, Percys, Dacres, and Howards each
ad several noble titles. The forms that feudalism took, however,
aried in different areas. The leading earls lived mainly in castles
round York. The Duke of Northumberland kept 165 retainers
1 his own household in Tudor times, and Lord Howard of
Jaworth still had sixty-five in 1640.[4] Much of Northumberland,
)urham, and Lancashire belonged to local squires. The hills and
arming dales of western Yorkshire, Westmorland, and Cumber-

2. *Victoria History of the County of Cumberland,* ed. James Wilson (2 vols
.ondon, 1902–05), 2, 268.
3. Daniel Scott, *Bygone Cumberland and Westmorland* (London, 1899). There
.ere no public carriages or stagecoaches in this area until 1649. Cf. Joseph Nicol-
)n and R. Burn, *History and Antiquities of Westmorland and Cumberland* (2 vols.
. p., 1777); *The Journeys of Celia Fiennes,* ed. Christopher Morris (London, 1947),
p. 194 ff., about a journey through the northwest in 1698; also many details in
ouch, and Victoria County Histories of *Cumberland, Lancaster,* and *York,* ed.
Villiam Page (3 vols. London, 1907–13).
4. Paul Van Brunt Jones, *The Household of a Tudor Nobleman* (Urbana, Illinois,
)17), chap. 1.

land, on the other hand, belonged to the great earls who rarely came to these estates. In the Middle Ages famous abbeys had developed there and owned large tracts of sheepland, though they also provided the only schools and hostels within miles. When all monasteries were closed in the 1530s, the great families annexed additional estates, but the tenants did not benefit.

In the central region of the North, the Pennine moorland, where Quakerism was strongest, the villages were mainly Norse in origin and name, and Norse had been spoken there in the Middle Ages.[5] From the Norsemen came the custom of moots, or assemblies in the open at a standing-stone or hilltop grave, which may have influenced the Quakers' love for such meeting places. The Norse custom was individual ownership of houses and fields: the Norman system of feudal manors imposed in the twelfth century was always resented.

The tenant farmers of Westmorland, West Cumberland, and the Yorkshire Dales had a reputation for independence. Except for the desperate poverty of those in the Lake District itself, their lives provided subsistence but, until Wordsworth came, no glamour. Houses were of stone with dark slate roofs. The family and farm hands all ate together: porridge, oatcake, meat and potatoes, and barley bread. Clothes were usually homemade, "the well-known 'hodden gray' of the Cumberland yeoman."[6] Sturdy furniture, often much carved and initialed; a chest of linen; a little pewter or brass among the more prosperous yeomen; and occasionally a book were bequeathed from father to son along with the farm, carts, and livestock. Flocks and herds were small, for winter feed was hard to get. Oats, barley, hay, and rarely flax, wheat, or hemp were grown. Most yeomen had necessarily several trades, and in the areas which became Quaker strongholds, these usually centered on wool. Kendal was a national market of the wool trade and sent trains of pack horses as far as Southampton.[7]

5. Bouch, pp. 17, 26; Norman Nicholson, *Cumberland and Westmorland* (London, 1949), p. 119.

6. Walter McIntire, *Lakeland and the Borders of Long Ago* (Carlisle, England, 1948), pp. 240–42.

7. Cf. John Somervell, *Some Westmorland Wills, 1686–1738* (Kendal, England, 1928); Bouch, pp. 240–42; *The Boke off Recorde of Kirkbie-Kendal*, ed. Richard S. Ferguson (Kendal, England, 1892); *Local Chronology, Being Notes of the Principal Events Published in the Kendal Newspapers* (Edinburgh, 1865).

Most yeomen held their land by customary tenure; though it was technically copyhold, rights to it could be inherited by the payment of a "fine" or "gressum" to the landlord. A few farms were freehold, owned directly by the men who worked on them. Yeomen held common rights in pasture or moorland which were often encroached upon when the landlord enclosed the land for sheep pasture. They also owed military service when the border was threatened.

Few records survive of the North before the Civil War. A glimpse is given into tenant life, however, by the "Pilgrimage of Grace" in 1536 and 1537, a rebellion of the entire North against Henry VIII.[8] The official bond of unity was the rebels' alarm for the old religion and, specifically, for the monasteries dissolved by the King. In the Yorkshire lowlands most of the lesser nobles, gentry, and clergy rose along with the tenants and assembled 40,000 strong under Robert Aske at Doncaster, a force to rank with any in the Civil War. Yet in the dales only the tenants revolted, under the leadership of "captain Poverty." It is surprising how few clergy or gentry in these areas took part in the rising (though the monks of Holm Abbey and the tenants of Furness abbey mustered out, and the priest of Brough was a leader).[9] The tenants suspected all landowners, and in fact the great Earls had not joined the revolt. "All commons, stick together, rise with no man till ye know his intent; keep your harness in your hands, and ye shall obtain all your purpose in all this North land." [10] The tenants rebelled mainly in protest against rising rents and paying tithes "impropriated" into the hands of gentry—who rarely paid the clergy, as was their corresponding duty. The northwestern tenants disliked absentee priests, and asked:

> 1. Thatt we may putt in thair rowmes to serve God, oder [priests] that wald be glad to keep hospytallyte. 2. All the tythes to remayn to every man his owne doyinge [i.e. church support to be voluntary. Also they asked] That the lands in

8. Madeleine Hope Dodds and Ruth Dodds, *The Pilgrimage of Grace, 1536–37, and the Exeter Conspiracy, 1538* (Cambridge, Cambridge University Press, 1915) is most enlightening on all aspects of this movement.

9. G. P. Jones of Sheffield, a scholar on northwestern regional history, disagrees. Cf., however, Bouch, pp. 181–87; Dodds and Dodds, *Pilgrimage of Grace, 1*, 360–75.

10. *Letters and Papers of Henry VIII*, ed. James Gairdner, *12*, 163, quoted in Tawney, *Agrarian Problem*, p. 324.

Westmorland, Cumberland, Kendall, Dent, Sedbergh, Furness, and the abbey lands in Mashamshire, Kyrkbyshire Netherdale, may be by tenant right, and the lord to have, at every change [of tenancy, only] two years rent for the gressum. . . . This to be done by Act of Parliament . . . and enclosures . . . since the fourth year of Henry VII to be pulled down.[11]

Evidently the abbeys were as unpopular as landlords as were the earls.

At Doncaster the Pilgrimage of Grace ended in a truce, after which King Henry broke all his promises and arrested and executed the leaders. The northwestern tenants disbanded reluctantly. Next year, the tenants of the dales rose again in riots, and some barns and enclosure walls were torn down. Even the Duke of Norfolk, who hanged them, felt pity: "the spoiling of them now, and . . . the increasing of the Lords' rents . . . all here think was the only cause of the rebellion." [12]

It is important to notice that the precise areas in which the Pilgrimage of Grace was basically a tenants' revolt were almost the only areas in which Quakerism became strong in the North. Many of the 1536 issues were echoed by the Quakers one hundred years later: the regional pride and the bitterness of the tenants toward noblemen, clergy, and tithes. Conversely, it is significant that when the great earls did finally revolt against Queen Elizabeth, the tenants of the dales took no part.

A few episodes over the next century suggest that little had changed. Bishop Latimer's royal commission against enclosures was blocked from holding hearings in the North. Archbishop Grindal wrote to Chancellor Cecil under Queen Elizabeth: "I have offte thought to make a generall sute to you for regard for that litle Angle where I was borne, called Cowplande, parcell of Cumberlande, the ignoranteste parte off this realme. . . . I . . . only praye you . . . nott to leave the poor tenantes suiecte to expilation off these countrey gentlemen." [13] In 1610 King James I united with Lord Howard of Naworth and the Duke of Norfolk in press-

11. Gairdner, *12*, 901, and *11*, 1080, 1244, quoted in Dodds and Dodds, *Pilgrimage of Grace*, *1*, 369, 370, 372.

12. Duke of Norfolk to Henry VIII, in Gairdner, *12*, Part I, 478, quoted in Dodds and Dodds, *2*, 121.

13. *Victoria County Histories, Cumberland*, *2*, 70. Cf. John Strype, *The History and Acts of the Most Rev. . . . Edmund Grindal* (Oxford, 1821), p. 2.

ng the claim that, since the Scots were now under the same crown,
he Border tenants were free from defense duties, and so dues and
ents could be raised or tenures ended. The king tried the same
maneuver again at Kendal in 1618. In both cases the tenants rallied
n protest, taking their case to Parliament and to the Court of the
Star Chamber. Though the King took countermeasures and some
enants suffered fines and imprisonment, the tenants' rights were
upheld. At Grayrigg, later a Quaker center, the tenants took a suit
against their landlord to the court at York and were forced to do so
wice again in the next fifty years.[14]

It is generally agreed that the northern counties, especially West-
norland and Cumberland, were at this time the poorest in Eng-
and. No doubt their representatives in Parliament exaggerated
conditions to win an easing of taxes, but men died of starvation in
Greystoke in 1623. During the Civil War also, conditions were
bad in the North: in 1649, 30,000 families in Cumberland were
said to be without bread, seed grain, or money; the tradesmen's
business had fallen by half, and tenants complained of raises in
rent and constant levies to the King.[15]

Another curse of the times was the plague. Typhus killed 8,150
in four moorland deaneries during the famine of 1623. The epi-
demic of 1597 seems to have been even worse. In 1649 the plague
spread north again from Manchester. The later years of the seventeenth century did eventually become a time of prosperity for the
farmers of the dales, but not until after 1660. A house-by-house
survey shows that with regard to dateable houses, house additions,
or sets of furnishings, twice as many survive from between 1660 and
1714, than from all the years before.[16]

During the Civil War the North faced confusion as well as
famine. There were, of course, outstanding families of local gentry
in addition to the absentee Earls, though some of them also aroused

14. Cf. Bouch, pp. 247, 250–52; McIntire, *Lakeland and Border*, pp. 230–40.

15. Cf. Tawney, *Agrarian Problem*, p. 188; Bouch, pp. 30, 169; G. P. Jones, *The
Poverty of Cumberland and Westmorland* (reprinted from *Transactions of Cumberland and Westmorland Antiquarian and Archaeological Society*, 55, Kendal, England, 1956).

16. Bouch, pp. 252–53. Cf. ibid., p. 248; Auguste Jorns, *Quakers as Pioneers in
Social Work*, trans. Thomas K. Brown (New York, Macmillan, 1931), p. 56. The
figures on the remarkable growth in prosperity after 1660 represent the author's
collation of *An Inventory of the Historical Monuments in Westmorland* by the
Royal Commission on Historical Monuments (London, 1936), which lists by parishes
all houses and structures built before 1725.

strong feeling. Impassioned statements still may be heard for o
against the Lowthers or the Stricklands in some parts of the North
west. Most of the gentry were royalist to the hilt, and at the end o
the war lost heavily in fines and seized estates.

The tenants, however, unlike those to the south and east, did no
enlist with their landlords. The banded yeomen of the two forests o
Pendle and Rossendale resolved "to fight it out against the King
rather than their beef and fat bacon should be eaten by papists"—
i.e. the Lancashire gentry. This sounds like the Pilgrimage o
Grace renewed. Yet, although Quaker references to similar "club
men" were disparaging, in later times this was the one area o
Lancashire where Quakers were not persecuted.[17] In most of th
Northwest the gentry did not risk forcing their tenants to choos
sides, considering them unreliable. Parliament, on the other hand
played for their loyalties by promising to maintain tenant rights
In 1642 the royalist Sir Philip Musgrave called out the Westmor
land tenants as a militia, who arrived with quarterstaves, pitch
forks, and a few pikes and muskets. He gave up hope of marchin
them against a much smaller puritan force besieging Thurland
Castle. The Parliamentarians then took their chance. Up to thi
time the Northwest had been considered royalist, and a "rascal
rout" of puritan tenants and a few West Cumberland gentry ha
been easily dispersed by royalist squires at Carlisle. Now the puri
tan detachment marched from Thurland to unite with a fev
Roundhead gentry (including Judge Fell) upon Swarth Moor, and
there beat a larger force of local Royalists. For the remaining year
of the first civil war and throughout the second civil war, the re
gion was mainly in Cromwellian hands, except when the march o
a royalist army temporarily shifted the balance. In 1645 the Round
heads completed their triumph by capturing the royal garrison o
Carlisle and wrecking many other castles, following vain efforts o
local royalist gentry to withstand siege.[18]

17. Here the gentry were royalist. Elsewhere, groups of "clubmen" stood ou
against both sides in the Civil War: cf. Trevelyan, *Stuarts*, p. 269, and Alan Cole
"The Quakers and Politics, 1652–60" (Cambridge University, 1955), p. 6, which cite
as Quaker references to "clubmen" Richard Hubberthorne, *The Commonwealths Re
membrancer* (1659), p. 16, and George Fox, *To Those That Have Been Formerly i
Authority* (1660), p. 5.

18. Cf. John Whitwell, *Kendal during the Civil Wars of the Seventeenth Centur
(Kendal, England, 1764), p. 5; Bouch, pp. 261–64.

The bitterness of the northern gentry against the Quakers was due to the decade of frustration they had known under puritan invaders, whom they considered beneath them. Friends, for their part, were teased as "Roundhead rogues" in royalist towns like Carlisle, yet few had been in the great centers of puritan idealism; those who had been Cromwellian soldiers were mostly Yorkshire-men. The Northwest had seen the less glorious side of both war and Parliament.

The dales of the North of England had been ignored by the church even more than by the state. Much of the region lay in the little diocese of Carlisle, founded in 1122. Most of the bishops, however, never made a visitation: the better ones (like Henry of Bolingbroke's adversary, Bishop Merke) lived at the royal court as statesmen or chaplains. If they proved earnest churchmen, they were moved away to become Archbishops of York. The diocese of Durham was better served but also isolated. Sedbergh and Rich-mond in the Yorkshire dales and the whole peninsula of Westmor-land and Furness fared still worse after Tudor times, since they were attached to the faraway diocese of Chester, whose bishops rarely crossed the Mersey.[19] In the North most of the tithes had been impropriated to the great abbeys; after these were closed, the income and the duty of appointing pastors were given to noblemen or to the universities, who kept the money. Little income came back to local curates, and hatred of tithes was the obvious result.

Northern parishes were hopelessly large. Kendal, which is now nineteen parishes, was then almost the largest in England and included half the Lake District. Ulverston parish in 1650 had nine villages, separated by distances up to thirteen miles; Dalton had twenty villages in an area twelve miles by four. Little chapels were often built in two, three, or four outlying villages in each parish, and these might serve also as schools. But they usually had only members' gifts of a pound or two a year to support the curate, usually a farmer serving as a lay reader and doubling as school-master during the winter. Of the parish churches themselves—

19. Cf. Bouch, pp. 101–06, on Merke; pp. 46 ff., on Bishop Mauclerc; and pp. 51 ff., on Sylvester. John de Kirkby (ibid., pp. 75 ff.) spent his whole episcopacy warring against the Scots. Most bishops of Carlisle spent more care on rebuilding Rose Castle than on the cathedral. As for the diocese of Chester, it was too far away; only under protest would some bishops visit even South Lancashire: cf. Halley, *Lancashire Puritanism.*

101 in Cumberland and Westmorland—only eight paid stipends of more than thirty pounds a year in 1535. Despite the steady inflation, these incomes may have been even *less* by 1650, for they grew smaller during each century after the thirteenth. There were always many parishes without pastors for as many as five years at a time, and others were served by absentees or pluralists living outside the parish. At all periods the clergy of the area were known as the most ignorant in the nation, and always the wretched stipends forced the bishops to admit mean scholars rather than have none.[20] In 1626, in the whole diocese of Carlisle, "there was never a doctor of divinitie . . . but eleven or twelve licensed preachers, three or four bachelors of divinity and eight double beneficed men." [21]

The religious changes under the Tudors all added to these misfortunes. The number of parishes and their total income had already shrunk by a quarter since 1291. In breaking up the monasteries, Henry VIII dissolved the chantries and the collegiate churches. The shifts to and from Catholicism under Mary and Elizabeth caused further drops in the numbers of clergy.[22] The new Prayer Book service in English was no help to men whose English was a dialect. The Elizabethan bishops found the churches dilapidated and the furnishings often gone, but many relics and superstitions from medieval customs remained: "They keep holy days and fasts abrogated; they offer money, eggs, etc., at the burial of the dead; they pray beads." [23] Few among them knew the catechism or the Ten Commandments. Nothing had been given anew to replace the broken remnants of medieval popular Catholicism.

20. *Cumberland*, 2, 90. The figures are based on the survey of the size, income, and needs of each parish in Furness by Oliver Cromwell's "Tryers and Ejectors" in 1650–55, as published in the *Record Society for the Publication of Original Documents Relating to Lancashire and Cheshire, 1* (Manchester, 1879), passim. For instance, two of the Ulverston chapel readers received £5 a year from gifts, and two apparently got nothing. The impropriators paid the vicar £10 a year, with no parsonage. Hawkshead, the biggest Furness parish, was 12 miles by six. Comparative figures for different periods are from Bouch, pp. 60, 68–69, 137, 156, 175, 319, etc. On absentee priests and empty livings, cf. John F. Curwen, *The Later Records Relating to North Westmorland or the Barony of Appleby* (Kendal, England, 1932), pp. 154, 377–80.

21. Bouch, p. 254.

22. Bouch, pp. 155, 220, quotes figures suggesting a drop in the Westmorland-Furness deaneries of the diocese of Chester, from 199 clergy in 1523 to 178 in 1548 and 113 in 1554.

23. Strype, *Grindal*, p. 243; cf. *Cumberland*, 2, 82–84; *York*, 3, 53–60.

The bishops in the fifty years before the Civil War were somewhat better. Under Queen Elizabeth, Bishop Henry Robinson at Carlisle reported:

> Most part of the . . . gentlemen are sound in religion, and the poorer sort generally willing to hear, but pitifully ignorant of the foundations of Christianity . . . many of them are without all fear of God, adulterers, thieves, murderers. The chief spring of all this wofulness comes of the weakness and carelessness of the ministry . . . the great facility of my predecessor in committing the charge of souls to such as were presented by [lay impropriators] who care not how silly the clerk is so long as themselves enjoy the fat of the Living.[24]

Bishop John Best also found his plans for reform hopelessly blocked by the desires of the local gentry. Just before the Civil War, another puritan, the saintly Barnabie Potter, was Bishop of Carlisle. Potter's High Church predecessor had asked his clergy to report whether they served Communion on an altar, used the sign of the cross in baptism, and whether their church members kneeled to receive the sacrament and uncovered their heads in worship. Bishop Potter, as a puritan, asked his ministers if they used any popish ceremonies and whether a bell was tolled when a Christian was dying.[25]

Bishop Best and Potter worked mainly to build up the quality of the clergy as preachers. They introduced a few brave puritans into the area who were startled by what they found. The pastor of Cartmel reported in 1625 that he had thousands of hearers and that his spacious church, though it had almost no seats, was "so thronged at nine in the morning, that I had much to do to get to the pulpit."[26] His people sometimes admitted not even knowing who Jesus was. By the time Fox came to the area, puritan pastors were serving in Kendal, Ulverston, Penrith, Cockermouth, Brigham, and six or eight other Cumberland parishes, and there were puritans eastward over the mountains in Newcastle, Richmond, Durham, and

24. Bishop Robinson to Cecil, quoted in Bouch, pp. 244–45.
25. Bouch, pp. 254–58. See Higginson, *Irreligion of Quakers*, pp. 33, 41; Nightingale, *Ejected of 1662*, 2, 879 ff., for some efforts to improve local preaching.
26. *Life of John Shaw*, as quoted in Benjamin Disraeli: *Curiosities of Literature* (4 vols. New York, 1881), *4*, 365.

towns down into Yorkshire. It was often such a puritan pastor
whose parishioners became the first Quakers in a new area.

Yet few of these puritans were writers or real scholars.[27] Some
had only recently been brought in by Cromwell's "Tryers and
Ejectors," who had no easy time finding substitutes for ministers
they ejected for immorality, pluralism, or royalist ties. They removed thirty-one ministers from the Carlisle diocese. Since at least
twenty-seven were forced out in 1660–62 when the puritans fell,
Cromwell's men must usually have found new men before remov-
ing old ones. But a surprising majority of parsons were kept in their
posts through all the changes in government, theology, and liturgy
from Laud through Cromwell to Charles II.[28] A few remained as
men beloved by their congregations, but most stayed only because
of their own indifference and the despair of governments that
knew they were inadequate. After the Restoration, another saintly
bishop, Edward Rainbow, found things little changed. A vicar was
reported as being given to drunkenness, and scandalous intem-
perance, and gambling at Penrith; many laymen were brought
forward for sabbath-breaking, for "going to witches and wizards,"
or for celebrating "handfast marriages"—a local common-law custom in which the couple took each other as man and wife before a
group of friends (perhaps foreshadowing Quaker customs). One
pastor was by that time rebuked because "his chancell is out of re-
pair . . . [and he] doth not use to catechize the young people . . .
nor doth . . . he labour to reclaime the Quakers." [29]

Even when an energetic puritan pastor arrived before the Quakers, it was often too little and too late. The people of the region had
learned to regard all their clergy as "cruel oppressors, greedy de-
vourers, Caterpillars, who have done no good at all, but kept the

27. Cf. Francis Nicholson and Ernest Axon, *The Older Nonconformity in Kendal*
(Kendal, England, 1915), pp. 12–27. Higginson himself was apparently the only
minister of Westmorland who published, though some preached effectively (cf.
FPT, Nightingale). As a "University Living," belonging to Trinity College, Cambridge, Kendal was more fortunate than most northern towns and obtained some
good puritan pastors.

28. Cf. Curwen, *Later Records of Appleby*, pp. 219–20. Dodgson of Ravenstone-
dale, though a puritan, was forced to conform by his congregation, to which he
remained loyal also, and which kept him as preacher from 1664–73.

29. Bouch, pp. 278–79. Cf. ibid., pp. 236–37, on the churches in general. On
"hand-fast marriages" cf. pp. 238–39.

People in blindness and ignorance." [30] Separatist congregations had begun to meet around Preston Patrick and Sedbergh; the best laymen and a pastor, Thomas Taylor, had joined them. A Lollard woman, Issabil Kendal, had lived in Pardshaw as early as 1508, and the Cockermouth area was a center for sectarianism. Other separatist groups were formed at Bolton and Wigton in Cumberland. Some of the puritan pastors, like Lampitt of Ulverston, reacted to these secessions with thunder, and some with despair.[31] Thomas Lawson and John Wilkinson gave up their ministry entirely and became Quakers themselves.

Much of the Quakers' bitterness against ministers and steeple houses, sermons and sacraments, must have arisen from the debased form in which these had been familiar for generations in the Northwest. Few of the hearers of the Quaker preachers had known vital religion in any form, unless they had made it so themselves.

Education was also short in the northern dales. Despite their quirks in spelling, most of the leading Friends had been through grammar school, but the region as a whole probably had fewer and poorer schools than any in England. Classes were evidently often taught by the minister or schoolmaster in his home or by a curate in the chapels. In Westmorland only twelve parishes out of forty-one had schools in 1645. By contrast, twenty-three more schools were built there in the next half-century. Cartmel Grammar School, dating only from 1598, was probably the oldest in north Lancashire. There were only forty-four schools in the whole Northwest before 1660. The Bible and a few other books were read at home, but a sampling of eighty-nine wills written in 1650–62 shows only twelve men who owned books.[32] The Quaker attitude to learning and to universities was again a reaction to their own futile experience.

In summary, the self-sustaining farmers and shepherds of the Northwest of England, where Quakerism took rise and gathered its special flavor, felt disinherited by their landowners and gentry, by

30. Camm and Audland, *Works*, p. 311.
31. *FPT*, pp. 63–64. Cf. Bouch, pp. 267–69; *FPT*, pp. 57–62.
32. Figures mainly from Bouch, pp. 37 ff., 240 ff., 236; personal collation for Kendal from Nicolson and Burn, *History and Antiquities*; Curwen, *Later Records of Appleby*. The wills are a group from Carlisle surveyed in Bouch, p. 230.

the church, and by the schools. Knowing all these at their worst, they considered them outright evils. In religion, in learning, and in moral and business practices they knew that they themselves could do better than their supposed superiors. They were individualists, with no abstract doctrines about equality, much less about socialism or class struggle, but they were thoroughly radical in their instinctive reactions to all the claims of the highborn and mighty. When this radicalism was focused and deepened by the religious experience of Quakerism within their own lives, it made them react explosively against the evils in the social order wherever they found them.

Other English regions reacted as a whole to Quakerism in characteristic ways, though in certain areas only knowledge of individuals or parishes would explain Quaker beginnings. The other parts of northern England followed the same general pattern as Westmorland and Cumberland. The area of northeastern Yorkshire from Cleveland down into Holderness, where the great Malton revival took place, was again an area of former abbeys and of rural isolation and poverty, with diffuse parishes where few puritans had come.[33] In the Northumberland moorlands on the Scottish border, feudal ties still bound the tenants in the valleys so tightly to the little "peel castles" and their lairds that outsiders, even Quakers, made little impact. In Durham and the Tyne valley, Quakerism made some headway, beginning in places where a foothold had been established by a few puritans and separatists, as around Darlington, Newcastle, and Sunderland. But Friends met opposition from pillars of town and church in these places and often preferred meeting in suburbs, though the purely rural Meetings later withered away.[34] In southern and central Yorkshire this pattern was even more marked: Puritanism belonged to the towns and Quakerism to the satellite villages. Quakerism there seemed less a regional movement than an awakening among the separatist congregations. Mass meetings were held only under heavy puritan opposition. Similarly, in southern Lancashire the puritan manufacturing centers like Manchester and Bolton were consistently unresponsive, despite many preaching assaults, whereas small

33. Cf. Newton, "Puritanism in York"; and *FPT*, pp. 295–301.
34. *JFHS, 48* (1957), 119–22, and diocesan visitation of Durham of 1662–71 as summarized in *Archaeologia Aeliana, 34* (4th Ser. 1956), 92–109.

Meetings took root in rural villages around Liverpool and Warrington. In Cheshire, Quakerism specifically centered on Seeker
groups in the villages of Malpas and Frandley, though mass meetings there were large enough to imply a regional awakening.[35] In
general, then, where Puritanism in the North was strong, Quakerism grew only on its separatist fringes; where Puritanism was weak,
the Friends often swept through the entire district and reached all
social groups and classes.

In the Southwest also, Quakerism had regional roots. The lack
of response in North Wales and the Welsh border is credited to the
work of Baptist revivalists like Morgan Llwyd, who pre-empted the
field without the difficulty of a language barrier. Where Baptist
groups were breaking up, as around Welshpool and Wrexham, and
in English-speaking regions such as those around Hereford and
Haverfordwest, Quakers came in. These districts were also rural
and beyond the zone of puritan consolidation, although the Baptist pastor John Tombes of Herefordshire became a national figure.
But the Quakers were strongest in Gloucestershire, Somerset, and
Dorset, an area that needs more study. A large proportion of anti-
Quaker literature in 1655 came from the Severn Valley. This region had strong local pride, and the Monmouth rebellion of 1685
was in some ways a southwestern uprising. Here also the country
gentry were royalist, but the people more indifferent. Gloucestershire had been Lollard country, and there was some tradition of
Puritanism, which had spread from Bristol and Plymouth, though
few strong puritan rural parishes are reported. The pattern here
is not so clear, for Quakers held few mass meetings outside Bristol.
The background of Friends in this region is fairly well divided
between country and town, and except for a high number of weavers, no trades were disproportionately represented. Here, at least,
"most weavers lived from hand-to-mouth upon the meagre wages
of the clothier" and had a reputation for corn riots, sectarianism,
and "turbulent and riotous behaviour." [36] Agrarian unrest in this

35. Swarth. 1/194 and 1/114 (*EQL* 207, 208); *FPT*, pp. 16–19, 147–51.
36. Alan Cole, "Social Origins of the Early Friends," *JFHS*, 48 (1957), 108, quoting
G. D. Ramsay, *The Wiltshire Woollen Industry in the 16th and 17th Centuries.* Cf.
FPT, pp. 16–19; *JFHS*, 35 (1938), 80; Braithwaite, *Beginnings*, pp. 346–49. On the
backgrounds of Quakerism in Wales see Nuttall, *Welsh Saints*, chaps. 1 and 3. A
forthcoming thesis of Miss Barbara Bowden for London University contains tables
classifying anti-Quaker literature by regions and years as well as by author.

area continued until the Tolpuddle martyrs of the nineteenth century.

It would be interesting to know why Quakerism did not become
a regional mass movement in Devonshire and Cornwall, another
area almost isolated from the rest of England and famous for
agrarian riots in Tudor times. In some backward districts like
Minver and Endellion on the Lizard cape, Quaker meetings swept
whole villages, as they had done in the North. Around Falmouth,
however, it was the Baptists in the garrison who responded; elsewhere those convinced were limited to a few educated families.[3]

The general coldness of the eastern counties to Quakerism was
related to the strength of puritan parishes. Local factors must have
been involved in the growth of the strongholds at Norwich, Cog-
geshall, and Colchester—famous for its radical sects, and its martyrs under Mary Tudor; weavers and separatists as usual played a
part. These and the patchwork of backgrounds and reactions in the
Midlands must be left to the expert historian.

The cities of London and Bristol were the third great source of
Quaker strength, and in the end they dominated Quaker organization. Both places had been puritan in sympathy during the Civil
War; the aldermen and merchants were Presbyterians, but the
craftsmen and apprentices were Cromwellians who had on more
than one occasion saved the day when Parliamentary armies fell
back. London and Bristol had been citadels of the Baptists, the
Levellers, and smaller sects, toward whom the orthodox puritan
ministers and men of substance were bitter. It is quite clear that
the Quakers were drawn from the working-class groups in both
towns. Though 10 per cent of Friends in Bristol and 15 per cent
in London called themselves merchants, only 3 per cent were
gentlemen or in the highly trained professions.[38] Quakers were at
all times identified with the radical puritans in these cities—even
with their political misadventures—and most London and Bristol
Friends probably came out of Baptist or separatist churches. When
conservative mayors and aldermen tried to suppress these sects,
Quakers made common cause with the sectarians.

37. Hodgkin, *Quaker Saint of Cornwall*, p. 8; *FPT*, pp. 20–29. The agrarian riot
ending in Blackheath near London, which began in Cornwall, nearly overthrew
Henry VII late in the fifteenth century.

38. Cole, "Social Origins" (*JFHS, 48*) presents detailed figures from all Meetings
where data is available from marriages, etc.

In most overseas areas where Quaker missionaries traveled, special situations limited their adherents to a few individuals or groups. In Scotland the espousal of radical Puritanism by Cromwell's army made Quaker ideas unwelcome to the Scots; young men and women who reacted against Presbyterianism would seldom join the new ultrapuritan movement. This was even truer in Ireland. Cromwell had tried to break resistance by banishing all Irish landowners to Connaught. Those Irish who remained had the status of squatters or tenants under 100,000 Scots and 200,000 English, half of them radical puritans whom Cromwell or his predecessors had settled in the north and east of Ireland. Most of the 800,000 Irish lived in windowless thatched cottages and were regarded by the English as brigands or "tories"; their resultant hatred for the English still endures. To the Quaker preachers, therefore, "our service laye only in great Townds and cittyes, for genrally the country is wthout Inhabitants ther, but bands of murderers, thieves and Robers," and "in this ruinous nation . . . it is very bad travelling every way afoot and also dangerous," on muddy roads without bridges or coaches.[39] In the isolated towns the little English garrisons or settlements welcomed Quaker missionaries enthusiastically, but Friends rarely preached to the native Irish. On almost the only occasion when a Quaker even tried to reach Catholics in Ireland, Solomon Eccles went naked as a sign, with fire and brimstone on his head, to condemn a celebration of the Mass outside the gates of Galway. Irish Quakerism was by no means concentrated within the old Ulster settlements of Scots and English, but probably no Friends Meeting exceeded one hundred members or could hope to grow much larger. In Ireland, and for that matter in Scotland, few opponents bothered to write anti-Quaker literature before 1658.[40]

39. On Irish backgrounds cf. Swarth. 3/16 (*EQL* 227), 3/17 (*EQL* 179); John M. Douglas, "Early Quakerism in Ireland," *JFHS, 48* (1956), 3–32; Olive C. Goodbody, "Anthony Sharp, Wool Merchant, 1643–1707," *JFHS, 48,* 38–49; Goodbody, "Ireland in the *Sixteen-Fifties: A Background to the Coming of Quakerism,*" *JFHS, 48,* 33–38.

40. Cf. Swarth. 3/134 (*EQL* 395), 4/24 (*EQL* 401); Douglas, pp. 30–31; ARBarc./65. Cromwellian officers who became Friends included William Ames, Edward Cooke, William Morris, Robert Turner, and Robert Malins, and the puritan colonists Edmondson, Perrot, and Luffe. When all Irish Friends were asked in 1680 to record their refusal to pay tithes, 780 did so, about half from Ulster. The largest Meeting, at Lisburn, recorded only 93, and 12 Meetings out of 28 recorded fewer than 15 adult members. On anti-Quaker literature cf. B. Bowden's thesis.

In the American colonies, on the other hand, there were many puritan settlers even outside the rigidly orthodox communities of Massachusetts and Connecticut. In Maryland and Barbados the puritan governors during the Commonwealth period tolerated the Quaker preachers. In back-country Virginia, Rhode Island, and the English settlements on Long Island and along the Delaware, there was no authority to resist the Friends. In such a "darke corner of the Earth and remote place, where the Lord hath scattered and some of us have had our natural birth," the colonists rarely had any religious guidance at all, and the Quaker minister worked in an untouched field. But in puritan Massachusetts, Meetings were small groups gleaned from among separatists, so that the English pattern was repeated in America. Colonists in America felt in no way divorced from English thought and ideals in this period, and, as far as the Quakers were concerned, this continued to be true until they migrated into farming areas beyond the Appalachians.[41]

The general relationship of Quakerism to puritan and separatist groups has been suggested, though in many individual towns and districts it remains obscure. It took deepest root in the regions where Puritanism and even the Baptists were weakest, but within these areas, in almost every case, Quaker groups arose near towns where there had been puritans and separatists. All over England, Quakers sought out Baptist congregations. Baptists and separatist groups sprang up on either the social or the geographical fringes of Puritanism. Where these churches were strong, especially in cities, Quakers might win only a few. Where they were in outlying rural regions—as in the Isle of Axholme in Lincolnshire, at Consett in Durham, or in the separatist gatherings of the Northwest—the entire puritan group might be won. A lone congregation of independent orthodox puritans might be broken into, as at Penrith, Bridekirk, and Cockermouth, but in the areas where outstanding puritan preachers had worked for generations, nothing of this sort was likely. Those who came to Quakerism were individuals who

41. Cf. Henry J. Cadbury's comments on the Laythes MSS in *JFHS, 33* (1936), 51. On the inadequate chaplains in Virginia and Maryland see William W. Sweet, *Religion in Colonial America* (New York, 1942), Chap. 2; on North Carolina see A. L. Drummond, *The Story of American Protestantism* (Edinburgh, 1949), p. 18. North Carolina, formally organized in 1672, did not have even an Anglican chaplain until 1700. Cf. also Tolles, *Atlantic Culture*, p. 19.

had known Puritanism and rejected it or larger groups that had known Puritanism only in fragmentary ways.[42]

The personal background of individual Friends gives further light on these matters. Most of the leaders and preachers had been through a series of churches and some years of religious experience before becoming Friends. Some had served in Cromwell's army: Crook, Billing, Bishop, Curtis, and others had been officers, and Ames, Dewsbury, Edmondson, Hubberthorne, Thomas Stubbs, John Whitehead, George Fox "the younger," and many others had served in the ranks. They had heard the puritan chaplains and attended prayer meetings and discussion groups. Nayler had been a lay preacher in the army himself. John Whitehead makes a typical report:

> I was . . . instructed in the strictest profession of Religion, that then was called by them Puritanism; yet notwithstanding, I lived without any true sence of my fallen and lost estate, until I was about 18 years of age, about which time I had a day of visitation, and God . . . did let me see that my heart was full of corruption . . . whereby my conversation became blameless to the world. . . . hearing sermons, reading the scriptures . . . I much frequented . . . until I was about 18 . . . about which time I went into the Army . . . but followed men zealously whom the world called godly Ministers. . . . But this faith was outward . . . for the root of evil still did remain.[43]

But Richard Farnworth, another leading Quaker, apparently did not enter the army. He had inherited a small farm at Tickhill, near Doncaster in Yorkshire, where he had been born, but he worked for seven years in the home of a puritan family some miles away, until he read the writings of Saltmarsh, a "spiritual puritan," and so "turned Antinomian and Perfectionist, pretended to internal Teachings and immediate Revelations, renouncing all outward publique Gospel-administrations, and refusing to joyn in Family

42. On Consett, cf. Swarth. 4/209 (*EQL* 54); on Axholme, 3/52 (*EQL* 36); on Chester 1/189 (*EQL* 55); also *FPT* on all counties.
43. John Whitehead, *The Enmity between the Two Seeds* (London, 1655), pp. 4 ff.

worship." [44] For this he was apparently fired, but he worked one year in the home of "Coronet Heathcote" in the neighborhood before becoming a Quaker preacher.

Though Nayler, Hubberthorne, Farnworth, and others considered themselves already convinced of the Truth and simply "joyned with it" when they heard Fox preach, even among these leaders many went through a new inner birth in the Quaker movement. Of the rank and file, not many had had deep religious lives before becoming Friends. Baxter reported: "very few experienced, humble, sober Christians . . . turned to them; but it's the young, raw professors [of Christianity] and women, and ignorant, ungrounded people. . . . And most . . . were Anabaptists or the members of some such sect." [45] Baxter is describing southern England where Puritanism had already won the elite and the Baptists had reached the remainder. In the North, individuals who had belonged to separatist congregations were much outnumbered by men who had known only the dead parish churches. A Cumberland man can stand as a representative:

> 1653: Christopher Wilson was one tht early embraced Truth in wch he lived & died. He was a man that had low thoughts of himselfe, although well Reputed of his Neighbors for his honesty among men & free heartedness. . . . His heart & house was kept open to entertain frds, and was belloved of them till his dyeing day . . . and a little before his death spoke of the goodness of god to him before some of his family.[46]

Wilson, like Camm and Howgill, was a leader in his community apart from his role as a Quaker, though the economic and social standing of early Friends as a whole was not high. Even the leaders were mainly farmers, "statesmen," or yeomen: James Nayler especially impressed Ellwood "because he looked but like a plain

44. John Stalham, *The Reviler Rebuked*, quoted in Geoffrey F. Nuttall, "Notes on Richard Farnworth," *JFHS, 48* (1956), 80. Farnworth's employer, Thomas Lord, was uncle of the Quaker Thomas Aldam and presumably owned the book by the spiritual puritan Saltmarsh. For Farnworth's break with orthodox puritanism see also *The Heart Opened by Christ,* cited in Watkins, p. 129.

45. Richard Baxter, *One Sheet against the Quakers,* quoted in Braithwaite, *Beginnings,* p. 194.

46. *FPT,* p. 40.

simple country-man . . . an Husbandman or a Shepherd." [47] To be sure, Anthony Pearson, Gervase Benson, and John Crook were justices of the peace, but Cromwell often had to reach far down among the ranks of gentry in royalist counties to find puritans to serve as his justices. In the South of England, the Penns and Peningtons also came into Quakerism from respectable backgrounds, as did Ellwood himself; indeed, Benjamin Furly was the richest merchant in his town and was called before the Privy Council by Charles II. Nevertheless the contrast of the Quaker leadership with the leaders of even the plebeian Baptists is quite striking: most of the Baptist leaders were high army officers, outstanding London merchants, or former puritan pastors from the universities. Of the few former pastors who became Friends, Samuel Fisher, Giles Barnardiston, Thomas Lawson, and Thomas Taylor had been to a university.

The main body of Friends in the North were rural people, about evenly divided between farming and the wool or clothing trades. A survey of seventeenth-century wills from the Kendal Friends Meeting (probably the biggest and most urban in the North) shows mainly simple farming backgrounds: out of seventy men, forty-nine listed themselves as yeoman or husbandman, but twelve were craftsmen as well. Their farms were small; the total livestock on eighteen farms adds up to only thirty-five horses, about a hundred cows, and ten flocks of sheep; only seven kept chickens and three had pigs.[48]

In the South of England the recent careful study of Alan Cole has showed more diversity. Twenty per cent of the Gloucestershire Quakers and 33 per cent in Buckinghamshire were farmers—with weaving and cloth trades, food-selling, and the group of "me-

47. Thomas Ellwood, *The History of the Life of Thomas Ellwood* (London, 1714), p. 19. For comparison of the social status of Baptist and Quaker leaders see Barbour, "Early Quaker Outlooks," appendix 2; also Cole, "Social Origins," *JFHS, 48,* 99 ff.

48. This material is collated from Somervell, *Westmorland Wills.* Cf. Cole, *JFHS, 48,* 103, who says that in the Kendal area 33 per cent of Quakers listed on marriage records were yeomen or husbandmen, 40 per cent were weavers, shoemakers, etc., and 17.4 per cent were in "mechanick" trades. Somervell lists 3 freehold farm owners, 14 who combined freehold and customary tenure, 20 who were merely tenants, several dozen holding no land at all, and only 8 who owned houses and workshops in town. Despite Ernest Taylor (*The Valiant Sixty,* London, 1947), these men were not well off economically, however sturdy and independent.

chanick" crafts each accounting for about a quarter of the total
(though cloth-workers made up 34 per cent in Gloucestershire and
only 16 per cent in Bucks). In both counties, and also in London
and Bristol, shoemaking accounted for 6 to 10 per cent, carpentry
and the building trades about the same; men from the highly cap-
italized industries such as soap-making or metal-working were
fewer. In towns, the biggest single occupation was tailoring; and
as Quakers became more prosperous toward 1700, a significant proportion of these men became drapers and cloth merchants.[49]

Of Quaker women who became preachers, a surprising number
had been domestic servants, and the prominence of such women
among early Quakers shows their indifference to social standing
and convention. Nevertheless, only one per cent of Quaker men
were willing to list themselves in Meeting registers as mere servants
or day laborers, and in no area did more than one per cent consider themselves gentlemen.

Thus early Friends were, in general, farm people or town craftsmen, often from poor areas or trades; few were either outright pro-
letarians or gentry. The strength of Quakerism among weavers in
the villages and among tailors and leather workers in the towns witnesses to their spirit of independence and self-respect. These
groups, especially the weavers, had been active in all sectarian
movements since Lollard times. Geographically, Quaker roots grew
strongest in just those areas where schools, landlords, and all other
religious movements had given least: the English Northwest and
Southwest and the American frontier. Within these areas the leaders and inner circles of Quakerism were men of independence, who
had been strongly reached but not claimed by puritanism. The
early Wesleyan Methodists and the New Englanders most active in
the Great Awakening had similar backgrounds. In each case the
rank and file had not been closely linked beforehand to either the
churches or the social order and felt disinherited by the wise and
prosperous who held prestige; hence they created new church denominations regardless of their leaders' intentions. The members
of all these movements were raised in Christian traditions, usually
Calvinistic, knowing the Bible and bearing a sense of sin. A dis-

---

49. Cole, "Social Origins," *JFHS, 48,* 99–119. Fuller figures are given in his "Quakers and Politics." Intensive work by Richard Vann of Carleton College may modify
these conclusions.

tinction remains between such movements of awakening and an ordinary revival within a pious church community. The deeper and longer-lasting transformation of life in a religious awakening stems both from the more radical social background of its members and from the freshness of their new experience.[50]

50. The clearest case of revivalism among non-Christians (with no Christian background to revive) was the nineteenth-century movement in Tonga: cf. K. S. Latourette, *History of the Expansion of Christianity*, 5 (New York, 1942), 221–22. There have been similar movements in West and Central Africa.

4

The Terror and Power of the Light

THE Lamb's War began for most early Friends with a hard, slow, inner conflict; only afterward could they call themselves the children of the Light. This opening struggle shaped the meaning of their new lives and gave color to all they thought or felt about the inward Light and the Spirit of God. The end of it was peace and joy, a sense of power to conquer kingdoms and demons, and a deep unity of love with other Quakers. The serenity and trust and the sense of daily direction from the Spirit finally became the most characteristic part of the Quaker way of life. Yet their actual ethical standards were based less on love and serenity than on the inward struggle they themselves had been through:

> God . . . doth nothing . . . but by his Son, the Lamb. . . .
> His appearance in the Lamb . . . is to make War with the
> God of this World, and to plead with his Subjects concerning
> their revolt from him their Creator . . . *The Manner of this
> War is,* first . . . he gives his Light into their Hearts, even of
> Men and Women, whereby he lets all see . . . what he owns
> and what he disowns . . . that so he may save . . . all that
> are not wilfully disobedient. . . . *They are to War against*
> . . . whatever is not of God . . . whatever the flesh takes De-
> light in, and whatever stands in Respect of Persons. . . .
> With the Spirit of Judgment and with the Spirit of Burning
> will he plead with his Enemies; and having kindled the fire,
> and awakened the Creature, and broken their Peace and Rest
> in Sin, he waits in Patience to Recover the Creature and slay

the Enmity, by suffering all the Rage and Envy . . . that
. . . the Creature can cast upon Him, and he receives it all
with Meekness . . . returning love for hatred.[1]

The same pattern of experience is described in dozens of Quaker
journals, though its form is so obscure in Fox's own that it is not
always recognized. Since the writing of spiritual diaries was a tradition in puritan England, the repeated pattern of events must be
treated with caution. But even in borrowed words each man speaks
for himself, often using familiar phrases because he knows no
others. A universal truth took on new meaning as a personal discovery even when individual experience was partly fostered by the
established ideal. A recent study of the diaries which were actually
published as autobiographical tracts in the 1650s shows that the
dozen Quaker examples have their own common pattern distinct
from those of Calvinists or Ranters.[2] This sequence of Quaker experiences is also found in the dozen most outstanding journals published after the writers' deaths.

Before analyzing the stages of a man's growth into Quakerism, it
would be well to present a typical story.

John Banks, who later preached in Cumberland and Dorset, was
mainly known by Friends as a beloved leader in his own moorland
Meeting:

> I came of honest parents . . . in Isell, in the County of Cum-
> berland; and my Father, having no Real Estate of his own,
> took Land to Farm; and by trade was a Fel-monger and glover.
> . . . And though my Parents had not much of this World's
> Riches, yet . . . they brought me up well . . . and was care-
> ful to Restrain me from such Evils as children and Youth are
> apt to run into . . .
>
> I was put to School when I was Seven Years of Age, and kept
> there until I was Fourteen; in which time I learned well both
> English and Latin. . . . And when I was Fourteen, . . . my
> Father . . . put me to teach School . . . at *Mosser-Chappel*
> (near *Pardshow*), where I Read the Scriptures also, to People

---

1. Nayler, *Works*, pp. 375–79, from "The Lamb's War."
2. See Watkins, "Spiritual Autobiography"; also Howard H. Brinton, ed., *Children of Light* (New York, 1938), pp. 383–406, where Brinton reports on stages of spiritual development in 100 Quaker journals, mostly from the eighteenth century.

that came there on the first Day of the Week, and Homily, as
it is called, and sung Psalms, and Prayed: but I had no liking
to the Practice . . .

And then I being Sixteen years of Age . . . in 1654 it
pleased the Lord . . . to reach my Heart and Conscience by
his great Power and pure living Spirit [while I was] by myself
alone in the Field, before I ever heard any one called a *Quaker*
Preach . . . at any of their Meetings . . . But the First Day
that I went to one, which was at Pardshaw . . . the Lords
Power in the Meeting so seased upon me, that I was made to
Cry out in the bitterness of my Soul, in a true sight and sense
of my Sins . . .

And the same Day at evening, as I was going to a Meeting of
Gods People . . . scornfully called Quakers, by the way I was
smitten to the Ground with the weight of God's Judgment for
Sin . . . and I was taken up by two Friends. And, Oh, the
Godly Sorrow that did take hold of me, and seised upon me
that Night in the Meeting. . . . So a Friend . . . being
touched with a sense of my Condition . . . read a paper in
the Meeting . . . which was suitable to my Condition . . .
I being very much bowed down and perplexed, by Sins being
set in order before me, and the time I had spent in Wildness
and Wantonness, in Vanity, Sport and Pastime . . .

Neither did I satisfie myself, that I was Reached unto by
the Power of God. But by taking True heed thereunto,
through Watchfulness and Fear, I came by one little after another, to be sensible of the Work thereof in my Heart . . . to
Wash Purge and Cleanse me Inwardly. . . . But before I
came to witness that Work Effected, the Nights of Godly Sorrow and Spiritual Pain, for many Months and some Years, that
I Travelled through, did bear so hard, both upon my Body
and Mind, that I was made to leave off . . . Teaching of
School . . . and did betake my self to learn . . . something
of Husbandry . . .

Keeping close unto the Power of God, in Waiting upon
him in Silence among his People . . . I came to more Settlement and Weightiness in my Spirit, and Peace . . . after
. . . I had passed through great Tribulation, in Weeping and
Mourning in Woods and solitary Places. . . . So that about

six Years after I had received the Truth . . . I had some
Openings in and by the Power and Spirit of Truth . . . and
with Fear and Trembling I spoke in our blessed Meetings.
. . . And Oh, the Days and Nights of Comfort and Divine
Consolation we were made partakers of in those Days to-
gether.[3]

John Banks' family background was typical, even in its unevent-
fulness, piety, and isolation from new ideas. Despite the convention
among all Puritan journal-writers of painting life before conversion in only the darkest colors, Banks' "wildness and wantonness"
were probably limited to bowling, shuffleboard, and boredom in
worship. There are few Quaker journals which fail to mention a
sober childhood and righteous parents. John Camm, for instance,
"from his Childhood was inclined to be Religious, and sought after
the best things; and . . . was one . . . that joyned . . . with
the most strict and upright in the performance of religious Duties." [4] Specifically, he became a separatist.

Like puritans, however, Quaker journal-writers also often
wanted to stress the outward, legalistic efforts at goodness that had
preceded the discovery of their inner inadequacy. Quakers, of
course, sometimes linked this legalism with their days as puritans.
Some diaries mention not only membership in puritan churches
but vital religious experiences and doctrinal truths found there.
Yet even those who, as leading separatists, had already accepted
ideas like Fox's, on entering Quakerism often went through times
of struggle as bitter as that of John Banks. Hubberthorne wrote to
Fox in 1652:

The hand of they lord hath bene mightly exersised upon mee
& his terrors hath beene sharpe with in mee. The consump-
tion determined upon the whole earth hath [been] & is passing through mee, wch hath bene terible unto the brutish nature wch could not endure the devouring fire, it being soe hote
& unquenchable that I sawe nothing that could live or pass
through it. . . . Judgment shall come forth to victory;

---

3. John Banks, *A Journal of the Life, Labours, Travels* . . . (London, 1712), pp.
1–10: John Burnyeat's account in *The Truth Exalted in the Writings* . . . (London, 1691) is very similar.
4. "Thomas Camm's Testimony" in Camm and Audland, *Works*.

> though the . . . end is not yet. In the midst of his terible
> judgments thear was a mercy hid wch I saw not, wch was the
> cause why I was not consumed; & his compassions failled not,
> though at that time I could see neither mercy nor compassion.
> . . . All things wch is pure and holy is hid from man, for he
> is seprate from god & knoweth not any of his wayes . . . Man
> must dye & know his own wayes no more, but must be led in
> a way wch he knoweth not, contrary to his will, contrary to
> his wisdom, contrary to his reason.[5]

The essence of pain was to know one's sins and self-will, but the
source of the pain was the Light itself. To modern Friends it is
startling to find the inward Light described in terms of such fierce
judgment. The Light that ultimately gave joy, peace, and guidance gave at first only terror. Howgill wrote:

> As soon as I heard one declare . . . the Light of Christ in
> Man was the Way to Christ, I believed . . . and then my Eyes
> were opened, and all things were brought to remembrance
> that ever I had done. . . . The Ark of the Testament was
> opened . . . and the dreadful power of the Lord fell upon me
> . . . Fear and Terrour . . . sorrow and pain. . . . mine
> Eyes were dim with crying. . . . All was overturned. . . .
> And then something in me . . . as I bore the indignation of
> the Lord . . . rejoyced . . . the Captive came forth out of
> his Prison . . . and the new Man was made. And so peace
> came to be made . . . through Death and Judgment.[6]

In such experiences the Quakers regarded the Light as being
God's own goad and probe, the truth. Margaret Fell wrote: "Now,
Friends, deal plainly with yourselves, and let the Eternal Light
search you . . . for this will deal plainly with you; it will rip you
up, and lay you open . . . naked and bare before the Lord God,
from whom you cannot hide yourselves. . . . Therefore give over
deceiving of your Souls; for . . . all Sin and Uncleanness the Light
condemns." [7] Here modern experience can recognize the experi-

5. Swarth. 3/1 (*EQL* 2), Hubberthorne to Fox, July 1652.
6. Howgill, *Works*, pp. 43–44. His autobiographical tract was *The Inheritance of Jacob Discovered* (London, 1655).
7. M. Fell, *Works*, pp. 95, 136. Cf. Fox, *Journal*, Camb., *1*, 28; Fisher, *Works*, p. 609; Wragge, *Barclay*, p. 43, etc.

ence of encountering inner truth. Even today, when our consciences are not honed on puritan commandments and the sense of the presence of God may be less fearful, few people can sit through an hour of silent Quaker worship without a wandering mind which dodges painfully away from steady reflection. The first efforts at stillness begin to show a person his inadequacy, emptiness of purpose, or well-buried guilt.

The pious, prim background of the early Quakers set them a moral standard that few men could live up to. The Christian ideal itself, especially in the Sermon on the Mount, is unlimited in its demands, and this was all the more true in puritan England. A bitter struggle was almost inevitable in the face of the puritan demand for inward as well as outward purity. The very harshness of the law added tension by provoking instinctive rebellions: "by the Law came Sin," and under the law a man knew himself to be "exceeding sinful." A Friend could report that the "Righteous Law of God is Rendered in fury & vengeance upon the transgresser in me," and that "in measure I see that Witness Raised that never Gives rest day nor night to that in me that Worshipps the beast." [8]

The quaking and trembling that gave the Quakers their name were the results of this inward experience. John Audland "sat down in silence and astonishment, like Job, for . . . he did Mourn and Weep bitterly." [9] Knowing "the terribleness of God's wrath," wrote Oxford graduate Samuel Fisher, "therefore no marvail if there be so much trembling in the true Church." [10] Quaker writers cited an impressive array of biblical tremblers to answer puritan scoffers. George Canby described how he himself, as a youth, was so struck down. He was

> Wild and Wanton at that Day, tho not Outwardly profane, but without God in the World; and the Power of God was mightily upon William [Dewsbury], & fixing his Eyes upon me, Declared what the Lord putt into his mouth to me in particular, and I did truly Witness the Word of the Lord to be Quick and Powerfull, which cut me to the heart, that I fell Down in the House ffloor as Dead. . . . When I came to sence again, he had got me up in his Armes . . . and my Beastiall

8. Dews./7 from Thomas Foster, June 7, 1655.
9. "Thomas Camm's Testimony" in Camm and Audland, *Works.*
10. Fisher, p. 16.

Fig. 3. Letter from George Fox to Benjamin Nicholson, 1653, with a message of guidance, perhaps for the Earl of Pembroke, who attended Quaker gatherings in London. Nicholson, from Tickhill in Yorkshire, was a prisoner with Aldam in York castle, where he wrote a tract supporting the "rule of the saints" desired by Cromwell's army, and joined in writing another pamphlet, against tithes. By the end of 1653 he was in the South. He died in 1660, in York Castle. Fox's letter to him reads:

der brother my care is over thee thou art amongst thorns least thou should be defild otake head of louking out at any thing that is visable least the safere be lost & the deserning but weak in that which is puer in thee to gid the to weat upon god for his pouer to order thee in all things that wisdom may be iustfied in all things of thee & keep to few wowords but weat in the pouer that the faeth of all may be brought in to the pouer & so god all mighty keep thee in his pouer to do his will i am in combarland yett & great workings the lord has this awayes

       Bengamen nickeles   Seand thiis with spead
& to the earl so caled withthe world theris a seeking deries in him in his will but bid him mind that which is contrare to his will which will leat him see all the deceats of his hart which light taking head to it will gid him to god loving it & teache him hole(?) & the feare of the lord & bring him from faros hous & out of egep to worship god mouw(?) now o man thout hast time pri. . it & thiis light is the ay to leet thee see all the deacets within & without & the wise mans ay is in his head which is krist who hat given him the light & the souels is abrod after many teachers without but hee that lovest the light which christ hath given him weath at wisdoms gat wich is not a steopell hous but at iesus who hath given him this light who is the tresher of wisdom & of knolg who with his pouer filleth heaven & earth & over all plesed for ever amen & that light with in thee will teach thee to know god & that light within will condam thee hateting it & loving it it will bring thee in to the narow way & out of the brod way from all the fashons & worships & costoms of the world & chroches of the world into the crouch of god & it will teach thee how to worship god fare well

FRIENDS' REFERENCE LIBRARY.

der brother my care is over thee thou art amongst these least thou should
be defild of all heed of looking out at any thing that is visable least
the safer be lost & the deserning but weat in that which is yours
tim thee to gid the to weat upon god for his power to order thee in all
things that wisdom may be iustified in all things of thee
& keep to few words but weat in the power that the faith of
all may be brought in to the power & so god all mighty
keep thee in his power to do his will i am in cumberland yea
& reall worke unto the lord hast this away es

benjamen nickles

seconi this with seal

& to the earst so colod with the word theris a seeking deriefs in him in his
will but bid him mind that which is compare to his will which
will leat him see all the occais of his hart which light
taking heed to it will yid him to god loving it & reade him hole
& the feare of the lord & bring him from faror house & out
of egyp to worship god no more now man that & times
it & third light is the ay to leet thee see all the deareset
with in & with out & the wis mans as is in his heart
which is crist who hat yiven him the light & the soues
is abod after many teathers without but hee that lovet
the light which christ hath yiven him weath or will
onis yat wich is not a steo el hous but at is is whoth hath
yiven him the light who is the wesher of wisdom &
of knols who with him power filleth heaven & earth &
over all blessed for ever amen y that light with in thee
will teath thee to know god & that light within will condam thee watering it & carry
it it will bring thee in to the narow way & out of the brod way from al
the fashions & wordslips & costums of the wold & churches of the
world into the croun of god & is will teath thee how to worshipe
ga fare wee

22781

Will at that time got a deadly wound that through the Loveing
Kindness of the Lord was never healed.[11]

Emotion spread among many listeners in a gathering and was
associated with the power of God. Group emotionalism had already been known among the Ranters and other small sects and is
found in pentecostal churches today; unsophisticated people express emotions freely. Even reluctant hearers might be carried
away: when George Fox "hearde of a great meeting of preists at
Ulverstone . . . and went into the steeplehouse in the dreade &
power of the Lorde & . . . spoake amongst them the worde of the
Lorde . . . the mighty power of the Lorde was soe over all that
preist Bennett said the steeplehouse shooke & hee was affraide the
steeplehouse would fall on his head." [12] As late as 1688 a preacher
reported an outbreak of the Lord's power in a meeting that brought
non-Quaker hearers from fourteen miles around. Such intensity
was more common in the early mass meetings. It was often linked
with the trembling of the Quaker preacher himself: Aldam, while
speaking at York, "was taken with the power in a great trembling
in my head and all of the one side all the while." [13] In fact, every
speaker was prepared for such experiences. Friends knew that
"though there was some mixture with it, yet there is true power." [14]
Jonathan Edwards realized that the value of such outbursts, when
they occurred during the American Great Awakening, lay not in
their intensity but in the changes in life and spirit that might result. Saint Paul had taught the same lesson when the church at
Corinth "spoke in tongues." [15]

In any case, the leaders warned Friends not to fight against the
power—"Many younge freinds wondred at it, the power is a strange
thinge amongst them in many parts of this Nation"—but an older
Friend writes: "think it not strange concerning the Fiery-trial which
is to try you, as though some strange thing had happened to you:

---

11. *FPT*, p. 290. Cf. Fox, *Saul's Errand to Damascus*, pp. 1–2.

12. Fox, *Journal*, Camb., *1*, 54. Cf. Nuttall, *Holy Spirit*, pp. 64–65; Tindall, *Bunyan*, p. 9; T. Edmund Harvey, *Quaker Language* (Philadelphia, 1928), pp. 23–27;
Fox, *Journal*, Nickalls, pp. 74, 79.

13. Swarth. 1/373 (*EQL* 4), Aldam to Fox, July 1652. Cf. ARBarc./131, William
Dingley to Fox.

14. Swarth. 1/78 (*EQL* 560), H. Fell to M. Fell, December 2, 1660.

15. Cf. I Corinthians 14; V. Ferm, ed., *Puritan Sage: The Collected Writings of
Jonathan Edwards* (New York, 1953), pp. 379–91.

Lincoln Christian College

but in the fear of the Lord keep down your Minds, that questions and stumbles at the power of God." [16]

The inward struggle was always harder to bear than the outward: "I am made to see there is nothinge for me to doe but to stand stel in the obedence to the light that doth decover & Judge; as I fathfull on my wach stand, I amm made so far sensesabell that there is no want in God but in my not abiding at home in my tent, wich is poisst in the lo vally." [17] Though there were a few sudden conversions, like Richard Beard's during a lightning stroke in Maryland, most Friends went through hard months when they felt entombed by "the earth with its bars." [18] "Start not aside from the judgments of the Lord," wrote John Audland; "for . . . if thou art brought as low as Hell; yea, if thou come to say there is no hope . . . a way will be made beyond thy understanding, for . . . deliverance . . . Abide in that which judgeth; do not labour to get peace. . . . He that comes to the Worlds end, comes to his Wits end, before the World be known which never shall have end." [19]

Today, so long and agonized a period of inward torture and guilt seems morbid to many people. Early Friends, however, felt they were facing truth under the judgment of the inward Light, and the reality of their actual lives and thoughts clashed with the objective moral standard. Similarly, the modern patient before a psychotherapist often takes several years to accept his actual motives and desires, deeply suppressed by their head-on collision with his conscious ideals. Many saintly men and women seem to have found humility and self-honesty without struggle and remorse; yet if a person's moral standard is high, even honesty will not remove the continuing tension between ideals and actual life. Some existentialists have achieved self-awareness only at the price of despair, and many men achieve peace simply by ignoring their childhood standards or by avoiding the truth.

A guide or a mirror may be needed to help a man see himself truthfully: the Jesuit "spiritual director" and the psychiatrist may provide this, as did the Quaker Meeting. The Quaker preachers,

16. ARBarc./57, Richard Waller to M. Fell, Waterford, August 10, 1657; M. Fell, *Works*, p. 69.

17. Dews./22, Katherine Bull to Dewsbury, June 30, 1656.

18. Swarth. 4/4 (*EQL* 1), Hubberthorne to Fox, June–July 1652.

19. Camm and Audland, *Works*, pp. 89–90.

like modern psychologists and novelists, knew the many ways the mind can avoid facing unbearable truths. They considered it evasion, therefore, when their accused listeners attacked the Friends' own social backgrounds and the strange workings of "the power," or even when they sought to be too friendly to the preacher of judgment. They also knew most of the theological devices by which men try to find release from judgment. The simplest is rule-keeping, or legal righteousness, the puritan's unremitting temptation to do good. The Saint's anxiety for righteousness, though in theory unnecessary because of predestination, was excused as being eagerness to obey God actively. But Quakers were harsh toward all such "Will-works," and knew that if the rule code is Christian, the chance of keeping it is small. Obedience must be deeper: "At this time I am oprest with in," wrote a newly convinced Friend, "but there is that stering that is willing to be what the Lord will in al things." [20]

Commitment itself, however, can also be too simple a way out. Although self-surrender is never easy, the self, once committed, need no longer ask what its own character really is. The revivalist who preaches only decision and commitment to Christ may in that very act protect the deeper shells of self-righteousness. The halo of the dedicated may be a good insulator. When Thomas Morford heard Audland preach at Bristol, he found his words like "the Arrows of God unto my heart. . . . For 4 or 5 days . . . no meate I did receive; and In that time I had amotion to go for Ireland." [21] Of such converts Will Caton said: "Now the Crosse is stumbled at." [22] Early Friends thus mentioned little about commitment in itself: they worked to open their minds to the Light. Thomas Taylor wrote, after some months of wrestling: "there is a great deale of mixture yet in me . . . and a storming heathenish head in the wicked nature that is loth to come under the yoke, Oh, the miserie of poor fallen man." [23]

A subtler way of escape is the process of confession so as to divide the self. Evil deeds and specific sins may be renounced, or even the whole self rejected in generalized remorse, but the inner

20. Dews./22. Cf. Swarth. 3/55 (*EQL* 146), Farnworth to Fox: "The Cross is that which must stay."

21. Swarth. 4/75 (*EQL* 355), Thomas Morford to M. Fell, Bristol, Jan. 4, 1656/57.

22. Swarth. 4/257 (*EQL* 269), Will Caton to L. Wardell, Edinburgh, May 20, 1656.

23. Swarth. 3/29 (*EQL* 24), Thomas Taylor to Fox, May 18, 1653.

self that confesses the sin can thus detach itself from the evil: "it is not I that do it, but sin that worketh in me." [24] Thus self-esteem is preserved. Albert Camus has shown in this attitude the fruits of the Fall. When Fox and Aldam arranged that Agnes Wilkinson be sent home from York to Westmorland after a moral lapse, they wrote to Margaret Fell:

> Agnes . . . hath beene made to Owne her condemnation divers times; But deare heart, it is not yet right: for the seale & the will speakes, from the sense of the Just in prison, & the will & seale Breakes out in passion, & soe the will getts ease, & the Judgement ceases; & the mynde turnes from the sword. But A subtill appearance in the Condemnation it is, to deceive the simple, [so] that she in to Unitye may Bee received. . . . See that shee Bee sett & kept to Labor, that flesh may be brought downe, & that wch would bee at ease in the flesh may bee brought to Judgement & the Life raised up to Raigne over her will, wch now doth her filthyness condemne.[25]

If even confession is self-righteousness, no wonder Friends were driven near despair before learning to depend on the Light, which alone could help them. "Oh my Frind," Dewsbury wisely counseled a woman, "look not so much at thy self for it begetts Unbelevfe." [26]

Even the acceptance of one's own total dependence on God's spirit can be used as an escape if it is only an intellectual grasp of the difficulty. Stephen Crisp discovered this when, to all appearances, he had been a Quaker for some months. After an adventurous pilgrimage through the churches of Colchester, he had become a Baptist, and then had heard and was convinced by Parnell:

> Here at the very first of my Convincement, did the Enemy of my Soul make Trial to slay me . . . seeing my Wisdom and Reason was overcome by the Truth . . . therefore I received the Truth . . . and defended it with the same Wisdom by which I had resisted it, and so was yet a stranger to the Cross that was to Crucifie me; and was at liberty . . . to lay out my Wits . . . for the Truth; but I soon felt my Sacrifice . . .

24. Romans 7:20.
25. Swarth. 4/89 (*EQL* 91), Aldam to M. Fell, October 30, 1654.
26. Dews./27, to Mary Smith, London, November 14, 1661.

was not accepted . . . and a Cry was in me which call'd to
Judgment. . . . In this state I continued a Month or two, but
then a swift sword was drawn against that Wisdom and com-
prehending mind . . .

Then . . . Woe, Misery and Calamity . . . opened upon
me . . . I am poor and blind and naked who thought I had
been rich and well Adorned. . . . After long Travel . . . and
many bitter Tears . . . I Waited as one that had hope that
God would be Gracious to me; yet something in me would
fain have known how long that should be; but a faithful Cry
was in me, which called that [also] to Death.

And, upon a time, being weary of my own Thoughts in the
Meeting of God's People, I thought none was like me, and it
was but in vain to sit there with such a wandring mind as
mine was. . . . At length, as I thought to go forth, the Lord
Thundred through me, saying, "That which is weary must
die;" so I turned to my seat.[27]

Augustine and Kierkegaard and perhaps the author of Job would
have recognized Crisp's discovery that neither hope nor weariness
can speed or remove God's hand.

At the end of human resources and evasions the classic discovery
for Christians has been the openness of God's love. Judgment remains sure and beyond begging or compromise, so that no man can
justify himself; nevertheless, God's loving forgiveness allows men
to trust him. This was Martin Luther's message, as it had been
Saint Paul's. Similarly, the standard experience of orthodox puritans, as repeated in hundreds of testimonies and autobiographies,
began with a period of moralistic effort representing a "legal call"
or religion under law, followed by the abandonment of self-righteousness and the acceptance of God's justification of men through
Christ. Martin Luther and John Wesley kept men aware of the
chasm between human character and God's absolute standard in
order to drive men into accepting themselves as forgiven sinners,
able to trust and depend upon God's love. The death of Christ was
for such men the evidence and means of this forgiveness.

The early Friends could not have faced God at all if they had
not believed that the God of Truth was loving and that they them-

27. Stephen Crisp, *The Christian Experiences* . . . (London, 1694), pp. 16–19.

selves were God's children, bought at the price of Christ's blood. Yet they could not accept mercy as enough. They felt that a forgiven man was not truly forgiven unless the evil in him was still recognized as evil and in need of removal. Quakers were shrewd enough to see that a man projects his own self-love and calls it the love of God: thus he may make peace with himself but not with God. No matter how much Christ and the Cross are invoked, self-forgiveness works to create God according to man's own image and imagination, and is the ultimate way one escapes from facing what he is and his need to be made over. God indeed "justifieth the ungodly . . . yet never in, but from their ungodliness." [28]

The Quakers lived in a puritan era even more passionate for morality than for love, and they did not grasp the puritan pastors' message that trust in God, if it be complete, will free a man to love, while love is the ultimate righteousness. Yet to a striking degree the Quaker message was like that of Jonathan Edwards, who was content to drive men to despair of salvation, with no mention of universal mercy, so that men might find the goodness and power of God directly for themselves. Friends, in any case, avoided any preaching of "imputed righteousness" and "substitutionary atonement," considering them "notions" by which a man escaped from facing his actual sin. For some Friends this was a final defense they had to surrender. John Burnyeat had held a "high profession of Imputative Righteousness, and that though I lived in the act of sin, the guilt of it should be . . . imputed to Christ. I found it otherwise, when I was turned to the Light . . . and my pretence . . . of Justification . . . was overthrown. . . . O the poverty and want that my Soul saw itself in." [29]

Fellowship in their common struggle, and the example and encouragement of older Quakers who had won peace, were crucial supports for most new Friends in the first dark months. Both loyalty and messages of warning within the group helped to convince new members that the truth was objective, despite the unlimited self-deception a man can uncover layer by layer within his heart. Emotional experiences that resulted from struggles with inner guilt, such as outbreaks of the power, expressed and heightened in

28. Fisher, p. 164. Cf. Burnyeat, p. 2; Nayler, *Works*, p. 338; Fox, *Great Mistery*, p. 90; Swarth. 3/160 (*EQL* 379).

29. Burnyeat, pp. 2–3.

the setting of the group, served to free men more easily from their old rigid patterns. "After we had meet together for some time," wrote Burnyeat, "in the living Judgment that sprung from the Light in our Souls, and looking for the Salvation of God, the wonderful Power from on High was revealed amongst us, and many Hearts reached therewith, and broken and melted . . . and great dread and trembling fell upon many, and the very Chains of Death was broken thereby . . . and some taste of the Oyl of Joy came to . . . the Hearts of many." [30]

The coming of peace and joy was usually gradual and intermittent at first, but unmistakable. "While I was waiting out of all visible things," wrote Francis Howgill, "the Lord opened the Springs of the Great Deep, and quite overflowed my whole heart with Life and Love." [31] That to which early Friends came is hard to put into words, as they themselves admitted, and less tangible than the experience of judgment that preceded it. One statement comes from Isaac Penington:

> Some may desire to know what I have at last met with. I answer, *I have met with the Seed.* . . . I have met with my God; I have met with my Saviour: and He hath not been present with me without his salvation; but I have felt the healings drop upon my soul from under his wings. I have met with the true knowledge, the knowledge of life, the living knowledge. . . . I have met with the true peace, the true righteousness, the true holiness, the true rest of soul . . . and I . . . am capable of no doubt, dispute or reasoning in my mind about them.[32]

The tone of certainty and powerful joy is convincing, but even if one's own experience can give a faint echo to this witness, Penington's description helps very little to explain it. Interpretation in terms of mystical intuition, direct knowledge of divine reality, while by no means foolish, is always inadequate to men without

30. Ibid., p. 7.

31. Francis Howgill, quoted in Will Hayes, *Grey Ridge* (Meopham Green, Kent, the Order of the Great Companion, 1942), p. 65. For a richer presentation of this serene and joyful phase of Quakerism, see Howard H. Brinton, *Friends for 300 Years* (New York, 1952), chaps. 1 and 2.

32. *Memoirs of the Life of Isaac Penington*, ed. Joseph Gurney Bevan (Philadelphia, Penn., 1903), pp. 26–27.

any such experience; nor is it quite appropriate in defining the specifically Quaker enlightenment. Penington was a mystic, but most early Friends were not. There were mystics in puritan England, such as John Everard and the Ranter Joseph Salmon, who was "as one confounded into the abyss of eternitie, nonentitized into the being of beings, my soule split, and emptied into the fountaine & ocean of divine fulness." [33] Quakers spoke not of such self emptying but of self-crucifixion. George Fox, Margaret Fell, George Bishop, and John Rous indeed had visions, and Humphrey Smith published an account of his, but no Quaker appealed to these visions as being the root of his life or doctrine.

There must always remain a depth of mystery about the warmth and power, the knowledge of being known and yet loved, which belong to true worship. Awe seems natural before any reality that in no way depends on oneself, especially if it be powerful and good, a *mysterium fascinosum et tremendum*. Yet it is striking that most early Quaker accounts do not treat their discovery of peace and joy as a mystery. The same Light that showed them their sins was the source of new life. This may correspond, in modern terminology, to the discovery that the truth is good even when it seems threatening. The God of truth is loving, or, in secular terms, the universe is trustworthy in relation both to man's intellect and to his inner self. These attitudes imply assertions about the ultimate reality: the Christian gospel itself, and even the involutions of Trinitarian theology, can serve to support such affirmations. More concretely, the Quakers affirmed that the same Light which condemned, judged, and wounded them was the source of their new power and joy. Friends did not merely believe that the Light existed in spite of darkness, or masochistically welcome pain and darkness for their own sakes; they accepted both struggle and joy as inseparable gifts of the truth that saved them. They cared more about salvation than religious peace or discovery. But truth can crush as well as liberate: humanly speaking, self-knowledge can only be creative if positive reactions to it can take place. In asking what happened within early Friends as their experiences led to new life, both religious and psychological perspectives are appropriate.

The surges of enthusiasm and joy that broke out in the early

33. Joseph Salmon, *Heights in Depths*, quoted in Watkins, p. 107.

Meetings partly reflected the sense of freedom following any act of decision or surrender. When the tension built up by the puritan sense of sin was broken, the results were usually dynamic, whatever the form they took. Even the Ranter Anna Trapnel, when convinced in 1642 that she was released from sin, found that "earth was now gone, and heaven come . . . every bit of bread I eat, how sweet it was to my taste. Christ sweetned every creature to me." [34] Certainly group emotion also augmented the joy of the "new man": the power of God was identified as often with outbreaks of singing or weeping for joy as with quaking for dread. But the steadiness of the Friends' new life cannot be accounted for as mere commitment or release from tension, since long periods of struggle preceded and interrupted the feelings of peace.

Another way to think of early Quaker experience is to see it as an example of conversion. In the classic analysis of William James, conversion ends a period of inward conflict of values, when the old ideals or focus of effort is broken down and a new center emerges. Newly convinced Friends in puritan England, however, did not simply abandon or change their professed moral values. They described instead the death of the "old man" within them, the conquest of the "bestiall" or "carnall" will. More helpful than James' conversion pattern is the modern psychologist's description of how an old self-image, with its narrow defense mechanisms and ways of self-fulfillment, can be broken open by a period of conflict. In such a breakthrough many previously buried impulses, appreciations, and creative abilities from outside the known limits of the old personality may be released. Friends, too, after emerging into joy, discovered the release within them of "Gentleness, Meekness, Patience and all other Vertues which are of a springing and spreading Nature." [35] They were more able than most men in times of conversion to set free previously hidden emotions, which gave them the strength to preach, to endure suffering, to be sometimes wildly antisocial, and to rejoice.

An experience of conversion goes beyond the breaking of the old self to the finding of a new personality pattern with a new central drive and focus. A new man is born as the old man withers. Friends preferred to say that the new man grows from the Seed

34. Anna Trapnel, *A Legacy for Saints*, quoted in Watkins, p. 74.
35. Nayler, *Works*, p. 370.

of Christ within him, or that they were able to "grow up in th
Eternal and Immortal Birth." [36] That Seed is within men, "some
thing in thee, that in all these Worldly delights, cries Vanity an
Emptiness . . . that cannot plead for Sin." [37] The inward search
ing and turmoil were the "threshing" or "ploughing up" of th
hard ground of the heart, by which the Seed is freed. When me
were "tender" or "broken-hearted," the Seed could grow in re
sponse to the Light. But it is no part of man's old self, no mustar
seed growing of itself. Following Genesis, it is "the seed of Go
which bruseth the seed of the serpent," the Seed of Adam an
Eve. It is the germ from which the new man grows in Christ'
image; or (as Friends sometimes quoted Saint Paul) Christ himsel
This was confusing, and careful Quaker writers were less likel
to confuse the Seed and the Light, i.e. Christ's Spirit; for the cente
of life within "the new man in Christ" was always the Light. Ce
tainly the Light came always as God's spirit, not man's: The Ligh
is, "though in men, yet of God, and no less than his own Law i
their own Hearts . . . and is not any meer Natural Faculty" no
a constitutive element in men.[38] The Light stands independen
from men, as truth is independent of self-will: it judges, condemn
and crucifies. The Light is the active power of the new life, an
the master that man obeys.

Friends spoke of Light, the Spirit, and Christ within so inte
changeably that no uniform distinction can be made clear. Friend
were not "Christ-mystics" any more than they were seekers of my
tical union with the Godhead. Their "unity in the Eternal Being
was their bond with other Friends, which set them off from th
disunited churches made by men. The sense of a personal presenc
of the inward fellowship of Christ's personality, was quite rar
among early Friends.[39] They called the Spirit "it" more often tha
"He." Yet Friends were not deists or pantheists, for they knew Go
in obeying him. The basically practical tone in which they matte

36. M. Fell, p. 93.

37. Nayler, *Works,* p. 333. Cf. ibid., p. 71; Fox, *Journal,* Camb., *1,* 142; J. White
head, *Two Seeds,* title page. Medieval thought had already developed the idea
Mary as the second Eve, basing it on Paul's description of Jesus as the Seed of Ada
who crushes the Seed of the Serpent (Rom. 5:14; Gal. 3:15).

38. Fisher, p. 37, cf. pp. 602–11; Wragge, *Barclay,* p. 43; Barclay, *Apology,* Propos
tion V.

39. Cf. T. Canby Jones, "George Fox's Teaching on Redemption and Salvatior
(Yale University, 1955). Fox was more Christ-centered than most early Friends.

>f-factly describe the Light by its "leadings," inward judgment and >ower, springs from their fundamentally ethical relation to God: 'God as he really is in himself is beyond all definition of ours at ıll. . . . But God, (whatever more he is . . .) is *really in himself* ∨hatever he hath at any time . . . revealed himself to be, *In* and *To* his holy Prophets and Children. . . . And if ye . . . Worship ın *unknown God . . . My Counsel* to you is, to stand still in *his >wn Counsel,* namely *his Light* in your own Consciences." [40] The eading, which Friends obeyed, came as a personal voice, yet one ∨ithout distinct personality: they reported that "it was said to me," hardly ever that "Christ spoke."

For Friends the experience of conversion could not be explained in human terms; events and impulses came either from God's will or from man's. In the intensity of the struggle to give themselves up, to let themselves be taken over by the Spirit, they gave up not only self-righteousness but every impulse they could identify as the product of their own will. The insight of Irenaeus, which affirmed that the Spirit would lead a man to become his true self,[41] was foreign to early Quakers. Still less could they think that God's love gave back to a forgiven man the freedom and responsibility to be himself, his choices bounded not by law but by forgiveness and grace. The most obviously human impulses, such as the ties to family, wife, and job, were often the most mistrusted among early Friends.

In our day it is necessary, however dangerous, to allow for human factors; but this need not disallow God's activity through such visible means. Since Friends experienced such strong judgment and guidance, insofar as any single human element served as the new focus of their life, it would seem at first sight to be the conscience. Indeed, some early Quakers do appear to have centered their lives on an overactive conscience, surrendering absolutely to its promptings, both positive and negative; but they insisted that the Light was not the same as conscience, which was a natural gift easily distorted, often misled, and capable of growth. The consciences of some careless people (such as the Quakers' more stubborn enemies) might be regarded as seared beyond further hope

40. Fisher, pp. 844–45. Cf. Nayler, *Works,* p. 32.
41. For Irenaeus on "recapitulation" see his *Refutations (Adversus Haereses),* 5.14.1.

of sensitivity. Nevertheless, the Quaker's appeal to his hearer was "to the Light of God in thy Conscience." He knew that the Light could shine through the conscience like a light in a lantern, though that conscience alone was not the source of man's power. Yet we must assume that something more creative than conscientiousness moved the early Friends.

Deeper than the conscience is the special thrill of fascinating horror that accompanies the sudden appearance of certain ideas contradicting the ordinary impulses of will or conventionality. The same compulsive, terrifying feeling evoked by "the Holy" may also be aroused by a sudden inward impulse from beyond the familiar boundaries of the conscious self.[42] Thus early Friends sometimes identified the Light, their focus and guide in life, with any positive impulses newly released. It expresses the unity of Quaker experience that both these unexpected impulses and the undesired warnings of conscience, preacher, or Quaker prophet were obeyed as leadings of the Light. The Lamb's War extended and integrated a man's personality both upward and downward; it gave his life a center which was permanently beyond himself, but also harnessed the full range of his own emotions.

The reader's faith must be his guide in deciding to what extent he believes God worked indirectly through the Quakers' psychological processes, and how far experience with the Light brought them into direct contact with God. In any case, they found a steady and growing strength and wisdom that went beyond sudden impulses. Many individuals often found themselves independently led in parallel ways and brought into a sense of unity, an aspect of Quaker life that came especially from waiting together in silence.

The daily actions of the convinced Friend centered on the Spirit, which often gave him an emotional tone of joy and power. The effort to respond to a great gift, to preserve one's joy by living up to it on tiptoe, comes naturally after many deep experiences. The puritan of any type, however earnest he had been in his younger years before his conversion, was likely to live a life doubly intense afterward, so as to be morally worthy of his Election. As John Burnyeat wrote: "O the pleasant dread that dwelt upon my Spirit,

---

42. Cf. Rudolf Otto, *The Idea of the Holy* (2d ed. London, Oxford University Press, 1950); Harry Stack Sullivan, *The Interpersonal Theory of Psychiatry* (New York, 1953), pp. 314–15.

. . . which filled it with living Joy . . . Then did I endeavour to keep down my Spirit to the meltings of it, and great was the care of my soul, that I might no ways ruin nor abuse this Power, nor let up a wrong thing into my Mind to be betrayed thereby." [43]

But impulses to specific acts were also given by the inward Spirit, as has been seen. These leadings, like those of the Oxford Group members in our time, might involve almost any form of action, including the trivial and the most technical, a word of greeting or the navigation of a ship. As time went on, such guidance became more and more constant in the daily life of each new Friend, but in the first few instances they renewed the challenge to his self-will. Stephen Crisp, even after surrendering his intellectual pride, found this test was still to be gone through:

> About the year 1659, I often felt the aboundings of the Love of God in my heart, and a Cry to stand given to his Will (which I thought I was . . .), but his eye saw further than mine. . . . And upon a time as I was waiting upon the Lord, his Word arose in me, and commanded me to . . . part with my dear Wife and Children . . . and bear Witness to his Name in Scotland . . . but when that came to pass, I found all Enemies were not slain indeed: for the strivings, strugglings, Reasonings and Disputings against the Command of God that I met withal." [44]

A new Friend's first clearly felt call was often to speak at the Meeting of Friends to which he belonged, and this in itself might create inner conflict. The emotional tension, evident when the speaker himself showed physical agitation by the power, presumably came from this personal involvement with the message given: similar turmoil is not always absent when Quakers speak at Meetings today. Soon after the first leading would usually come a call to speak elsewhere, to confront a non-Quaker group. Not only the summons but the place, time, and actual words spoken were given by the Spirit. John Banks' first such adventure was typical:

> Upon a time, as I was Sitting in Silence, waiting upon the Lord, in a Meeting of Friends upon Pardshow-Cragg, a weighty Exercise fell upon my Spirit, and it opened in me, That I

43. Burnyeat, pp. 17–18.
44. Crisp, *Christian Experiences*, pp. 21–22.

must go to the Steeple-House at Cockermouth; which was hard for me to give up to. But the Lord by his Power made me to shake and tremble, and by it I was made willing to go. But . . . I would have known what I might do there . . . and as I was going, it appeared to me as if the Priest had been before me; and it opened in me [to say] "If thou be a Minister of Christ, stand to Prove thy Practice, and if it be the same [as] the Apostles' . . . I'll own thee; but if not, I am sent of God this Day to Testify against thee." And so soon as I entered the Place, where the Hireling Priest, George Larcum, was Preaching, he cryed out, "There is one come into the Church like a Mad-Man, with his Hat on his Head, Church Wardens, put him out." . . . And after some time . . . I was moved of the Lord to go in again, and had strength given me to stay until the Priest had done: (But Oh, it was burthensome confused Stuff). . . . And then with the Words aforesaid I opened my Mouth, in the Dread of God's Power. . . . And the People were in a great uproar, some to Beat me, and some to save me from being Beat. . . . And having obey'd the Requirings of the Lord, I came away in sweet Peace.[45]

In some ordinary activities no special guidance was looked for, and it was enough that Friends found within themselves no contrary balks or "stop to their minds." Special actions like preaching trips needed specific and positive commands, and on such missions early Quakers tried to go and to speak only as they were led: "Thou that calls thy selfe a prophett & speaks with thy owne will, thy words comes not to pass."[46] A pair of young Quakers in the garden at Swarthmore felt a call to deliver a warning to a landowner in Cumberland, but the message itself was not given to them. They went in any case, but the inner voice still gave them no words upon their arrival. They stayed overnight, refusing the offer of meals from the landowner, and then went home again.[47] Will Caton was preaching in Cumberland when "it came upon mee to goe into Scotland, and the thing fell very heavy upon me . . . being I had determined to come Southwardes . . . but, however I gave up to

45. Banks, pp. 10–11.
46. Swarth. 3/3 (*EQL* 8), Nayler to M. Fell, rebuking Richard Myers.
47. Higginson, *Irreligion of Quakers*, pp. 7–8.

the will of the Lord in the thing." [48] Perhaps the most dramatic of all such examples was James Nayler's first call to preach after becoming a Quaker in 1652. He was then at his home in Yorkshire:

> I was at the Plow, meditating on the things of God, and suddainly I heard a Voice saying unto me, "Get thee out from thy kindred and from thy Father's House" . . . And when I came at Home . . . I began to make some Preparation, as aparel and other necessaries, not knowing whither I should go; but shortly afterward, going a-gate-ward with a Friend from my own House, having on an Old Suit, without any Money, having neither taken Leave of Wife or Children, not thinking then of any Journey, I was commanded to go into the West, not knowing . . . what I was to do there, but when I had been there a little while, I had given me what I was to declare; and ever since, I have remained, not knowing to Day what I was to do tomorrow.

Poor Mrs. Nayler next saw her husband in jail.[49]

The Friends themselves knew that not every leading came from the Spirit of God. In addition to following impulses directly from the devil or the old self, they knew that a man might become "very much coloured" [50] and partially deceive himself. He might easily outrun his inner guide. Nayler wrote to Swarthmore about a young man who at "about midnight . . . had a voyce, which said, up, get the hence, & he did arise, and went forth, but the mind not waiteing to be guided, but runing before, he lost his guide, & soe returned home againe, & the tempter got in, and tempted him strongly to destroy himselfe, biding him cast himselfe into the fire, persuading him he should not burne, but at length he grew soe high, that he prevailed with him to put his hand into a Cetle full of boyling lickquor." The margin reads: "The young man is nowe

---

48. Swarth. 4/267 (*EQL* 493), Caton to Fox, Swarthmore, October 23, 1659.

49. Nayler, *Works*, pp. 12–13. Cf. Swarth. 3/66 (*EQL* 21), Nayler to Fox, Appleby jail, January 1653. Nayler was seldom home again. Dewsbury mentions one visit to Mrs. Nayler in 1656: Swarth. 4/137 (*EQL* 280); otherwise, she hardly appears in Quaker literature. Between the summer of 1652 and Nayler's arrest in 1656 he preached or was in prison in the northwest and northeast, then in London, then in the southwest of England. Whether he made a visit home during the London imprisonment is not clear. Cf. Braithwaite, *Beginnings*, p. 273 n.

50. Swarth. 4/232 (*EQL* 111), John Grave to M. Fell about Robert Benn.

recovered out of the temptation & his hand recoverd very fair, wch is . . . a mighty wonder." [51]

Friends knew also that a man might receive direction through another person, though they waited anxiously for the man himself to be led to concur. Samuel Fisher was gradually convinced by John Stubbs to accompany him to Venice, despite the opposition and illness of Fisher's wife. When Fisher first declined, Stubbs wrote that he

> gave upp to the will of the Lord, Notwithstanding his gratious promisse to Mee when I was in Ireland; I was not to dispute wth him about it, but was brought to say lord thy will bee done." But later, "Comeing to his house I gave him thy Bookes. . . . I durst not Mention any thing of it till he spoke . . . and then in the feare, I told him, and it sunke deepe & departed not, and still I begged & doe beg to be kept out of the will of the flesh wch remaines, and as aforesaid it pursues him soe tht hee sees hee cannot avoide it, and nowe my humble breathings to the lord of the harvest is that his Call may be Cleared upp to him . . . that he may goe forth Clearely, with joye and not wth griefe, for truely . . . his goeing wth mee was made as Cleare to mee as any Command or promisse I have had hitherto.[52]

Friends believed that a leading could come directly from God, precisely like the inspiration of the Hebrew prophets. If clearly heard and heeded, no human impulse was thought to be involved. In fact, if a consciously selfish motive opposed the impulse, this provided all the greater reason for proceeding. The deed asked for might be dangerous or repulsive to the social standards of the day. Friends read that the prophet Isaiah "went naked for a sign" to Jerusalem: any impulse to do likewise they would react to with terror, and then conclude that their resistance was self-will. The example of one Friend who made such a sign, and the simultaneous ridicule of the world, would prompt other Quakers to do the same.[53]

51. Swarth. 3/192 (*EQL* 61), Nayler to M. Fell, Durham, April 1654.

52. Swarth. 3/160 (*EQL* 379) John Stubbs (and Hubberthorne) to M. Fell, April 1657. On the same events see also Swarth. 4/14 (*EQL* 373), Hubberthorne to M. Fell.

53. Examples are given eagerly by Higginson, *Irreligion of Quakers*, p. 30; also by Thomas Weld, Richard Prideaux, Sam Hammond, Will Cole, and Will Durant

To us it seems clear that some of these impulses came from the subconscious minds of the Friends themselves, though they were treated as leadings of the Spirit because they were not consciously willed. The most famous example was Fox's reaction to the spires of Lichfield cathedral when returning on foot from Derby prison in 1651:

> I espyed three steeplehouse spires & they strucke att my life; & I askt ffreindes what they was & they saide Lichfeilde & soe the worde of the Lord came to me: thither I might goe. . . . Soe I went . . . till I came Into the townde, & . . . the worde of the Lorde came unto mee againe to cry: "Woe unto the bloody citty of Lichfeilde;" and being markett day I went Into the markett place & went upp & doune in several places of it . . . cryinge "Woe unto the bloody citty of Lichfeilde." . . . Soe when I had declared what was upon me . . . I came out of the tounde in peace . . . And when it had donne, I considered why I should goe & cry against tht city & call it tht bloody citty.[54]

Fox himself was later satisfied by hearing a legend that a thousand Christians were martyred at Lichfield in the reign of the Roman Emperor Diocletian. A likelier reason is that Fox's emotional explosion at the sight of any steeple was in this case reinforced by an unconscious memory of the martyrdom at Lichfield, in Mary Tudor's time, of Joyce Lewis (perhaps Fox's ancestress) and that of Wightman, the Unitarian, in 1612.[55]

The receptivity of some early Friends to impulses, it must be admitted, bordered on insanity:

> I, Jane Withers, was moved of the Lord to go to the Steeplehouse of Kellit, to speak to Priest Moor these words: "Thou art the beast that all the world worships and wonders after; the plagues of God must be poured upon thee." When these words first came to me, the power of God seized upon me, but

---

(puritan ministers of Newcastle) in *The Perfect Pharisee under Monkish Holiness* (London, 1654), p. 48. See also *FPT*, pp. 364–69.

54. Fox, *Journal*, Camb., *1*, 15–16.

55. Braithwaite (*Beginnings*, p. 56) reports a similar suggestion by Neave Brayshaw. Paul Lacey considers Fox's kinship in spirit as being directed toward martyrs of the early church.

. . . I did not obey at the first movings; but the power of the Lord so seized on me again, that I was bound about my body above the middle as if . . . with chains, and it was said to me, "That if I went not I should repent it" . . .

And in the afternoon, I was forced to go, and as I went in at the [Church] door, I should have said, "the plagues of God must be poured upon thee;" but I did not speak the words then; and then the power of the Lord came upon me: but in that priest Moor sayes, I was in a trance, it is a lye, for I was as sensible all the while as ever I was.[56]

John Gilpin of Kendal heard the first Quaker preachers in 1653, and after learning that quaking was the mark of the Spirit's coming, waited anxiously until he himself was finally seized with it while home in bed after his fourth attendance at a Quaker meeting. Present at a meeting soon after, when John Audland spoke, Gilpin was thrown from his chair, lay on the ground all night, moving from one position to another, unable to resist the power that acted upon him. Somewhat later, Gilpin felt commanded to cut his own throat—"open a hole there and I will give thee the words of eternall life"—but he rejected the impulse, and the idea soon came to him that his previous leadings had all been demonic. Feeling now that his demon had been cast out by the Spirit, he set out to reverse his previous deeds, and so began another round of adventures with a second disillusionment. A third seizure seemed to him to be the indwelling of Christ himself. Finally, he began to doubt all his impulses, and returned to the Bible and the Presbyterians. He wrote out his story to show that Quakerism was the product of Satan—a testimonial endorsed by the mayor, the vicar, and the schoolmaster of Kendal, and quoted along with other lurid reports by many anti-Quaker tracts of these years.[57]

The local Quaker leaders were themselves watchful over Gilpin and men like him, not wanting to crush whatever might be good in the most tormenting experiences. Nayler wrote to Margaret Fell about a struggling woman: "Judge the death, but save the little

56. Jane Withers is quoted in James Nayler, *A Discovery of the Man of Sin* (London, 1656), p. 45, one of his best controversial tracts, without disapproval of Jane.

57. John Gilpin, *The Quakers Shaken* (London, 1653). Cf. Higginson, *Irreligion of Quakers*, p. 30; Weld et al., *Perfect Pharisee*, p. 26; Ralph Farmer, *The Great Mysteries of Godlinesse and Ungodlinesse* (London, 1655), pp. 81 ff.

:hing wch I have seene moveing and show her the way of love wch is much lost in the height." [58] Friends expected the inward con-licts of the Lamb's War to drive many to their wits' end before the old man was broken. It was, moreover, common for puritans to come close to suicide before conversion, as their diaries often reported. Even the leaders hardly knew how dangerous it could be to bring a man's subsurface impulses and guilt to light, but they usually knew insanity when they saw it and accepted it with-out much psychiatric subtlety. Thomas Willan described objec-tively and dispassionately the case of William Pool at Worcester, a young Quaker convert who became insane and drowned himself. An overeager Friend, Susanna Pearson, tried in vain to revive Pool miraculously, and was ridiculed by writers against Quakerism, as well as by a Friend who wrote in the margin of Willan's letter: "mad whimesye." [59]

Friends, however, faced the daily job of recognizing the true from the subjective when they were led to speech and action. From Jeremiah's time to the present, men have known no absolute or easy way to tell a genuinely divine message from wishful impulses and false prophecy. Early Quakers were regularly labeled by men of their time as "Ranters." The actual Ranters claimed that since they were redeemed and led by the Spirit, they could do no wrong, and so followed impulses into all kinds of immorality and anarchy. Some went further, saying that no man could be freed from a sin until he had committed that sin as if it were not a sin. Most of them felt they had found true faith or had been given a special prophetic call by God after a period of frustration in orthodox churches. Some were clearly psychotic, like John Toldervy, "led with flies to crucifie himself, and to burn his legs & prick Needles in his Thumbs, and such filthie bewitched stuff." [60] It was there-fore important for Quakers to know themselves and to explain to other men the ways in which they differed from Ranters.

The Quakers' first test for the genuineness of a leading was moral purity. Friends said that the Ranters "fled the cross," and

58. Swarth. 3/2 (*EQL* 27), Nayler to Fox about Ellen Parr, July 26, 1653. Was she perhaps related to the puritan Parrs of Kendal and Henry's queen?

59. Swarth. 1/217 (*EQL* 368), Willan to M. Fell, February 1657.

60. James Nayler, *The Foot Yet in the Snare* (London, 1656), p. 16, in answer to John Toldervy; cf. Ralph Farmer, *Great Mysteries*, p. 58; Lawrence Claxton, *The Lost Sheep Found* (1660), p. 25.

that the true Spirit was always contrary to self-will and led to righteousness. They applied this test within their own Meetings, and their austerity was certainly in contrast to the libertine habits of the Ranters. Even condemnation of the impure was part of this test, "for the word of the Lord is puer, and Answers the puer in every one . . . itt is as a hamer to beat down the transgresor." [61]

As a second test, Fox, Margaret Fell, and others warned the Friends to sit with their leadings for a while in patience. Self-will is impatient of tests; to wait was to "be patient & still in the power & still in the light that doth convince you, keepe your mynds unto god. . . . If you sitt still in the patience which overcomes in the power of God, their will be no flyinge." [62]

The third and most important test was likely to be the self-consistency of the Spirit. The Light should not contradict itself, either in history or among the members of the Spirit-led group. Even the senior preachers submitted their directives to each others' testing. In 1659 Aldam and Dewsbury wrote to Fox and Burrough: "take into your consideration the thinges written downe in that Power which came to mee & W. Dew at Yorke & lett mee have an answer, how the Large wisdome of god in you doth aprove of the particular thinges to bee done, & what it disabroves of, that in one Mynde wee may meete." [63] From these casual ways of verifying each others' leadings, there grew up in turn the uniform and practical organs of Quaker group life in Meetings for Business. When Quakers were led in diverging directions, the leadings of Fox and other "Weighty Friends" came to have increasing authority. In later years undue pressure was imposed to heed these guides, and innovators were taught to question and restrain their private doubts and impulses to originality, but in the beginning the constant danger was anarchy. When leaders like Fox and Nayler disagreed, or even when a solid cluster of lesser Friends felt led to reject the uniform traditions of Quaker conduct, there was no external standard for imposing judgment.

One strong means, however, for using the consistency of the Spirit as a test for the validity of leadings was to compare them with

61. Fox, *Journal*, Camb., *1*, 319, referring to Jer. 23, 28.
62. Fox, ibid., pp. 224–25.
63. ARBarc./73, Warmsworth, October 13, 1659.

biblical conduct. Friends were never willing to use the Bible directly as a guidebook or rule book lest it substitute for each person's own direct experience of the Light. In every area of life the Spirit must be absolute. But Quakers, of course, believed that the biblical writers were also divinely inspired and that biblical teachings and prophecies were therefore proper to use for comparison. They were also willing for their opponents to test them by the Bible. This agreement of the Spirit with the Bible was achieved more easily then than it would be now, since early Friends were steeped in the Bible, quoted it unconsciously, and felt that it was the Spirit's characteristic vocabulary.

Sometimes on the basis of these tests Friends acted to discipline each other. Christopher Atkinson and Agnes Ayrey were severely treated for acts of immorality. Agnes Wilkinson was sent home to Margaret Fell's care, as was noted, in disgrace and with a guardian.[64] Thomas Ayrey, after his retreat from hostile reactions to his preaching in Plymouth, was told harshly in his home Meeting in Westmorland that his testimony could not be borne. But warning was often given gently: "Rich. Mires, thou getts above thy Condition," wrote Nayler; "mind the babe in thee and it will tell thee soe. And freind, thou tht calls thy selfe a prophett art run up into the ayre; lowlie consider it. . . . I saw many dangers cominge through looking out, but if you waite upon the Lord to be guided by his feare, all will be well, husht and Calme." [65] There was a significant contrast between the sternness with which the early leaders judged moral offenses and their caution in condemning Friends whose leadings seemed confused or products of their own minds: "Take heed of Judgeing any one openly in your meeting Except they bee openly prophane Rebellious Such as bee out of the truth; that by power and life & wisdom you may stand over them . . . soe tht there in the truth stand Cleare & single. But such as are Tender, if they should be moved to bubble forth a few words

64. Swarth. 4/89 (*EQL* 91), Aldam to M. Fell, York, October 30, 1654. Cf. 4/1 (*EQL* 65).

65. Swarth. 3/3 (*EQL* 8). Cf. Swarth. 4/202 (*EQL* 99) on Anne Wilson's brutal rebuke to Ayrey, in which the writer, Thos. Robertson, concurs. A similar case is Swarth. 4/232 (*EQL* 111). See also 4/177 (*EQL* 532) by Henry Halls the younger, about Mary Howgill: "for the worlds sake she is borne; it were well she were stoped."

& speake in the seed & lambs power, suffer & beare that, that is the tender." [66] Nayler and others went too far in their hesitancy to condemn the leadings, messages, and signs of other Quakers, but they stood in great awe before the Spirit and feared crushing its least or strangest workings, for they suspected that self-will might be involved in judging anything except clear immorality: "It is speaking in the Imaginations of Truth, both in your Speaking and Judging, that causes Divisions and Strife among you; and all this is cursed from God, and shut out of the Kingdom for ever. Therefore in that which is Pure and Eternal, which is one in all, which leads into love and Unity, dwell and abide faithful." [67]

The power of the Spirit to bring men into unity was one of the happy discoveries of the early Friends, and served as a final test of the guiding of the Light. For example, Thomas Stubbs, though his own work kept him in Northampton, spoke of feeling the call which had brought Burrough and Howgill to Ireland, and at the same time he wrote to Dewsbury in prison that he felt united to him, also, in the will of the Lord.[68] Out of this sense of unity came some of the remarkable friendships that developed between pairs of Quaker preachers in their work together. These partnerships often lasted for years and involved both practical balancing of individual skills and the constant checking of one another's leadings. But the deeper roots of their unity showed themselves when couples were forced by their work to separate, as Burrough and Howgill needed to do at Dublin:

> We have been heare about 3 weekes & we have pretty mettings on the first day but they are a carlesse desolut proud people. . . . But now . . . my beloved yockefelow and I now must parte who hath borne the yock so longe togither which was pretiouse one to the other as our one lives. The Crose is greate in so strange & barboriouse a nation, yett it is nott so greate, as if any other had parted us: my very life I have with him whose bow, sword and speare never returned emptie from the slayne of the mighty [as David had sung over fallen Jonathan] and often we have sunge togither att the deviding of the spoyle. But in the will of god is peace: I ame moved to goe a hundred

66. Fox, *Journal*, Camb., *1*, 222.
67. M. Fell, p. 56.
68. Dews./13, T. Stubbs to Dewsbury, Olney, August 4, 1655.

miles west in the nation towards Corke . . . & E. B. must stay heare, for this citie we cannott leave yett.[69]

Sharing the Spirit of God within them led Quakers in the outbursts of their affection to express some very fuzzy theology, and this extravagance of language accordingly became a cause of persecution and an issue in their debates with the puritans. At the same time, it underlay the deepest of all Quaker experiences, the unspoken awareness of the unification of the group by the Spirit in the silent Meeting, where the whole body, and not primarily its individuals, received power, wisdom, and joy from the Light. This "group mysticism," as Thomas Kelly calls it, has rarely been better described than in the sober theological "Apology" of Robert Barclay, the first systematic treatise about Friends:

> We judge it the duty of all to be diligent in the assembling of themselves together . . . to wait upon God, and returning out of their own thoughts and imaginations, to feel the Lord's presence. . . . And as everyone is thus gathered, and so met inwardly in their spirits, as wel as outwardly in their persons, there the secret Power and Vertue of Life is known to refresh the Soul, and the pure motions and breathings of God's Spirit are felt to arise; from which, as words of declaration, prayers or praises arise, the acceptable worship is known. . . . And no man here limits the Spirit of God, nor bringeth forth his own conned and gathered stuff. . . . Yea, though there be not a word spoken, yet is the true spiritual worship performed. . . . Yet . . . as our worship consisteth not in the words, so neither in silence as silence; but in an holy dependence of the mind upon God.[70]

In times of persecution the refusal of Quakers to give up meeting was more than stubbornness and more than sheer obedience to what seemed God's command: "Those that have seen the sweet lovely precious state of Unity and Concord, that the excellent Power of the Lord God Almighty gathered into, in the blessed

---

69. ARBarc./118, Howgill to M. Fell, Dublin, September 3, 1655. Cf. Burrough's account, Swarth. 3/17 (*EQL* 179) and the parting of Briggs and John Braithwaite in Somerset, Swarth. 3/128 (*EQL* 415).

70. Barclay, *Apology*, Proposition 11, §§ 6, 9 (pp. 248–49, 254). Cf. Wragge, *Barclay*, p. 107.

morning of our day, and the spiritual advantages, comforts, joy, refreshments and divine satisfaction that attended in this true and spiritual Unity with the Lord Jesus and one with another . . . cannot but . . . greatly dread the turnings aside, and goings out of it." [71]

The early Friends seem to have continually deepened and enriched life and worship in their Meetings, despite nostalgia for the first great days. It is hard, however, to find in their writings a clear picture of the ways in which a man might grow in spiritual life once the first decisive struggle was past. This lack arose partly from the assumption that the Spirit was infallible and that perfect Christianity was simply perfect obedience; even though obedience in all aspects of life was not attained at once, they felt that in each situation a man was either completely obedient or not at all. Nevertheless, the Spirit clearly did not impart all truth at one time, and "Christ requireth obedience according to the knowledge that is given or increased. That is many times required to be left, upon a further degree of knowledge given, which was not required to be left before." [72] Nayler is almost the only early writer who describes the continuing inward growth that results from following the Spirit: "Every good work of God in his Saints, who become obedient to his working . . . begets the Creature nearer to God, and into his Likeness and Nature, and this is the reward of good works to every one who are exercised therein, that thereby they are wrought out of the World's Likeness, and Conformity, and . . . Friendship." [73] Outward pressures of persecution sobered Friends, and the needs of ministry to others made them more loving, quite apart from their growth due to inward experience. Yet even epistles of those converted late in life or late in the growth of Quakerism speak more and more of peace and strength of spirit as their years passed. Francis Howgill early in the 1650s and Robert Barclay in the 1660s both went from a period of fiery conflict to one of in-

71. "Testimony of Christopher Marshall Concerning the Unity of the Spirit," in Camm and Audland, *Works.*

72. Isaac Penington, quoted by Ruth L. Armsby, "The Quaker View of the State, Its Nature, Powers and Limitations, with Special Reference to Isaac Penington" (University of Birmingham, 1932), p. 16. Cf. Nayler, *Works,* pp. 304–05.

73. Nayler, *Works,* p. 308. Cf. Nayler, *Man of Sin,* p. 26; James Nayler, *A Discovery of the Beast . . . An Answer to T. Winterton* (London, 1655), p. 7.

tense activity, and finally came to a time of serenity when conscience gnawed less and love was easier.

But before 1688, the sense of the Lamb's War was never entirely absent. Quaker life was not complete without sharing the work of the Spirit in the world as a whole. Most Quakers took some part in preaching to the unredeemed world and saw their own lives in relation to this campaign. It is possible to regard their aggressive attacks against non-Quakers simply as the negative side of their intense dedication to the Spirit and the Quaker life. The man who has given everything to a cause is likely to release his suppressed regrets by denouncing the men who belittle it as wicked yielders to temptation. It may also happen that the remnants of hostility in a man committed to loving his brethren will be diverted quite forcefully against a convenient nonbrother. Many strong and growing sects have reacted in just such ways. But these were not the primary motives in the Lamb's War, as one may see by the lack of emphasis in their writings on temptation or on the reprobate. The preaching of judgment involved the Quaker directly and personally with his fellow men, and for their sake he would undergo suffering and hardship himself and give up all wealth and any other work.

The willingness to antagonize peaceable men by open condemnation was developed by most preachers only after further inward struggles of their own. But seen either psychologically or theologically, it was a major achievement. Psychologically, it can be both easier and more unwholesome to suppress resentment than to express it. Any man's trust that his aggression will produce no catastrophe, and perhaps even a creative result, implies a very fundamental faith in himself and other men. Most early Quakers came out of the youthful period when they, like Fox, became ardent separatists and shunned all wicked men, into a time of ministry, when they feared no one and considered no felon or American savage beyond the reach of their message. From the bitter background of the North of England, the ruthless morality of Puritanism, and, most of all, the intensity of their own inner fight, the early Friends could not but carry strong hostility and pent-up driving power. But these were channeled almost completely into the hope of transforming the world, for within this hope lay the faith that inner judgment and outer suffering such as they had been through would also be God's way of redeeming other men. The highest sign of their faith that the power of God had worked through their own suffering and self-judgment was their willingness to urge the Cross upon others: "Being faithful to the Light . . . it will lead you to the Death upon the Cross, and Crucifie you unto the World and wordly things, and raise you up into the pure Life, to follow the Lamb whethersoever he goeth . . . and therefore all come to the Cross and love it, and rejoyce in it." [74] The Quakers took this militant faith in the goodness of God's power into all their work and ministry.

74. Camm and Audland, *Works*, pp. 257–58.

5

Debate with Puritan Pastors

I do witness that Christ Jesus is the light of the world . . .
and his light . . . lets you see that you should not live in
covetousness, pride . . . lust & uncleanness. . . . And I do
stand a witness against you that make a profession . . . of
faith in him . . . and yet say that not any can be made free
from sin. And I do witness that not any Minister of Christ is
made by the will of man, nor fitted for his Ministry by hu-
mane learning. . . . And I do stand a witness against all those
that say they are gifted to Preach the Gospel, & limits themselves to a particular time, people, and place.[1]

THE early Quakers preached to transform the world, as they themselves had been reborn through their inward struggle. Their sermons on ethics were often very detailed, but the aim was always
total conversion. Though sensitive to specific injustices, they were
at first little interested in any reform which did not turn their
hearers toward complete obedience to the Light.

This campaign to bring the world under the conquest of the
Light was built upon fierce judgment and condemnation. The
puritans rebuked the Friends for saying so little of the love of
God and showing so little love themselves; Nayler's answer was
simply that "this is pure Love to the Soul, that deals faithfully
therewith, in declaring its Condition; and that was the great Love
Christ showed the Jews, when he told them they were Hypocrites,
Blind Guides, Lyars, and said . . . "Ye Generation of Vipers." [2]

1. J. Whitehead, *Two Seeds,* pp. 10–17.
2. Nayler, *Works,* pp. 288–89.

The loving surgeon cuts out the cancer: peace was only possible through judgment. This had been the Quakers' own experience. Thomas Taylor wrote to Fox: "Blessed be the Lord that he did not suffer thee from the beginning to flatter me, but to deale faithfully with me in that great businesse of my soul." [3] Friends felt that it must always be so: "If ye will reckon Wrath, Judgment and the Ministration of Condemnation none of the things of God . . . but reckon it to the Law or Old Testament . . . I answer that . . . the Righteousness, Salvation, Mercy & Grace of God in Christ . . . is preached in the same Light in which Judgment and Wrath is revealed." [4] For Friends the message of judgment and the experience of God's love were not two successive experiences, as they have been for most other Christians, but simultaneous actions of the same Light. It is not possible, therefore, to separate sermons of judgment from messages of positive hope in their preaching. Even in a personal warning the two were always combined. Fox wrote to the Ranter John Toldervy, who had passed briefly in and out of Quakerism: "It will be hard for thee, John . . . when the fire and heat enter into your flesh . . . then remember, every word that ye have given forth will come pat upon you [as] a burthen. . . . Now come to the just principle in thee. John, thy flight was in the winter." [5]

The Quaker appeal consistently implied that all men are by nature evil and that the essence of hope lay purely in the Light. They believed that that which was of God in men's Conscience would condemn them. At times Fox sounded neither loving nor hopeful: "To the light in thy conscience I speake, thou child of the devill, . . . which will witness me eternaly and thee condemne eternaly: and when thou art in thy terror & torment remember I warned thee in love to thy soule in thy life time." But more often he showed concern and love, however desperate: "Prize your tyme while you have it . . . O why will you dye, why will you chuse your owne waies. . . . Christ Jesus hath given thee as much light as will let thee see this is evill." [6]

3. Swarth. 3/29 (*EQL* 24), May 18, 1653.
4. Fisher, *Works,* pp. 605–06.
5. Fox, *Great Mistery,* p. 35. This personal note in the middle of a huge theological tract is quite typical.
6. Fox, *Journal,* Camb., *1,* 90, 99–100. Cf. M. Fell, *Works,* pp. 49, 79, 86.

The Quaker preacher's technique was a massive assault on any
point of guilt in his hearers. Robert Widder, when at Embleton,

> spoke to the priest & people in publick, [and] Charged them
> in the presence of God that if any of them Could tell what
> would become of their souls if they shou'd be cut of[f] at that
> present, let them speak. But never one of them durst open
> their mouths in answer to him. Then stood up one Bayliff
> Pearson, & sd,
> "You Disturb us from hearing the word of god."
> R W: Replyed again, "Thou never heard the word of god
> in all thy life; thou art but a sinfull man." To the wch the
> Bayliff answered, "God forgiv us, wee are all sinfull enough." [7]

A good preacher felt a human delight in the consternation he
caused when "babels high walles are terribly shaken." But he also
knew that his hearers' salvation depended upon this attack on
their conscience. Camm and Howgill thought they had failed when
on their first visit Oliver Cromwell received them politely! They
took it as a sign of his depravity that they could not get anything
"fastened" upon his conscience so that he would confess his guilt.[8]
Howgill reported a still more revealing dialogue with Lampitt,
the puritan pastor of Ulverston:

> We met at the litle gate that goes to the steple house. . . .
> At the first I tould him he was a persecutor of Ch[rist]; he
> denied & sayd he witnesed Ch[rist] in him: I asked him
> how . . . he cam to haue Ch[rist] in him, he sayd throug
> Death. [I] asked hast thou pased through Death: he answered
> yea twenty yeare since. I sayd, but whear art thou now: Death
> reules [thee]; thy actions demonstrate playnely. . . . Then
> I tould him he was an enemy to the Crose of Ch[rist], & then
> he playnly descovered himselfe: & sayd: I live vnder no Crose.
> . . . I sayd to him, Is all subdued: thy will & all sin in [thee?]
> He sayd by Christ he was compleat; I tould him . . . thearin
> he was deseved . . . but he would have bene gone, he sayd:
> I hop you will alow me the same liberty you have—that was

---

7. *FPT*, p. 35.

8. Swarth. 3/192 (*EQL* 61), Nayler to M. Fell; ARBarc./127, Howgill and Camm
to Fox about their interview with Cromwell, March 1654.

that none should Speake agaynst his deseite; I tould him
playnly: thear was no liberty to that nature he lived In.[9]

It would be wrong, however, to think that the Quakers' preaching sought only to prod human consciences to repent. The Light
to which Friends appealed was the power of God; and the result
of their message was a direct and growing experience of that power
by those who heard. Human actions of either the preacher or the
repentant hearer were intended only to prepare the way for what
God would do. Thus ministry, whether it was to judge the world
or to encourage Friends, was always a temporary step. If the
preacher was genuinely led by the Spirit, he knew his hearers were
brought directly before the same Spirit. He turned them to the
Light of Christ within them: the role of the preacher was to be
not a priest but a matchmaker. Despite the adulation some women
felt for Fox and Nayler, Friends knew that the preacher's own
personality and feelings ought to be kept down; he had to restrain
himself even in his hatred of sin. In a beautiful address to the
Quaker leaders in 1658, Fox said:

> ffrends take heed of destroying tht which yee have begotten.
> . . . In the livinge unmovable word of god dwell . . . & re-
> maine in the pure. . . . And take heed of many words; but
> what reatcheth to the life, tht settles in the life. & soe frends
> must be kept in the life . . . soe with tht they may Answer
> the life of god in others.
>
> Itt is the greatest danger to goe abroad, except aman be
> moved of the lord . . . for then he keepinge in the power
> is kept in his Jorney, . . . Soe if any one have Amovinge to
> any place, & have spoken what they were moved of the Lord,
> [they should] returne to there habitation againe. . . . And
> preatch as well in life as with words . . .
>
> In tht waite which . . . cooles . . . The power of the
> lord god hath bene abused, & the worth of truth not bene
> minded; there hath bene atramplinge on & maringe with
> your feet . . .
>
> Now itt is amightie thinge to be in the worke of the min-
> istery of the lord god & to goe forth in tht, for itt is not as
> acustomary preatchinge, but to bringe people to the end of

9. ARBarc./75, 1652, Howgill to M. Fell.

all preatchinge; for your once speaking to people, & then
people com into the thinge yee speake of. . . . Now if words
be rashed out again unsavory, then they . . . may hurt again
that which he hath gott upp . . . And soe walke in the love
of god.[10]

Quakers watched themselves. They knew that not every word they
preached came from the Spirit; subtler misunderstandings than
mere impulsiveness or self-will could corrupt the message. A genuine leading, for instance, might be intended for the individual's
own help and not as a message to be shared, yet the tension in facing it might be interpreted as the power impelling the receiver
to speak; and by the act of speaking he avoided the need to face
the truth in himself. Margaret Fell advised against

> speaking Words at random, when the Power moves, under
> pretence of a Burthen, which Burthen is the Earthly Part
> of yourselves, and the Words that you speak belongs to your
> own Particulars: This being spoken out to others . . . then
> others take it, and Judge it. So I warn you to be silent, and
> to wait low in the Silence, until the Word be committed to
> you to minister . . . that you discern what you speak from,
> and what ye speak to; and who speaks here, is a Minister.[11]

A Friend who felt he had been given a genuine message for the
group, or for non-Quakers, but failed to present it at the right
time would pray afterward that a new chance be given him. But
if he tried to speak anyhow, out of his own anxiety, he might realize his mistake: "when . . . the well was sett oppen then I did
not speake," but later "in the dread I spoke, but the life was shutt
upp." [12]

A clear difference in tone separates the fiery warnings of
preachers, who "threshed among the world" at great public meetings, from the gentle ministry within Quaker Meetings. But in
both situations every message was prophetic, in theory a direct
word from God, not given at the behest of the hearers. Even the

10. Fox, *Journal*, Camb., *1*, 317–21.
11. M. Fell, p. 55.
12. Swarth. 4/25 (*EQL* 272), John Stubbs to M. Fell. Burnyeat. p. 23, also describes
feeling God's wrath for failure to present a word when commanded.

ministry delivered to fellow Quakers within a Meeting was un-
planned. To Friends the greater responsibility was the taking of
the word of the Lord to the men in the world. Thus their ministry
was in principle itinerant, recognizing no geographical limits. It
was also free: the logical people to support the Quaker prophet,
since support was often needed, were not his hearers but the Meeting of Friends from whom he was sent out. Those at home supported not the man but his mission, after feeling a call to share
in it; yet the preacher spoke not on behalf of Friends but for the
Spirit. Within the Quaker fellowship a man might be set aside
as a teacher but never as a priest to lead their own prayers, for God
alone could lead worship.

Despite any distortions or confusions in their message, their ministry expressed a spirit of finality. As a word from God, it required
the hearer to respond to the message by immediate decision.
Quaker preachers, "being . . . divinely inspired, their Doctrine
is to be received by you as from God, and . . . it will be found
in due time to be your sin, even Unbelief and Rebellion against
God, not to submit to what they speak in his Name." [13] To doubt
the inspiration of the Quaker prophet, knowing what he had passed
through before receiving it, seemed blasphemy.

The importance of women among preachers was connected with
the primacy of the Spirit and not with any deliberate campaign
for feminine equality. The orthodox puritans, and even the early
separatists, had ruled that women were not permitted to speak
in the church at the "time of prophecy" after the sermon or in
Bible study sessions. If they were confused or doubtful about anything spoken at that time, they were to ask a man to teach them
in private.[14] Ann Hutchinson was banished from Massachusetts
over this issue. But when the minister of Hawkchurch, Dorset,
quoted St. Paul's dictum against women to the Quakeress Dewens
Morry, she denied that it was the voice of a woman who spoke,

13. Fisher, p. 559. On Ministry, see Nayler, *Works*, p. 353; Barclay, *Apology*,
Proposition 10. On funds raised to support Quaker ministry see "Minutes of North-
ern Counties Yearly Meeting and General Meeting, 1658–59 and 1671 ff.," now in-
cluded as No. 103 of the manuscripts in the strong room of Kendal Monthly Meeting,
Westmorland. Cf. Harold E. Walker, "The Conception of a Ministry in the Quaker
Movement" (University of Edinburgh, 1948) for a more pastoral view.

14. Cf. John Smyth, *Principles and Inferences Concerning the Visible Church*,
cited in Burrage, *Dissenters, 1,* 233.

but said that it was the voice of the Spirit of God.[15] Friends themselves had much trouble with slightly hysterical women ministers who tended to be, like Elizabeth Leavens, "of no great parentage, but of the lower ranks in the world."[16] A Quaker preaching to villages in Devonshire wrote to Swarthmore for help, asking for men rather than women Friends, "ffor they do not Care to here any women Friends."[17] Quaker women made more outlandish mission voyages and acted out more provocative signs than did the men. But the authority of the Spirit could not be denied even in women, and, in reply to non-Quaker critics, there were the biblical prophetesses for analogy.

The dependence of ministry upon the Spirit, not upon the hearers, also explains the willingness of Friends to give their message only once or to speak in English before foreign hearers or to repel bystanders by their signs. In general, Quakers ignored the obvious, practical results. The response to their preaching could come only by the Spirit's work, and once the witness was faithfully borne, the outcome could be left to God.

Puritan ministers, on the other hand, were by vocation pastors. The orthodox preachers also thundered for repentance, especially from the great pulpits of Cambridge and London, for they were as zealous for the authority of God's word as were the Friends. Though trained in Calvinist theology, the puritan ministers took pride in "unshelling their controversies out of their hard school terms, [and] made thereof plain and wholesome meat for the people."[18] The puritan struggled against the temptation to "tickle the itching eares of his auditorie with the fine ringing sentences of the Fathers." The minister "must privately vse at his libertie the artes, philosophy, and varietie of reading whilest he is in framing his sermon, but he ought in publike to conceale all these."[19] Such men worked hard: Richard Greenham preached seven sermons a week, besides making pastoral calls and giving time to generous care for the poor and prisoners, official duties to super-

---

15. *FPT*, p. 87. Cf. Fox, *Great Mistery*, p. 153; John Whitehead, *A Manifestation of Truth in the Written Gospel-labours* . . . (London, 1704), p. 142.
16. *FPT*, p. 260.
17. Swarth. 4/163 (*EQL* 334), Arthur Cotten to Fox (November 18, 1656).
18. Thomas Fuller, *The Holy and the Profane State*, p. 90, quoted in Louis B. Wright, "William Perkins," *Huntington Library Quarterly*, 3, 173.
19. William Perkins, *Works*, 2 (Cambridge, 1604), 670.

vise public food prices and farm conditions, and writing often and at length for publication. These ministers had developed a century of tradition in pastoral counseling, in keeping spiritual journals, and in expecting from the preachers' wives a self-sacrifice equal to their own, a tradition maintained through the Wesleys, Edwardses, and Beechers down to our own day.

The key point is that the puritan ministers expected to work mainly with people already converted. They realized the danger that a man might relapse from conversion, because he "never smarted for sinne at the first." But "God knowes that as wee are prone to sinne, so when the conscience is throughly awaked, wee are as prone to despaire for sinne." [20] Their counseling involved the guidance of laymen in moral judgments of daily life, but often laid bare a deeper anxiety: "In God's Church, commonly they who are touched by the spirit, and begin to come on in Religion are much troubled with fears that they are not God's children." [21] The Calvinist doctrine of Election only made more miserable many an earnest churchgoer who had no clear sign "that there was a change wrought in my heart, will and affections, notwithstanding the remainders of sin." [22] Many overconscientious young Puritans like John Bunyan had stumbled upon Mark 3:28–29 and feared they had committed the unpardonable sin against the Holy Spirit. Wise pastors like Perkins and Greenham assured them that the elect cannot commit this sin, and therefore that such a man, whose struggle against sin was already a sign of God's intervention in his life, need not despair "The excellencie, goodness and dignitie of conscience stands not in accusing, but in excusing . . . an infallible certenty of the pardon of sinne and life everlasting." Puritan pastors spoke to their hearers of God's love more often than of his judgment, and gently reminded them that "it is by the Spirit that we cry: *Abba,* Father," and that "the Spirit himself beareth witness with our spirit that we are children of God." [23]

Thus the Quaker preacher and the puritan pastor worked in

20. Richard Sibbes, *The Bruised Reede and Smoaking Flax,* p. 15 and signatures a+6–a:6r, both quoted in Watkins, p. 11. Cf. Marshall M. Knappen, *Tudor Puritanism* (Chicago, University of Chicago Press, 1939), p. 386.

21. Perkins, *Works, 1,* 420.

22. Edward Staunton, *A Sermon Preached at Great Milton,* quoted in Watkins, p. 36.

23. Perkins, *Works, 1,* 538–40; Romans 8:15–16; cf. Perkins, *Golden Chaine,* p. 197.

opposite directions and never understood each other's basic purposes. The orthodox ministers tried to keep their parishioners from "the gulfe of desperation" as well as from "the rocks of presumption," but Friends would never risk giving the slightest foothold to man's pride. Instead of making sinful Christians aware of their dependence on God, the pastors seemed to make them self-satisfied. Friends attacked the ministers as "pleading for sin" in saying that any man, though he still sins at times, may go to heaven. They had found such compromise in their own experience to be a temptation to escape from the Light. The puritan pastor, said Friends, was "never without his Cordialls and Pills to purge the head and heart from all sense of judgment." [24] Behind this scorn lay their confidence that they themselves had overcome evil after the fiercest battle of their lives, and that nothing else would be true freedom.

The puritan leaders, by contrast, were men who had known life in its complexity. They knew the ambiguous mixture of sin and grace in their own best actions and in the motives they least admired. They had discovered new levels of sin and evil in the moment of seeming victory, when Cromwell and the forces of Parliament broke apart in the struggle to remake England. Inevitably, they regarded the Quakers as self-righteous and unrealistic. Both groups actually stemmed from the same traditions, and most of their crucial doctrines were the same: man's dependence on God for both righteousness and salvation, inward conversion by the Spirit, the crucial importance of daily effort by each Christian pilgrim, and the possibility of actually transforming the world by God's power. Seeing the similarities, many puritan pastors began by receiving Quaker preachers with tolerance and discussing differences of doctrine in a fairly open spirit. But as it became clear in almost every case that they were entirely different in mood and method, the lines were drawn. A great minister like Baxter felt man's unending need of God's love and forgiveness. Those who had really seen God, he said, would not speak of sinlessness, but would abhor themselves like Job. Throughout human life, "Christ's Kingdome is an Hospitall." [25] Nayler and Fisher replied

24. Fisher, p. 173. Cf. Nayler, *Works*, pp. 294, 399; Nayler, *Foot Yet in the Snare*, p. 10; Fox, *Great Mistery*, p. 183.
25. Baxter, as quoted in Fox, *Great Mistery*, p. 79.

that those to whom Christ came had been fully cured. When Baxter admitted his own imperfection, Nayler exulted. While Baxter was daily praying to receive God's Spirit, Friends insisted that they had it.[26]

When the prophet met the priest in actual debate, each thought he was fighting for what he most deeply believed. To Friends, the pastors seemed to thwart the Lamb's War and hence God's Spirit itself. To the puritans, the Quakers not only were intruding illegally but were committed to breaking up the most godly order in church and state that England had ever seen.

The gusto with which puritans and Quakers argued has seldom been equaled in religious history. One or more Friend challenged almost every English pastor in his own pulpit, and debates were held wherever both sides would accept the terms—before packed houses or Cromwell's Major Generals.[27] A flood of pamphlets repeated and continued the verbal arguments. Every important Quaker writer in the 1650s produced up to a dozen such tracts except for Ellwood and the Peningtons. The leading puritans joined in the fray. Richard Baxter and the radical Baptist Feake wrote in 1653 before any Quakers had yet come south in person. Outstanding Presbyterians such as Prynne, Danson, and Firmin wrote, as did Independents like Chancellor Owen of Oxford. The Baptist leaders were drawn in almost without exception: Henry Denne, Roger Williams, John Tombes, Vavasour Powell. Many wild sectarians and dozens of little-known pastors whose parishes had been invaded also burst into print. The list included men of letters such as Henry More of Cambridge and Lord Saye and Sele. Anti-Quaker tracts averaged a fairly steady twenty a year up to

26. Nayler, *An Answer to a Book . . . by Richard Baxter* (London, 1655), pp. 27–36. Cf. his *Works*, pp. 277–78, or Camm and Audland: "They . . . say . . . they are a company of miserable Sinners, that err and stray like lost Sheep from the ways of God, and are Grievous Offenders of Gods holy laws . . . therefore, say we, unredeemed yet" (*Works*, pp. 247–48).

27. Cf. Swarth. 1/1 (*EQL* 248) to Fox, March 7, 1655/56, on the debate of Alex. Parker and other Friends against Lancashire puritan clergy before Major-General Charles Worsley. See also debates with Baptists at Chichester (Swarth. 4/216, *EQL* 471) and at Bedford (3/159, *EQL* 476), both in the crisis year of 1659, and the later Barbican debates in London in 1674, on which see Fig. 4, and Jeremiah Ives and Thomas Plant, *A Contest for Christianity, or a Faithful Relation of Two late Meetings . . .* (London, Oct. 1674). The printer of the anonymous *Quaker's Ballad* seems to have used older woodcuts of Nayler and of the meeting of a shepherd and a gentleman (a Jesuit?).

The Quakers Ballad.

OR,

a Hymn of Triumph and Exultation for their Victories, at the two late great Disputes by them held with the Baptists; the first in *Barbican*, on the 9th. the second in *VVheeler-street*, on the 16th, of the Eight Month, 1674.
To an excellent new Tune, called, *The Zealous Atheist.*

YE she-friends and he-friends whoe'er inherit
Infallible light in dark-lanthorn of Spirit,
Come prick up your ears, for behold! I will fit ye
With an Hymn that is cal'd by the wicked, a Ditty

In the Scuffle we late have had with the Baptists
Wherein both our honour and intrest wrapt is,
Though our logick perhaps be too weak to dispute
We hope by a Ballad at least to confute um. (um

For though Fiddle & Organs are both Babilonish
Wherewith the prophane delighted alone is;
Yet in such a case inspiration may haunt
Even us which are perfict to warble a Chaunt.

Then let us a while our tremblings lay by,
And quit our still Meetings to set up a cry,
Lets challenge, and rant, talk loud and be bold,
For the Spirit at present doth move us to scold.

'Tis time to exclaim, as receiving the wrong,
And take up that carnal weapon the tongue,
For if we delay our whole party must sink,
And our long-boasted light go out in a stink.

Our juglings so plain will appear that each eye,
Through the mask of our holy pretences will spy,
And see that a Quaker, when stript of his paint,
Is nearer of kin to an Athiest, than Saint.

Then let us equivocate neatly and lap
A plausible meaning on all that we say,
And the very same art that serves to excuse us,
At once shall condemn all those that accuse us.

This being done, we point time and place,
And come full prepared to bandy the case,
In the Barbican first we gave them a meeting,
And never was seen such a Bear-garden greeting

A Rabble thrust in from each end of the Town,
And before half an agreement cou'd be laid down
In less time than a man can a pot of Ale swallow,
'twas confirm'd with a hoop, & deny'd with a hallow

The place like an Hot-house appear'd, and by hap
Some Friends might be cured here of a clap;
And if it were so I cannot but say,
'Twas the best effect of our meeting that day.

Fig. 4. *The Quaker's Ballad,* an anti-Quaker tract of 1674, with a woodcut of Nayler's entry into Bristol. The doggerel verse refers to the Barbican debates against the Baptists.

1660. Blow and counterblow would continue for three or four rounds, as when John Bunyan publicized a charge of witchcraft against two itinerant Friends.[28] Though Fox and Fisher issued works of 750 pages apiece, most tracts were ten to twenty-five pages. The method was in any case not systematic but consisted of taking sentence after sentence from the opponent's tract and answering or ridiculing it, quite in the manner of Origen and Celsus. The language was full of scriptural epithets about sinners and deceivers, with only emotional relevance. Fox wrote: "O Lawson, oh Blood sucker, oh Esau, who would slay the Righteous and slayeth them in thy hart . . . thou cunning ffox who seeks to devoure the lambs of Jesus Christ . . . oh thou serpent who are painted outwardly with the saints words, but a murtherer and killer of the Just, oh thou viper. . . . Neither count this hard language nor rivile at it, its the love of the lord god to thee." [29] Men as gentle and saintly as Nayler and Baxter flung at each other pamphletsful of biblical billingsgate, because they dared not refuse the challenge: "You accuse me with *horrible rayling,* to which I answer, What language have I used against you, except such as the Spirit of God in Scriptures gives . . . but deceit is got into such fine colours that it cannot bear a plain language . . . that must . . . cal him that vents his lies, a lyar. . . . You instance thes words: *Thou art damned and I see the devil in thy face,* and this you say is [our] first salute to all we meet: to which I answer: Thousands . . . we have met with, past by, and spoke not one word to them." [30] The emotional intensity of the Quaker experience carried even men like Fox to the edge of unbalance at times: "I wish that these outward powers of the earth were given up. . . . Oh Hypocrisy It makes me sicke to thincke of them. I have given them a vissitation and as faithfull a warneing as ever was: There is an ugly a slubering hound an ugely hound an ugely slobering hound but the Lord forgive them—destruction—destruction." [31]

---

28. See Barbara Bowden's data on other anti-Quaker authors. Richard Baxter (*The Quakers Catechism,* Preface) complained that he "offered to come and answer all there Queres" in the Quakers' Assembly if they would consent that he might do it without interruption. But they had refused to promise silence, so he sent them written answers; upon hearing that Friends had decided to publish them with attacks upon him, he beat them to the punch. A long duel of pamphlets followed.

29. Fox, *Journal,* Camb., *1,* 116.

30. Nayler, *Man of Sin,* pp. 3, 46.

31. Fox, *Journal,* Camb., 2, 172.

For their part, the puritans were often genuinely convinced that Friends were led by the devil. They had stories to prove this, not only Gilpin's firsthand narrative but a report that Fox himself had admitted such an alliance. There was the painfully clear fact that some earnest neurotics burst into obvious insanity on becoming Quakers. The puritans, like the Bible, ascribed such seizures to demon possession. Sane Quakers were also accused of deliberate witchcraft in Ireland and Barbados. Fox's power to overcome opposition with his piercing eyes and friendly handshake was cited as evidence even within England.[32]

In many places Quakers were simultaneously suspected of being Catholic agents, since they wandered without credentials and attacked orthodox ministers and predestination. In reality, the Jesuits had known Friends only from puritan anti-Quaker literature and a few wild missions by men like Perrot. But even Baxter believed some tall tales linking the Quakers and papists:

> Deposition . . . of Geo. Cowlishaw of the City of Bristol . . . 1654 . . . who informeth on his Oath that in . . . September last [he] had some Discourse in Bristol with one M. Coppinger an Irish man, formerly a Schoolfellow of his, . . . who told this Informant that he had lived in Rome and Italy eight or nine years, & had taken upon him the Order of a Friar of the Franciscan Company. . . . He had been at London . . . and that none came so near him as the Quakers. And being at a Meeting of the Quakers he there met with two of his Acquaintance in Rome . . . (of the same Franciscan Order . . .) that were now become chief Speakers among the Quakers.[33]

Neither Quaker nor puritan was above fogging the issues. Baxter was willing to call the Friends papists, with or without evidence, "because they do the Papists work. . . . [and as for] under-

32. Cf. Higginson, *Irreligion of Quakers*, p. 18; Swarth. 1/66 (*EQL* 329); notes in *EQL*, p. 207. Douglas, in *JFHS*, *48*, 26, quotes a gay yarn from *Irish Witchcraft and Demonology* on Quaker witches.

33. Baxter, *Quakers Catechism*, p. C-5. Both he and the Newcastle pastors (Weld et al., *Perfect Pharisee*) also cited a Catholic agent who had pretended to be a converted Jew and linked him with Quakerism. For other accusations of Catholicism see Fisher, pp. 109, 122, 191; Swarth. 4/145 (*EQL* 416); ARBarc./61. Titus Oates, however, knew better than to confuse Quakers and Catholics: cf. Dews./32. So did the Jesuits: cf. *JFHS*, *31* (1934), 37.

mining the sufficiency of Scripture, the denying of the Ministry [and] the slighting of Justification by Imputed Righteousnesse . . . who do you think should reveal all this Poperie to the Quakers? Not the Spirit of God. . . . And whether it were Friars or Devils or both, that make Quakers, its not worth the while to dispute." [34] After all, Rome was Antichrist, and Antichrist was an incarnation of Satan, from whom Quakerism arose. But a Quaker in the same mood, when asked "whether Christ be in his Saints in . . . that nature wherein he suffered at Jerusalem," answered: "What hast thou to do to querie after the divine nature, who art the natural man, that knows nothing of God but what thou knows naturally as a bruit beast." [35]

Beneath all the misinformation, misunderstanding, and baroque imagery, there were very solid issues in debate between Quakers and puritans. The pastors were the most articulate defenders of the established church. In Cromwellian times, when outspoken Anglicans had been ejected, the puritan clergy was a pillar of established social order as well and this made the clash more bitter. But the ministers also had the knowledge to see and pin down the real theological issues. Some few Quakers were able to meet them on this ground.

The basic area where real discussion was most needed was the nature of the Light itself. This issue was sometimes wrongly narrowed down to a clash between the authority of the Bible and the authority of the Light in men; both sides should have been able to go deeper than this, and occasionally did. Quakers accepted the Bible's inspiration, though they did not depend on it. The puritans likewise accepted the need of inward conversion and the work of Christ and the Spirit within men's hearts (though never, said the orthodox, in the total absence of the outward Word). The argument about the Light had two main points of issue: first, to clarify whether the ordinary indwelling of the Spirit in the Christian was the same as the extraordinary inspiration of the prophets and apostles, so as to evaluate the divine authority claimed for Quaker messages; and, second, whether the Light of Christ found in every man was enough to save him, or corresponded only to

34. Baxter, *Quakers Catechism*, p. C-4.
35. E. Burrough and F. Howgill, *Answers to Several Queries . . . by Philip Bennett*, as quoted in Farmer, *Mysteries of Godlinesse*, p. 45.

God's self-revelation in the Creation of the world, through which men might have known God but had been unable to since Adam's Fall.

The argument, of course, had little to do with the nature of man, though some modern Quakers may wish it had. Friends were as certain as any Calvinist that human nature "while in the Fall . . . is . . . only Evil, Vanity and Deceit." [36] Their basic objection to puritan pastors was in fact that they allowed men to think too well of themselves. In spite of the puritans' many efforts to identify the Quaker Light with the purely human or natural element in reason or conscience, Friends denied this consistently. "This Light is not Natural . . . it comes from God and Christ into every Creature not by Creation, as the rational Soul and . . . Conscience itself do." [37] In their own lives Friends knew the difference between the thoughts of the natural man and the leadings of the Light, even if the outsider could not distinguish.

In the same way, the Quakers could quickly brush aside puritan claims that they sought salvation by human effort or good works. Though a man had to keep himself constantly open to the Light, to God alone belonged all credit for the deeds into which the Spirit led him, for "That righteousness which God accepts . . . is his own . . . as the Measure of the Light of Christ is received. . . . Who abides in that Righteousness, abides in that which denies Self." [38] Friends were so far from urging men to make their own way to heaven that they accused even the puritans of willworks, "Religious Performances in my own Will, in my own Time, and in my own Strength," since the pastors did not constantly depend on the Spirit's leadings. [39]

The Quaker doctrine of Election may be mentioned in this context. Friends rejected predestination, since they asked for every man's repentance, and this confused the issue for both puritan and modern critics. Fox indeed blamed the Presbyterians for having "frightened people with the doctrine of election & reproba-

---

36. Fisher, p. 814. Cf. ibid., pp. 668–69, 672, 849–50; also Nayler, *Works*, p. 362; Fox, *Great Mistery*, pp. 91–99; Fox, *Journal*, Camb., *1*, 132. On all these issues there is careful discussion in Bohn's thesis "Puritans and Quakers."

37. Fisher, p. 609. Cf. Wragge, *Barclay*, p. 43.

38. Nayler, *Works*, pp. 265–66. Cf. Fox, *Great Mistery*, pp. 46–48.

39. Ellwood, *Life*, pp. 29–30.

tion, [who] saide the greatest part of men and women, God had ordained . . . for hell, lett them pray or preach or doe what they
coulde. . . . And God had a certain number which was elected
for heaven, lett them doe what they woulde." [40] To Fox this
sounded immoral as well as snobbish. Therefore, he and Nayler
made generalities out of these Calvinist terms by saying that "Election and Reprobation are in the two Seeds, that after the Flesh
and that after the Spirit." [41] Election "stoode in the second birth
and reproobation stoode in the first." [42] Quaker teachings on Election were nevertheless an outgrowth of Puritanism. The Seed of
the Spirit and the Second Birth came by God's power and not
from men, who by the nature they "are now Universally Degener-
ated into . . . all are the children of wrath." [43] The frequent
Quaker mention of the "Everlasting Covenant" was also significant. By 1620 William Ames (not the Quaker but a puritan theologian) had set down a "Covenant Theology" in which God, as
he elected the Saints, foresaw the good works he would empower
them to do. Thereby predestination became less arbitrary, and the
justice of God and the moral sense of the puritan were affirmed.[44]
Once Election had been linked inseparably with the moral transformation of men by God's power, it was a logical step for radical
puritans to assert that all men could accept or reject this power.[45]
As the actual mission of Puritanism became more universal, and
all men were called to repent and accept God's glory, the doctrine
of Election was inevitably universalized.

Thus it is obvious that the area in which the basic conflict of
Quakers and puritans really lay concerned the *nature* of God's
power and its relation to the human personality and to decision.
All Calvinists, puritans, and Quakers had already (unlike other
Churches) identified the grace of God mainly with power to over-

40. Fox, *Journal,* Camb., *1,* 293.
41. Nayler, *Works,* p. 310.
42. Fox, *Journal,* Camb., *1,* 27. Cf. ibid., *2,* 151; *Great Mistery,* p. 16.
43. Fisher, p. 813.
44. See Knappen, *Tudor Puritanism,* p. 395; Perry Miller, *The New England Mind*
(Cambridge, Mass., 1954), pp. 366–67, 371–97. An example of Quaker "covenant"
language is Dews./2. Cf. also Herbert Schneider, *The Puritan Mind,* Chap. *1.*
45. Tolles (*Atlantic Culture,* p. 106) compares the theology of Quakerism and the
Great Awakening and shows how the same needs led to the same doctrines. Friends
and the General Baptists in the 1650s, like Methodists a century later, were Armin-
ians but not Pelagians.

come sin.[46] Augustine and Saint Paul described how God overcomes sin by working upon the human will. But as Baxter saw, although the Quakers said that the Light within was sufficient if obeyed, the crucial uncertainty was whether it was sufficient to bring men to obey it. Against this a yeoman Friend like Hubberthorne could only reply that if every man was not led to God by it, it was because he did not sufficiently obey the Light, which was no answer to the problem.[47] The paradox is just here: this first step of faith seems for some men impossible without God's special help. The difficulty was inherent in Puritanism. Paul, Augustine, and Luther had seen the problem of man's will as his inability to love without first knowing God's love. But the puritan tradition spoke more of man's unwillingness to give himself to God's glory and service; thus the grace of God conquered and enlisted man's will, enabling a man above all to strive incessantly against evil in himself and others. The Elect was known—although not saved—by his effort. Quakerism took this outlook to extremes. At times early Friends seemed to consider God's grace simply as the granting of the ability to recognize and resist sin: "For want of Faith . . . it is, that so many perish in Sin, and yet seem to strive against Sin, even because they cannot believe that to be sufficient to save from Sin, which manifests Sin. . . . If they did but in Faith joyn with him to condemn Sin . . . it would die and wither." [48]

Yet the Quakers had also concluded that the essence of sin is self-will, and here too they were following puritan premises. The wiser puritans knew that at this point the answer is not simple either, for man's surrender of will is an act of will. The obedience that both Quakers and puritans stressed requires a positive activity of the whole personality, yet an act of self-giving. The only adequate Christian conversion is one which can by love transform or realign a person's will, love, and desires, rather than destroy

46. Power over sin has always been one aspect of grace in Christian thinking. Yet some churches have emphasized other aspects: Eastern Orthodoxy tends to see God's grace in the overcoming of man's mortality and finiteness; the Lutherans have known grace most strongly as forgiveness; Roman Catholic doctrines of grace involve the metaphysical power of the sacraments and the Church's ability to cancel men's debt or penalty for sin before God.

47. Baxter, as quoted in Fisher, p. 692; Hubberthorne, *The Light of Christ Within Proved Sufficient* (London, 1660), p. 9. As Bohn says (p. 90), the issue may be called one about prevenient grace.

48. Nayler, *Works*, p. 365.

them. But Friends realized that the way lies through the death or crucifixion of the "old man." Their attack on self-will meant that for them the power of God displaced the human will and personality permanently, so that a man saw himself as possessed by the Spirit of God almost as a demoniac is possessed by an evil spirit. These problems about man's will take other forms for liberals today. Man's freedom to surrender spontaneously is expressed by saying that "the Choice is always ours"; [49] the attack on self-will has become the effort for unselfishness. But the early Quakers' difficulty in seeing the nature of the conversion of the will came not from liberalism but from its opposite. Their radical dualism of human and divine was not a split of spirit versus matter but a projection of the intense struggle of the good and evil they had been through.

The puritan pastors in general made conversion too easy: they tried by encouragement to build up a man's will to obey, love, and serve, and they made obedience simpler by presenting biblical commandments which could be followed. Early Quakers wisely would not protect a man's self-will by reassurance or by making obedience external. Insofar as one believes sin and redemption are matters of the self and the will, one must respect the Quakers for insisting that a man's surrender be complete and that each man find God's power for himself, solely from within.

Both the strength and the weakness of their understanding of God's grace are clearly shown in their teachings and experiences regarding worship. Friends were too little aware that a man is not a lone individual but a physical being responding to gestures and beauty and an intellectual being drawing strength from ideas. For these reasons, the fellowship of the church, the physical sacraments, the beauty of rituals, and the teachings of ministers and sacred books have been treated by most Christian groups as "means of grace." Throughout history, men have witnessed the receiving of power from God by means of group worship, the service of Holy Communion, and the Bible. But the early Quakers, believing that it is in the heart and will of a man that God's power and salvation are most deeply needed, insisted on finding these in the most direct way possible: in silent worship.

49. Nayler's phrase has become the title of a modern devotional anthology edited by Dorothy Berkley Phillips and others (New York, 1948).

Early Friends broke with all Christian tradition in rejecting the outward use of baptism and the Lord's Supper. Tradition itself had little hold on them, because the churches they had known had been mainly dead and the sacraments associated with popery. On puritan principles they were justified in their stand. Quakers did not make the ascetics' separation between the physical and the spiritual, but contrasted the inward and the outward. The essential baptism is that of the Spirit which "washeth the inside and cleanseth the Heart." [50] The same doctrine had been taught by William Dell, Winstanley, and other spiritual puritans. The puritans in general had much trouble in interpreting baptism. They saw salvation as the establishing of an inward and personal relationship between man and God, a realignment of man's will to God's will. Into such a bond baptism could bring nothing but the supporting faith of the parents. The Baptists, as has been shown, preferred to make baptism a symbol by which the church brought into its covenant those whom God had already converted as adults. Early Quaker writers, who joined them in condemning the "sprinckling" of infants, instead proclaimed the Baptism of Fire, and the washing of the Water of the Word, the inward "Water of Life." [51] But except in anti-Catholic pamphlets, a Quaker in puritan England found few occasions to argue the matter.

In the same way, Quakers interpreted the Eucharist symbolically: "the true Supper of the Lord is the Spiritual eating and drinking of the flesh and blood of Christ spiritually," [52] and Fox carefully distinguished the physical Last Supper before the Crucifixion and the inward "marriage-supper of the Lamb" that followed. Some could discern the Lord's body in the Christian community, and most talked of the inward cleansing by Christ's blood,[53] but on these points, too, the puritans gave them little

50. Howgill, *Works*, p. 424. Cf. Barclay, *Apology*, Proposition 12; Nayler, *Works*, p. 322 (from "Love to the Lost," the most systematic Quaker theological work before Barclay, but not Nayler's best).

51. William Dell, *Select Works*, pp. 377–402; Howgill, *Works*, p. 424; Fox, *Doctrinals*, pp. 104 ff. See also Swarth. 1/4 (*EQL* 504), *EQL* p. 271 nn., and Braithwaite, *Beginnings*, pp. 392–93, about the consternation among Friends when Humphrey Wolrich baptized a convert in 1659.

52. Nayler, in preface to Fox, *Saul's Errand*, p. 17. Cf. Nayler, *Works*, pp. 22, 326–32.

53. Fox, *Doctrinals*, pp. 933–53; Howgill, *Works*, pp. 436 ff. (a particularly good treatment).

rgument. To the puritans the communion service was a "seal
of faith" rather than an essential means of grace, and most of them
ound the spiritual presence of Christ more real through the word
of God than through the Eucharist.

The weakness of the Quaker ideas about God's grace in relation
to men can be seen in their statements about Jesus Christ. They
equated the Seed of God, or the Spirit of God within man, with
Christ; they spoke of Christ within. Better-schooled Friends did
not go as far as Fox, who merged Christ and the Spirit and asserted
that Christ was not distinct from the Father.[54] But the imperson-
ality of the Inward Christ [55] is noteworthy from the beginning.
This reflects the basic Quaker experience, which was surrender to
God's will rather than discipleship to a risen Lord. Most Quakers
were vague about the Trinity, and called the term itself unbiblical: "God and the Spirit hath no Person, nor cannot truly be distinguished into Persons." [56]

They recognized the importance of the historical death of Jesus
as an atonement for past sins. Consequently, Fox presented to the
Assembly of Barbados a creed in which he used traditional and
orthodox language and ideas about Christ "Crusified for us in
the flesh," who "shed his blood for all men." But the actual conquest of evil was more central: "there was need of a Saviour to
save from sin, as well as the blood of a Sacrificed Christ for the
remission of Sins past." [57] In other words, acceptance of Christ's inward Light was the ultimate necessity for salvation: "Without
the Sufferings or Death of Christ at *Jerusalem*, no Man can be
saved, justified or sanctified, though . . . that can [not] save any
man without feeling of his Spirit, Power and Life made manifest
within." [58] This was linked to the puritan and Quaker attitude
that God's grace is primarily moral power rather than forgiveness;
for "if we be not *renewed by the Spirit*, and *saved from Sin;* then

54. Fox, *Great Mistery*, p. 142. Cf. Fisher, *Works*, p. 782.

55. Edward Grubb, *The Historic and the Inward Christ* (London, Headley
Brothers, 1914), pp. 52–53. This book is still valuable on Quaker Christology.

56. Burrough, *Works*, p. 484. Cf. Fox, *Great Mistery*, pp. 99–100. For such language about the Trinity in *Sandy Foundation Shaken* (London, 1668), Penn was
prosecuted after the Restoration, along with his printer, John Darby: cf. *JFHS*,
16, 64.

57. Fox, *Journal*, Camb., 2, 198; Burnyeat, p. 2. Cf. pp. 136, 153–54.

58. J. Whitehead, *Written Gospel-Labours*, pp. 134–35. Cf. Fox, *Great Mistery*,
p. 13; Nayler, *Man of Sin*, p. 20; Fisher, pp. 138, 151.

. . . *grace* is no more use . . . to us." [59] Yet Friends never really made clear the connection between the death of Jesus and their inward obedience to Christ the Spirit. In fact, the puritan doctrine of Election and conversion was also vulnerable here: it made the need of atonement for the Elect somewhat arbitrary (God could have pardoned the Elect in some other way without altering the process of salvation). The puritans, at least, were usually aware that the highest mark of the Spirit within was the childlike faith which cries "Father" to the God whose love is known in Jesus. But most early Friends linked their own inward experiences not with Jesus' love but with his ministry and cross. The effect was to make the actual historical events of Jesus' life mainly an example, at times only a symbol or type, of the recurring events on every Christian's pilgrimage.[60]

The inadequate Quaker theories of will and personality added to their difficulties here, for they tended to make Jesus' life simply the ultimate instance of a human life and a human body taken over by the power of God: "Distinguish . . . between that which is called Christ, and the bodily garment which he wore. The one was flesh, the other Spirit. The flesh profiteth nothing. . . . The body of flesh was but the veil." [61] Friends insisted that Christ's soul was not human, and that his human body was not in heaven. His earthly nature did not share in the Resurrection. This Christology was similar to that held by Saltmarsh, Dell, and many General Baptists, and to the "Hoffmanites" in Germany.[62] It had the effect of breaking up the unity of Christ's personality, and it re-

---

59. Fisher, p. [162] (misnumbered).

60. Cf. *FPT*, p. 121: John Moone told Baptist minister John Tombes that the True Cross was not a piece of wood outside Jerusalem but the power of God by which Paul was crucified to the world. Such symbolic use of scriptural events as "types" was common among puritans (cf. Haller, *Puritanism*) and had begun with Calvin himself (cf. John T. McNeill, in *Church History, 28*, 1959, p. 36). Fox, however, insisted also on the reality of Jesus' historic life, especially against the Ranters: cf. Fox, *Journal*, Nickalls, p. 63; Jones, "George Fox's Teaching."

61. Isaac Penington, *The Works of the Long-Mournful and Sorely-Distressed Isaac Penington* (2d ed. 2 vols., London, 1761), *1*, 360.

62. Robert Barclay maintained that Friends were not Apollinarian or Eutychean, but early Quakers perhaps verged on Nestorianism if he is right: both heresies tried to avoid linking too closely the human and divine in Christ. On this see also Fox, *Great Mistery*, pp. 99, 103, 113–14, 130–31, 159 ff., to which Bohn adds 71, 101–02, and 322.

flects again the Quakers' experience of being taken over by the power of the Spirit.

An immediate result of this Christology was to allow statements about themselves for which Quakers were accused of blasphemy. To those modern Friends who regard God as a diffuse, pervasive spirit or power, "Christ within" them presents few problems. To the orthodox puritans, however, Christ was a person, sharply distinguished from God the Father; both were of a substance different from the human. The claim that Christ dwelt in individuals was to them startling; and though they knew the biblical phrases which Quakers brandished, about "Christ in you the hope of glory," they understood them symbolically. If Quakers had "the Spirit of God as they pretend abiding in them *personally* and *essentially*, this blasphemy must necessarily follow, that they are equal with God." [63]

Friends, on the other hand, identified Christ with the Light which they were certain was within them, using many biblical passages (mostly from John's Gospel) to support it. They also felt, in their newness of life, that "the Saints are Temples of God, and God dwels in them, and walks in them; and they come to witnesse the flesh of Christ, and they glorifie him in their souls and bodies." [64] It was hard to pin them down on this, since they had minimized Christ's own physical body.

Moreover, Friends had strong experiences of sharing the inward Spirit within each other, which led to other extravagant phrases about themselves and their leaders that upset the soberer puritans. The first sentences of every letter were likely to be expressive. A fairly innocuous and typical introduction to a letter from Stubbs to Dewsbury runs: "Deare brother: In the eternall unchangeable love of the Liveing God our heavenly Father in Jesus Christ, with you I have unitie which bonds in body cannot Separate." [65] But toward Fox and the pioneer Quakers, language was stronger: "Deare Geo. ff. who art the father of all the faithfull . . . I know thee whome thou art, who was ded and is alive & for ever lives . . . thy right hand hath preserved me, therefore thy Child keepe

63. Richard Sherlock, *The Quakers Wilde Questions*, quoted in Braithwaite, *Beginnings*, p. 109.
64. Fox, *Great Mistery*, p. 135.
65. Dews./12, from Thomas Stubbs, Northampton, July 25, 1655.

me in thy feare continually, and it shall be my meat to doe thy
will." [66] Fox himself was so alarmed that he cut away or altered
the openings of many letters, especially those from Thomas Holme.
"My deare life" was amended to read "my deare frend" and so
on.[67] Nevertheless, Fox made statements about the power of Christ
in him which brought him under actual arrest: "It was not so
spoken, as George Fox was equal with God," explained Fox, but
"he that sanctifieth and they that are sanctified are all of one." [68]
Nayler was clearer: "Geo. Fox was denied as dust, but the Spirit
that spoke in him is equall with God. . . . As to the calling
George Fox the Son of God, you know nothing of this Son of God
as he was revealed in the Apostles." [69] Soon after, Thomas Holme
was banished from Chester, allegedly for claiming to be "coe-
equell with God, and the eternall Judg of the world, and the Son
of God." [70] When Nayler's ride into Bristol finally forced Friends
to face the issue squarely, Margaret Fell wrote: "This is narrow
and deep to discern, betwixt him that sheweth himself as God,
and is not, and him that is the true Image indeed." [71]

The Quaker view of the indwelling of the Spirit could never
take seriously enough any personality as a whole, either Christ's
or the Christian's, to make clear theology possible. Perhaps
a symptom of this was the frequent habit among early Friends
of disowning their own names when the old man in them was
replaced by the new birth. A letter to Margaret Fell was signed

66. Swarth. 3/87 (*EQL* 470), Thomas Curtis to Fox, January 5, 1658/59; these
words were crossed out later, probably by Fox. For other similar examples see
Braithwaite, *Beginnings*, pp. 105, 244–51.

67. ARBarc./41, Mary Howgill to Fox, 1656. For other such letters to Fox see
Swarth. 4/193 (*EQL* 234), Mary Fisher; 4/58 (*EQL* 293), Mary Prince; 4/211 (*EQL*
192), Richard Sale; 4/180 (*EQL* 219), Sarah Bennett; 4/249 (*EQL* 78), Thomas
Holme. For a similar address to Margaret Fell see 1/186 (*EQL* 453), Walter Somers;
1/192 (*EQL* 77), Holme; 3/49 (*EQL* 75) Farnworth. See also Nuttall, *Christian
Enthusiasm*.

68. Fox, *Saul's Errand*, pp. 5–6. Cf. Braithwaite, *Beginnings*, p. 107.

69. Nayler, *Man of Sin*, p. 13. Later the roles were reversed at the time of Nayler's
fall. Bishop wrote: "I have read J. N.'s Conceited answers & Cant but Commend
and Prefer G. ffs who had such things Buzed about Concerning him, & The Judg in
a Court, puting this Question to him, are you Jeasus Christ, Said, 'No, I am Geo.
ffox.'" (From a manuscript note on tract in Birkbeck Library, York quoted by Cole,
"Quakers and Politics," p. 48.

70. Swarth. 4/250 (*EQL* 105), Thomas Holme to Fox.

71. M. Fell, p. 193.

by him who is "named by the world by the nam of Alexander Parker, but hath a new name wch the world know of not, wreten in the booke of life." [72] A much more serious symptom of this problem was an atomistic approach to ethics in terms of obedience moment by moment. This—like modern existentialism—achieved a sense of urgency at the expense of undermining the sense of unity and responsibility within individuals and ran the risk of dissolving sin into a repetition of sins.

The relation of Spirit and personality in Quaker thought came to its acute focus in the idea of perfectionism, the issue for which puritans took Quakers to task more often than any other. Two assertions were involved in this doctrine: the infallibility of the Spirit and the possibility of perfect obedience. Since they felt the Light of Christ within men to be the Spirit of God himself, Friends said that those "who have the spirit of Christ have that which is infallible." [73] Only in part should this claim be ascribed to the very human hunger for certainty which leads other Christians to insist that God must establish an infallible Bible or an infallible Papacy, "for if there be no certainty or assurance given to any man . . . wherein he may be assured of the certainty of God's will, then whither should any go." [74] Quaker preachers, who condemned men in God's name, especially needed to be able to claim unquestionable authority when a man resisted being judged. Much more basically, however, they stressed the infallibility of the Spirit, because they would not recognize any sin or evil which the Spirit might not overcome. Quaker perfectionism, like the "Holiness" doctrine of modern American sects (which it only partly resembles), rested on personal religious experience. Many puritans never believed that Friends had felt the power of the Spirit. On the contrary, Quakers (who read puritan claims that the early Christians' writings in the New Testament were infallible) felt that the Spirit was no less powerful within the Quaker movement than within the primitive church. The puritan doctrine seemed *"rea-*

72. Swarth. 1/356 (*EQL* 110). Cf. 3/16 (*EQL* 227): "knowne to you in the new name, Edward Burrough beeing the old"; also Fox's custom of reversing his initials. It is possible that Friends used initials instead of names for this reason, just as Henrik Niclaes, the Familist, used his initials to stand for *homo novus.* Cf. Rev. 2:17.

73. Fox, *Great Mistery*, p. 28. Cf. Nayler, *Works*, pp. 293, 304; Fisher, pp. 38–39.

74. Howgill, *Works*, p. 618.

sonlessly to *restrain* . . . the *Spirit of the Lord* . . . and to pound him up into such a small point and pittance of time." [75]

The possibility of perfect obedience was also an answer to all talk of compromise with evil. How could men be urged to strive endlessly against evil, if at the same time they were taught they could never succeed? "Now examine yourselves, doth not something let you see . . . this thing, or the other thing, that you continue in the practice of . . . which you know you should not do? . . . In words you desire pardon for them, but you still continue in the same practice. . . . And therefore are not free, and in your principles conclude you never can be, while you are in this world." [76] It was never claimed that any specific Quaker individuals were infallible, except in the moment of following the leading of the Spirit. They rejected the Calvinist doctrine of the perseverance of the Elect and considered even David only a saint by turns. They allowed for growth in human understanding and assumed that men might have different measures of the Spirit or the Light.[77] Yet even in its opening stages Quaker life demanded perfect obedience to the Light as far as it was known. When Fox was offered freedom from prison in 1656 if he would return home at once, he refused: "to say we will goe to our outward habitation if it be according to the will of God, when we knowe it is the will of god otherwise, now we cannot speake soe truely." [78] After returning from the risk of death in Boston, Joseph Nicholson wrote: "If He call us againe to goe there we must goe whether we dye or live." [79]

The attitude toward learning shows in a fascinating way the practical results of the Quaker expectancy about the infallibility of the Spirit. Quakers, of course, like the radical puritans, were suspicious of worldly knowledge. "Take heed of your wisdom which is from below," [80] they warned. Feed not on knowledge.

75. Fisher, p. 566. Cf. Boisen, *Religion in Crisis and Custom*, p. 77.

76. John Crook, *The Case of Swearing (at All) Discussed* (London, 1660), pp. 25–26.

77. Fisher, pp. 40, 718, 720, 721. Cf. Howgill, *Works*, pp. 617–46. Fox stressed degrees or growth in Light less than did Nayler and Fisher: Bohn, "Puritans and Quakers," p. 240 n.

78. Fox, *Journal*, Camb. *1*, 239. Cf. ibid., 238.

79. Swarth. 4/107 (*EQL* 520), Jos. Nicholson to M. Fell, Boston, April 3, 1660.

80. Camm and Audland, *Works*, p. 259; a sermon of Nayler cited in John Whiting, *Persecution Expos'd* (London, 1715), p. 176. Cf. Braithwaite, *Beginnings*, p. 242.

"Who feeds on knowledge dies to the innocent life." They made clear that the authors of most Greek and Latin classics, as medieval Christian tradition indeed affirmed, were in hell, and their works therefore hardly merited the time spent on them in schools. "The tongues of Hebrew, Greek & Latin were set up over Christ by Pilate who crucified him." [81] But this rejection of learning came partly from a more central distinction between intellectual knowledge and the transforming knowledge of personal experience. The crucial issue was the use of knowledge in ministry.

Friends, however, expected to be divinely provided with the equivalent of book-learning: "That which gives to understand the Creation . . . is the wisdome of God . . . who counts the Stars, and numbers them in their kinde. . . . Now who understands these things, it is by the spirit of wisdome." [82] The orthodox puritan, following Augustinian doctrine, expected the mind of a Saint to be straightened by conversion for practical use in God's service, but Quakers expected men to set reason aside and let the Spirit lead: "Neither are Omnisciency and Omnipotency themselves as to all those things that are to be known and done . . . so altogether incommunicable to spiritual men as our Academical Animals imagine." [83] Fortunately, only a few Quakers relied on this completely in practice. A witty diplomat in 1657 described two Quaker missionaries who, knowing no French, "past lately by Paris; they were found in the streetes soe starved wth cold & hunger, that one would have thought the Spirit had beene dead in them; the charity of some English gentleman relieved them, not knowing [yet their] religion; but the fire & a supper revived itt; & would you know their buisenes, they were Ambassadors from the Ld to the Duke of Savoy; wt thr message was is unknowne, but they despayrd not of the gift of tongues." [84] The sense of power within, in Quaker experience, made all things seem possible. Fox, when he had "come up through the flaming sword into the paradise of God," found "the creation was opened to me; and it was showed me how all things had their names given them according

81. Fox, *Great Mistery*, p. 70. Cf. George Fox, John Stubbs, and Benjamin Furly, *A Battle-Door for Teachers and Professors to Learn Singular and Plural* (London, 1660), appendix, p. 25.

82. Fox, *Great Mistery*, p. 125.

83. Fisher, p. 575.

84. *ESP*, p. 24, Charles Perrott to Joseph Wilkinson, Paris, January 17, 1656/57.

to their nature. . . . I was at a stand in my mind whether I should practice physic for the good of mankind, seeing the nature . . . of the creatures were so opened to me." [85]

The Quaker outlook was part of the whole puritan assumption that the world was in God's hands; that miracles could be as common as in biblical days, since the physical world was ruled by the Spirit; and that Christ within was truly the Word, that Word, "which we have seen, which we have heard . . . by which Word the World was made." [86] If inner transformation into the innocence of Adam was possible for Friends, then the physical world could again become like Eden. When a Quaker woman gave birth without long labor on the day Fox was freed from Launceston jail, it was understood in this light. They expected the power within themselves to produce tangible miracles, and Fox kept a book to record them. Some of these were merely catastrophes visited upon persecutors of Quakers, which seemed providential. Friends, like puritans, expected God to work within laws of science as well as beyond. Some "miracles" seem now mere feats of strength, like Nayler's repeated attempt to prove that, being sustained by the Spirit, he could fast without food for weeks: "ungodly Murtherous Fasts," [87] the puritans called these. Some of the episodes do show, however, the remarkable power of Fox and early Quaker leaders over the hearts and bodies of men. John Banks tells of being healed by Fox in 1677:

> A Pain struck into my Shoulder, which gradually fell down into my Arm and Hand, so that . . . my Pain greatly encreas'd both Day and Night; and for Three Months I could neither put my Cloaths on nor off my self . . . until at last as I was asleep upon my Bed . . . I saw in a Vision, that I was with dear George Fox, and I thought I said unto him, "George, my Faith is such that if thou seest thy way to lay thy Hand upon my Shoulder, my Arm and Hand shall be whole throughout." Which remained with me . . . that I must go to G.F. . . . he being then at Swarthmore . . . on the first day. . . . And sometime after the Meeting, I called him aside into the Hall, and gave him a Relation of my

85. Fox, *Journal*, Nickalls, p. 27; cf. Roberts, *Flaming Sword*, p. 43.
86. M. Fell, p. 127.
87. Higginson, *Irreligion of Quakers*, p. 20.

Concern as aforesaid, showing him my Arm and Hand; and in a little time, we walking together Silent, he turned about and looked upon me, lifting his Hand, and laid it upon my Shoulder, and said, "The Lord strengthen thee both within and without." And so we parted, and . . . went to Thomas Lowers of Marsh-Grange that Night, and when I was sate down to Supper in his House, immediately, before I was aware . . . my Hand and Arm restor'd to its former use and strength, without any pain. And the next time that G.F. and I met, he readily said, "John, thou mended, thou mended;" I answer'd, "Yes, very well, in a little time." "Well," he said, "give God the Glory." [88]

When Burrough and Howgill, in an equally tender spirit, tried to heal a lame boy, they reported their failure to Fox with great perplexity, and partly in cipher.[89]

Fox and other early Friends also recorded visions, most of which were dreams, often interpreted symbolically. Some were subconscious intuitions, as when in 1658 Fox sensed the approaching death of Cromwell on seeing his face. A few men announced daylight visions, and Fox and Humphrey Smith thought they had foreseen the plague and Great Fire in London in 1665 and 1666 as judgment for the preceding years of persecution. More closely linked to Quaker preaching was Fox's belief that he could "discern the spirits" within men he met, since "the spiritual man discerns and Judgeth all things." [90] Examples of this now sound like mere suspiciousness: "there was some wicked women in a feilde

88. Banks, pp. 66–67. Cf. ibid., pp. 137–38. On Mary Clement's childbirth see Swarth. 3/158 (*EQL* 311). On Nayler's fasts see Nuttall, *James Nayler*. See also Swarth. 1/12 (*EQL* 303), Audland; 4/88 (*EQL* 157), Killam. The fullest discussion of all these is in *George Fox's Book of Miracles*, ed. Henry J. Cadbury (Cambridge, Cambridge University Press, 1948).

89. ARBarc./21 (1654).

90. Fox, *Great Mistery*, p. 69. On Fox's visions concerning Cromwell and the Fire of London see *Journal*, Camb., *1*, 327; *2*, 89–90. For Smith, see *The Vision of Humphrey Smith Concerning London* (London, 1660). Some "visions" were symbolically interpreted dreams. See M. Fell, p. 90, and "Ann Camm's Testimony" in Camm and Audland, *Works*. John Rous wrote from Barbados (Swarth. 1/82, *EQL* 454) that he had seen Margaret Fell and her family in a dream. Since Rous later married Margaret Fell, Jr., this has been interpreted as "the first vision of his future wife," but it remains to be proved that he had not met the Fells in England. See Nuttall, *Letters*, p. 253.

. . . & I saw they was witches & I was moved to goe unto them and declare unto them . . . that they were in the spiritt of witch craft." [91] But many men felt that Fox had truly seen into their hearts.

The early Friends did not entirely despise knowledge, certainly not that of a practical kind, for later they became pioneers in developing trade schools and scientific education. Thomas Lawson turned schoolmaster and studied Hebrew when he resigned his parish ministry; John Stubbs, Fox, and Furly produced the *Battle-door,* a book in which the correctness of saying *thee* and *thou* to individuals was demonstrated by examples or parallels from Latin, Italian, Greek, Hebrew, Aramaic, Syriac, French, Arabic, Persian, Aethiopic, Samaritan, Coptic, Armenian, Welsh, Portuguese, Cornish, Saxon, German, Danish, Slavonian, Bohemian, Polish, and Irish. Among early Friends, Samuel Fisher, Willem Sewel, and Albertus Otto Faber were trained language-scholars. Hilary Prache and one or two others gave up their libraries on joining the Friends; but Fox himself had collected 108 books by the time of his death, and when a company of papists affirmed that the Pope was infallible, he quoted Eusebius to show them that one of the Bishops of Rome had denied the faith.[92] Later, Robert Barclay and William Penn also joined the roster of Friends with university educations. Like Crook and Fox himself, Penn knew enough law to win lively arguments in law courts.

Nevertheless, Quakers constantly said that "hireling preists . . . made at schooles and colledges and not by Christ . . . was to be denied." [93] Many fierce arguments with puritan pastors began over this direct challenge. Friends maintained the social radicalism of the Baptist "mechanick preachers." God prefers to "chuse out foolish, weak, base things and persons, even Laicks, Mechanicks, Russet-Rabbis . . . to confound and bring to nought these mighty wise and prudent," wrote Fisher.[94] The "foolishness

91. Fox, *Journal,* Camb., *1,* 110. Cf. ibid., *1,* 271–72; James Nayler, *Discovery of the Beast,* p. 9.

92. Fox, *Journal,* Camb., 2, 95. Cf. Howgill, *Works,* p. 644. On Lawson cf. ARBarc./42. On Sewel see *JFHS, 31* (1934), 57. On Faber see *ESP,* pp. 214 ff. On Prache see Cadbury in Brinton, *Children of Light,* p. 144. Fox's library is catalogued in *JFHS, 28* (1931), 3 ff., though clearly many of these books were bought late in his life.

93. Fox, *Journal,* Camb., *1,* 258, cf. *1,* 35–41, 384.

94. Fisher, pp. 588–89.

of God" in choosing the Quakers was tied up with their North Country origin as often as with their lack of education. But the basic protest of Friends against the parish ministers was that "they have run, and never were sent": after a "certain time of . . . studying in the University, these hasty Hirelings run abroad before the word of command be given them from the Mouth of the Lord." [95] Quaker ministers knew they had been called by God before they preached, yet many puritans—even Bishop Latimer —were equally sure of their own divine call before entering the ministry. Quakers wanted converted ministers, but in practice usually condemned any minister who took tithes or accepted an appointment to a parish.[96]

The actual sermons of the pastors were the subject of still more fierce debate. Puritans agreed that the message had to come from the preacher's own experience, but Friends tested the success of puritan ministry by its ethical fruits, and judged severely: "Had you but in any measure stood in the Counsel of God, and caused his people to have heard his word of faith in their hearts, they had been turned from the evil of their wayes long ere now." [97] Quakers evidently used as a measuring-line the explosive inward experiences that followed their own messages. The famous Quaker distinction between a religion of "notions" and a religion of "experience" specifically tested whether the ethical battle of the Lamb's War had been fought within.

Quakers insisted, of course, that the direct source of any sermon must be God. Puritans preached what they had studied out of books and "old Authors . . . by an hour glasse, and not as the spirit of God gives . . . utterance." [98] To Baxter the attitude of Quaker ministers was simply inverted pride, and he ridiculed their claim that God would reveal to them without study the truths which demanded all the scholarly diligence of the pastor.[99] Baxter claimed no special inspiration.

95. Burrough, introductory epistle to reader, in Fox, *Great Mistery.*
96. Fisher, p. 226. Cf. Tindall, *Bunyan,* chap. 1; Nuttall, *Holy Spirit,* chap. 5; Nayler, *Answer to Baxter,* pp. 33–34. Cf. Dell, *Select Works,* pp. 447–54, 555, 588–89.
97. Ambrose Rigge's broadside *To All Hireling Priests* (London, 1659). Cf. Fisher, pp. 226, 260–63, 553. However, Weld and his cronies, in *The Perfect Pharisee* (p. 20), made fun of Fox for asking to have a biblical concordance sent to him and asked (p. 40) if Paul's learning had really made him mad.
98. Burrough, in his epistle introducing Fox, *Great Mistery.*
99. Baxter, *Quakers Catechism,* p. B-3.

The Friends' ministry, however, was meant to lead men to the true source of power in worship, through silence. Human ministry was out of place, for "you must not create that which must stand before God, for he will be served with his own begettings in you. . . . Therefore . . . as you come into a patient stillness, you will feel the begettings of the Father moving in you to be brought forth." [100] To worship in any other way was to make God man's servant, and thus to practice idolatry. Puritans broke statues and stained glass all over England, but the Friends accused them of worshipping inner idols.[101]

The Quaker stand against tithes caused more suffering in the long run than any other. Unlike the modern voluntary tithe, these were a pattern of universal taxes by which all European national churches had been supported since medieval times. Many English tithes had been impropriated into laymen's hands when monasteries were closed, but it was not against this that Friends protested, for they paid their taxes to the civil government. Rather, they resented the Catholic background of tithes, and they knew how often in the North they supported vicars in a lazy life. But the insuperable objection to tithes and to a national church sprang from their belief that there could be no true worship led by the decisions of ungodly men: "their is no justice in it . . . that any should be caused by force to uphold a house, for other men to commit . . . idolatry in; if the house were for any good purpose . . . as for poor or impotent people to dwell in . . . then that were a deed of charity to uphold it." [102] Like the radical puritans and separatists, Friends wanted no worship but pure worship; no matter what it cost them they could not come before God otherwise.

The attitude of Quakers toward hymns, liturgy, and the Bible can be understood from this standpoint. Like the puritans, they suspected men of singing words or reciting prayers they did not believe, and made fun of "singing David's Psalm with Saul's Spirit, in such Meeter as . . . Q. Elizabeth's Fidlers have moulded

100. Nayler, *Works*, pp. 371–72.

101. Edward Burrough, *Trumpet of the Lord Sounded Out of Zion* (London, 1656), p. 17; cf. *Works*, p. 100.

102. Edward Burrough, *A Message for Instruction to All the Rulers* . . . (London, 1658), p. 7; cf. *Works*, p. 743.

them into, and . . . as some Priest, Clark or Saxton sayes them
lineatim." [103] But whereas the puritan was satisfied that only the
converted could truly worship, Friends insisted that each act of
worship should be led by God directly.

The Bible was of necessity placed in a secondary role lest it sup-
plant the initiative of God's Spirit and the absolute need of obeying the Light within. Theologically, the puritans and Quakers
were not as far apart regarding the Bible as is often assumed. The
puritans knew the need for the inward Spirit and conversion, and
the Quakers, for their part, considered biblical writers inspired,
though they themselves were also. Most of their characteristic
phrases were drawn from the Bible. "The Light," "the Children
of Light," and "the World" can only be understood in terms of
their derivation from John's Gospel and Epistle and from Ephe-
sians 5; "Friends" came from John 15:13–15; the "Seed" from
Genesis 3:15; the "Lamb's War" from Revelation, and "Christ
within" from Paul's letters. In many Quaker tracts, letters, and
even journals, 70 per cent of the phrases are biblical quotations or
paraphrases.[104]

Friends argued repeatedly, in answer to puritans, that only
through the Spirit could scripture be rightly interpreted; in
practice, however, this usually meant that they sensed vitality
in those passages which corresponded to their own vivid experiences and felt coldness when puritans expounded them. Their
use of scripture was often obstinately literal ("take the scripture
in plain words") and they made fun of the biblical study of which
puritan pastors were so proud: "so many Years at Oxford and
Cambridge . . . to know what unlearned men, Fishermen,
Ploughmen and Herdsmen did mean when they spoke forth the
Scriptures." [105] On the other hand, Friends believed that their

103. Fisher, p. 92.
104. On the leading of the Spirit see Matt. 4:1; Acts 2:4; 4:8; 8:29, 39; 10:19;
11:12; 11:28; 13:2, 4; 16:6; 20:23; 21:11; 23:8. From the Book of Revelation came
"the Great Beast," "the Lamb," "the Harlot," "the Mystery of Iniquity," "the
eternal gospel," and "plagues" in a symbolic sense, and Quaker apocalyptic ideas
in general. For other beloved passages, see John 1:1–9; 3:19–21; 15:19, 26; I Cor.
2:5, 10–16; II Cor. 3:6; 10:3–4; I Tim. 1:19; 4:2; II Tim. 3:1–4; Titus 1:11; James
4:1–3; 5:12; I John 2:15–17; 3:9; 4:1, 6. Surprisingly few are from the Synoptic
Gospels.
105. Nayler, *Works*, p. 43. Cf. Burrough, *Works*, p. 143; Fisher, pp. 588–91.

own experience of God was like that of the authors of the Bible, and this allowed them to suggest a richer view of biblical inspiration than the puritan idea of divine dictation. In line with much modern biblical higher criticism, Fisher wrote: "Such Prophets, Apostles, Evangelists, as wrote their own Prophesies, Epistles, Histories, Proverbs, Psalms, etc., with their own Hands, as they were moved by the Spirit . . . had, both then and long before also, an Active concurrence thereof, and . . . active Obedience to God. . . . They became first Holy men before they were used by God in such an holy work." [106] If the Bible is the transcript of man's experience of the Spirit, its human flavor, the varieties of its styles, and even its textual corruptions did not upset the Friends as they did the puritans. Despite endless fighting over single verses, however, they did not at this time produce any actual interpretations of scripture that brought more light from it than the puritans had already found, nor did attempts to argue about the role or authority of scripture produce much clarity. Friends conceded that the Bible was authoritative and then talked about the Spirit.

The key difference between puritan and Quaker attitudes was in their ideas of the *relationship* of the inward Spirit and the outward Word in the life of Christians. Where Quakers made these independent, the puritans saw them as working together: "Ordinarily, the Spirit maketh use of the written word in this way of witnessing; he maketh the word without, a voyce within, by the effectual application of it unto a particular soule." [107] The crucial "openings" or inward leadings of puritans like Bunyan also took the form of biblical quotations. To Quakers, however, the scriptural message and the leadings of the Light were parallel: scripture was the record of the work of the Spirit in other lives. They denied that the Spirit worked through the Book. Quakers could even be bitter about Bible-buying, wondering why one would give money for anything other than bread. They were dis-

---

106. Fisher, pp. 418–19 (cf. pp. 422–33). Fisher was the most thorough and imaginative Bible scholar among early Friends, being an Oxford man. He runs wild and spends 160 pages attacking the inerrancy of scripture by skillful but redundant argument about Hebrew vowel points and Greek manuscript variants. Yet he presents the meaning of the biblical canon and sources in mature ways which anticipate modern scholarship.

107. Petto, *The Voyce of the Spirit*, quoted in Nuttall, *Holy Spirit*, p. 31. Cf. M. Fell, p. 134.

turbed, however, when some overeager Friends in Kent "had given occasion to the world against the truth with burning their bibles." [108]

Though it was supported by much word warfare about the Letter which killeth, the claim that the Spirit worked independently of the Bible was at heart an affirmation that the crucial work of the Spirit occurs when each man individually faces truth about himself before God, when he subdues his individual will and sets free the Seed within: "In the Scriptures . . . you may read the Right of things, and what you should and should not be and do, but the Light within is larger than that . . . showing not only the Right . . . but also the Fact, even what we do and are." An instrument "may be good to Cut and Kill, that . . . can't quicken nor heal . . . The Letter kills . . . but the Spirit only gives Life." [109] Even at this point of harshest debate, the Quakers showed themselves puritans in their ideas of how God works in remaking men. Puritans had known such inward change while opening themselves to the biblical message; Friends had known this more radically in baring themselves to the Light within them. Consequently, repeated attempts then and since to discuss whether Quakers received new truths from the Spirit that were different from or beyond scriptural revelation have usually ended in frustration. Friends did not expect the Spirit to contradict its past revelations. They did expect it to work with power apart from the Scriptures, to lead men into truth, and to lead them personally as they carried their witness out into the whole world.

108. Swarth. 4/14 (*EQL* 373), Hubberthorne to Fox [March 20, 1657].
109. Fisher, pp. 13, 253.

6

Customs as Witness to the Unconvicted

YOUR life and your Words are a Terrour to all that speak
not Truth; in your dealings . . . your lives do judge them;
and through your Constancy, Faithfulness and Life, which is
Everlasting, you bring many to Amendment: For both Life,
Actions, Words & Conversation preach . . . to the unright-
eous world.[1]

THE CHANGE in daily life required for those who became Quakers,
even though many had been puritans already, was probably as
drastic as that in any religious movement in Protestant history.
Obedience to the Light meant giving up every habit or custom
considered even partly evil. Specific new customs resulted among
the Quakers and have become famous. Obedience to the Spirit,
however, led primarily to campaigns rather than to moral codes,
for early Friends worked to change the world as they had been
changed. Their way of life was part of their warfare and a demon-
stration of their message. Standards were aggressive, not defensive;
they were called Testimonies and were seen as instruments of conversion.

Quakers felt that they could not be instruments of the Spirit if
they did not obey the Light in their own daily living. Bitter examples were cited of Friends like Thomas Ayrey who had compromised and then lost spiritual power. An absolute obligation
was therefore involved in even the most limited ethical issues.
For example, Humphrey Bache, having already given up his profit-

1. George Fox, *A Line of Righteousness Stretched Forth* (London, 1674), p. 8.

able job as excise collector out of a burdened conscience, met a Quaker. This relentless spirit, rather than congratulating him, pressed him onward and "asked . . . if I believed that thee & thou to one perticular Person was truth; I said yea; said he then, if I did not come into obedience to what I was convinced of to be Truth, I must come under condemnation." [2] Bache became a Friend.

It was not easy to be known as a Quaker. For the socially respectable like Thomas Ellwood, even a refusal to remove his hat could lead to family disownment and ridicule. He once visited Oxford, where he had attended Court with his Justice father:

> A Knot of my old Acquaintances, espying me, came to me . . . and . . . saluted me after the usual manner, putting off their Hats and Bowing, and saying "Your Humble Servant, Sir," expecting, no doubt, the like from me. But when they saw me standing still . . . they were amazed: "What? Tom, a Quaker?" To which I readily and cheerfully answered, "Yes, a Quaker." And as the words passed out of my Mouth I felt joy spring in my Heart . . . that I had Strength and Boldness given me, to Confess my self to be one of that despised People.[3]

Richard Atkinson and Ellis Hookes were shut out of their homes by their fathers, and many others were disowned by their relatives for at least some years. As apprentices, Alexander Delamain and Richard Davies were under pressure from their masters, and other men were rejected for refusing their apprenticeship oaths. Three nursing sisters in St. Thomas Hospital in London were fired for refusing to give up Quakerism.[4] To join the Mormons or the Jehovah's Witnesses in our time demands no more decisive a break with past life and social ambitions.

The uncompromising sternness with which a few Quakers respected a single point of conscience seems to us now an obsession: Solomon Eccles renounced music teaching and sold his virginals and viols, but feeling guilty, bought them back and burned them.

2. Humphrey Bache, *A Few Words in True Love Written to the Old Long Sitting Parliament* (n.p., 1659), p. 9.

3. Ellwood, *Life*, pp. 33–34.

4. Braithwaite, *Beginnings*, pp. 488–95; Swarth. 4/166 (*EQL* 464), Thomas Ollive to Fox (Nov. 9, 1658); *JFHS, 31* (1934), 39; ARBarc./109.

Quakerism produced no musicians or painters before the eighteenth century. But this same sensitiveness later drove John Woolman to refuse all compromise about slavery. Out of their absolutism, Friends were able to make firm their new standards about war and mental illness when they became convinced of them.

Each specific stand against a social evil was justified independently in their writings, but it is nevertheless useful to group them according to basic issues such as simplicity and equality. In addition, three interacting factors should be noticed as contributing to each of these Testimonies: the role the standard held as part of the total Quaker war against the world; the special concern of one or more sensitive Friends who first laid each issue upon Quaker consciences; and the social or regional background which often focused their awareness upon one evil rather than another.

Concerning the time when these customs arose and their individual relation to events in the Quaker movement, little is known except in regard to the rejection of war and slavery after 1660 and the stands first taken in the eighteenth or nineteenth centuries. Fox, Penn, and other writers took for granted that the other basic Testimonies were all understood and obeyed from the beginning of the Quaker movement.[5] In fact some of them already seemed axiomatically right to all radical puritans. In proportion as this was so, the question of origins is irrelevant. Against war and tithes, a general principle felt from the beginning was only later formulated in terms of patterns of conduct, and in these cases the pressure of social forces and political events was the catalyst. The stages in developing a standard are well documented for the role of Meetings in marriages; probably similar steps occurred in formulating less discussed norms. Such an issue was opened by a few Friends' sense of concern, and then grew through a period of "advices" between Friends, given either as leadings or as mere personal opinions. The movement as a whole then came to agree that the new position was the teaching of the Light. One individual's conscientious conviction pricked and unsettled the consciences of all Friends. The classic example of the process was the role of John Woolman in the abolition of slavery, in the eighteenth century.

5. Penn, in preface to Fox, *Journal*, 1694; Fox, in *Journal*, Nickalls, pp. 30–39.

The most prominent Testimonies in the first years were those concerned with social inequality: the Quaker *thee* and *thou,* hat honor, the refusal of titles and of courteous greetings, and the social standards implied in dress and furnishings. Nevertheless, these ways of behaving were intended by Quakers not to exalt the humble but to break down the proud. The judgment and condemnation of pride and self-will were at the heart of the Lamb's War. Social inequality was also a constant issue in the whole Cromwellian revolution, but most radical puritans thought of equality in terms of brotherhood and love between all classes of men. A few, like the Levellers, explicitly agitated about wealth, freedom, and legal rights. The "mechanicks" were also glad that God had in battle humbled the noble and mighty. But love outweighed social planning or class warfare in puritan hopes for the future. For the Quaker, however, love was expressed through judgment. The issue was the spirit of "lordship," which had to be broken down for the proud man's sake if he was to surrender to the Light. Every protest in regard to equality was meant fundamentally as an assault on pride and a means of conversion, not as social reform. Yet in their concrete attacks on pride and lordship, the Quakers used habits and attacked patterns which were at the same time directly involved with their own regional and social background. While there is no way of knowing how widely these customs had been practiced earlier, by Fox and others, it is clear that they were crystallized as distinctive Testimonies during or before the great Quaker awakening in Westmorland and Cumberland in 1652 and 1653.

Friends were known by *thee* and *thou* throughout England well before 1662, and the whole history of the English language was involved. Friends insisted that to say *you* to one person was permanently incorrect grammar and contrary to usage in the Bible and in other European languages (of which Fox and Stubbs had dredged up twenty-three examples).[6] In England, by Shakespeare's time, however, the use of *thee* (and also of *ye* instead of *you* in the nominative) had dropped out of polite speech. There were exceptions to this: as is still true of the French *tu* and *toi* and the German *du,* seventeenth-century English used *thee* and *thou*

6. Fox, Stubbs, and Furly: *A Battle-Door* is the fullest presentation.

within the family, among intimate friends, and to social inferiors, and this form was common among farmers.[7]

The stigma of social inferiority was the real issue behind the Quaker testimony: "for amongst the Great and Rich ones of the earth, they will either *Thou* or *You* one another, if they be equal in Degree, as they call it; but if a man of low Degree . . . come to speak to any of them, he must *You* the Rich Man, but the Rich Man will *Thou* him. . . . If a poor labouring Man come before one that you call a Minister . . . he must *You* the Priest and the priest *Thou* him." [8] It was an accident of history that the use of *thou* continued to shrink and finally dropped entirely out of English speech, leaving Friends clinging to a curious vestige. But given their own situation of two levels of speech, the early Quaker reaction was characteristic: Abraham Lincoln or Oscar Wilde might have said *you* to honor a charwoman as much as a Duchess; the Friends leveled downward to humble the pride of all men, for they felt it was only "corrupt Men for Corrupt Ends, in later and Corrupt Times, [who], to Flatter, Fawn and Work upon the Corrupt Nature in Men, brought in that false . . . Way of speaking *you* to One." [9]

It is curious, then, to find how deeply regional custom was also involved. *Thee* and *thou* were much more often used among farmers than among courtiers, but regional dialects also varied. When systematic dialect grammars were first compiled in the nineteenth century, *thee* forms were standard in the North and West of England, especially in Yorkshire, Lancashire, Westmorland, and Cumberland, and in Devon and Somerset; presumably they had been even more common two centuries earlier. Judging, however, by the regional grammars, they were not used in the South and East, even in rural Essex, Buckingham, and Wiltshire.[10]

7. Cf. Leon Kellner, *Historical Outlines of English Syntax* (London, 1913); A. C. Baugh, *History of the English Language* (New York, 1935), p. 300; W. Franz, *Shakespeare-Grammatik* (Heidelberg, 1924), p. 261; *Oxford English Dictionary* (under *Thou*).

8. Parnell, *Several Writings*, p. 94.

9. Ellwood, *Life*, p. 27. Cf. Fox, *Great Mistery*, p. 73; Nayler, *Man of Sin*, pp. 42–44.

10. See the following dialect grammars: on Westmorland: Hirst, also Wheeler; on Cumberland: Borje Brilioth, also Dickinson and Prevost; on Yorkshire: J. Wright; on Cheshire: Egerton Leigh; on Worcestershire: Jesse Salisbury; on Devonshire: Sarah Hewitt; on Wiltshire: G. E. Dartnell; on Buckshire: H. Hartmann; on Essex: Edward Gepp.

It was precisely in the areas where Quakerism arose and was most strong that men used *thee* forms instinctively between equals, whereas in other parts of England *thee* was an insult except to inferiors. The same regional isolation that encouraged the rise of Quakerism in the North by keeping out puritan churches and schools may have protected the older forms of speech. But the Quaker custom was natural to those who first used it; it was Truth, whereas in other parts of England it had to be learned as a Testimony and was subject to ridicule.

American Quakers have fallen into a curious usage, saying "thee is" (in place of "thou art") or "Will thee go?," and so on, which may also stem from the dialect of northern England. Two centuries before Fox, the old form "he goeth" had been replaced, in that region before other parts of England, by the modern usage "he goes," which apparently is of Scandinavian origin. In the North also, as many quotations in this book have shown, it was common to say "I is," "they was," "we was," of which customs only "says I" crept into standard English. The North of England, moreover, still uses *tha* or *ta* (and Somerset and Devon use *thee*), where correct pronounciation would be *thou*. Thus *"haes ta?"* (how is thee?), "thaul want" (thou will want), and "es that thee?" were common until recently. "If thee will thee may send itt," when "thee findes freedome," wrote an early Cumberland Friend,[11] like his American descendants.

In line with their use of *thee* and *thou,* early Quakers refused to give men hat-honor, thereby attacking lordship and social inequality but, above all, pride. Hats were universally worn at this time, even indoors, and this was surely as true among farmers as in King Charles' Court, and in the wet North more than in the gentle South of England. The hat flourishes of Ellwood's friends or of *Hamlet's* Osric show the hypocrisy in customs of courtesy then current, but southerners and gentlemen did customarily take off their hats to friends and equals. North-Country farmers probably did not, and Friends refused to "be charged with flatter-

---

11. Dews./15, 16, Stubbs to Dewsbury. Cf. A. Wheeler, *The Westmorland Dialect in Three Familiar Dialogues* (Kendal, England, 1790); J. Close (pseud. of Sam Dowell), *The Book of Chronicles or Winter Evening Tales of Westmorland* (Appleby, England, 1842); William Dickinson and E. W. Prevost, *Dialect of Cumberland* (London, 1899).

ing of any man." [12] There, inequality was again involved, just a
to this day custom expects a Negro to uncover his head before a
white Mississippian, but not vice versa. When Friends were brough
before judges, "if they give them the hat, it is a civil thing; it pac
ifies the rage of the transgressor . . . but break down his Idol
and bring him . . . to seek the honour which comes from . .
God . . . and not give him this the hat honor . . . and he wil
rage." [13] Though it often cost fines or jailing, Friends kept up
this form of assault upon pride in order to subject men to the
Light.

Another infuriating habit, which William Penn listed among
the twelve key Testimonies of the Quakers, was their refusal to
salute or greet anyone they met in passing, even by " 'Good night
good morrow, Godspeed,' for they knew the night was good and
the day good without wishing of either." [14] Friends said it was
doubly hypocritical to wish such things to the unconverted, and
so again showed the cleavage they set between "Children of Light'
and the world. Yet again this attitude was more natural for la
conic Dalesmen, who expressed truth by "having very few words
upon all occasions." [15]

Testimonies for social equality were thus no sign of any effort to
create a new social order by custom or by law (as with the Level
lers), let alone by revolution. The loyalty of Friends was given to
the Spirit and to the Spirit-led community. This indeed disrupted
their already tenuous ties to the social hierarchy in general and to
their absentee landlords. Their ideas about the relations of fathers
to children, of masters to household servants, and even of colonial
planters to their Negroes and Indians were still paternalistic:
"Now consider, ffriends," wrote Fox to Barbados Friends in 1671,
"that it is no transgression for a master of a family to instruct his
family him self. . . . Now Negroes and Tawney Indians make
up a very great part of ffamilies here in this Iland, for whom an
account will be required by him who Comes to Judge both quick

12. Samuel Fisher, "Episkopos Aposkopos" (in *Works*, but paginated separately)
p. 51.

13. George Fox, *An Instruction to Judges and Lawyers That They May Act and
Judge as the Judges Did of Old* (London, 1659 or 1660), p. 6.

14. Penn, *Witness*, p. 24.

15. Ibid. Cf. Weld et al., *Perfect Pharisee*, pp. 33–34; Higginson, *Irreligion of
Quakers*, p. 28.

& dead." Fox considered it a "slander & Lye" [16] when Friends were said to incite Negroes to rebel, and he himself never clearly attacked slavery. The rather Whiggish paternalism that William Penn showed later in his colony and in his family, though it owed much to Locke and Sidney in words, was in spirit no treason to early Quakerism. Yet even within the Quaker household lordship was denied, since Christ was Lord over master and servant alike, as Paul had written:

> By God's Ordinance, some have a Superiority given them, for the Punishment of evil-doers, and a Praise to them that do well . . . the Husband over the Wife . . . the Parents over the Children, the King over his Subjects. . . . [But the] Honour due from Inferiors . . . consists not in vain Ceremonies . . . such as uncovering the Head, and bowing the Knee . . . neither in vain Complements . . . but in . . . speedy Obedience to all just commands. . . . We design to level nothing but Sin. . . . And therefore we cannot call any Man . . . "my Lord," because God is the Lord.[17]

The positive fruits of this Quaker attitude were less obvious in cautious letters to King Charles than in the support of Quaker household-servants who became preachers: Jane Waugh, William Caton, and Richard and Anne Cleaton.

The Quaker testimonies against war may be kept for later discussion in connection with Quakers and the state.

The standard of simplicity stands next after these as a major social challenge. As with social equality, several motives acted upon Friends. Simplicity was a witness to the world, and especially to the proud, against all self-love and vanity. Simplicity echoed the puritan fear of luxury and waste, and the details in practice followed specific puritan codes. Lastly, simplicity was a reminder that many would be poor if a few possessed too much.

Friends knew that English law and tradition, even among conservative puritans, specified differences of dress to mark the upper, middle, and lower classes. All such badges of status—especially the courtly cavalier costume—called forth the Quaker's judgment so as to crush the self-esteem of the "proud and lustful . . . who

16. Fox, *Journal*, Camb., 2, 200, 201.
17. J. Whitehead, *Written Gospel-labours*, pp. 142–43.

. . . deck your selves in your proud Attire, inventing New Ways and Fashions to make yourselves glorious in the Sight of men, that they may bow down and worship you." [18] Many burned their laces and finery upon becoming Friends, some in emotional bonfires, as in Bristol, and some, like the midwives of Barbados, only after earnest discussion. Many a Friend also gave up any job involving luxuries, such as that of goldsmith, toymaker, court tailor, or excise collector.[19] Friends were warned to beware of the world's fashions and to keep to their own, so that they "therein . . . may judge the World." [20] Evidently, however, the need to bear witness against the pride of the outside world was here secondary to the need of inward discipline for the athlete or soldier in the Lamb's War. With inward detachment from the world, the heart was freed; simplicity of spirit therefore became one of the permanent marks of Quakerism. When Ellwood had been convinced as a Friend and first returned to visit his old guardians, who were Quakers, "Isaac Penington and his Wife . . . received me courteously: but not knowing what Exercise I had been in . . . were not forward at first to lay suddain Hands on me; which I observed and did not dislike. But as they came to see a Change in me, not in Habit only, but in gesture, Speech and Carriage . . . they were exceeding kind and tender towards me." [21]

The pattern of the Quakers' plain dress was at first simply puritan daily clothing with a working-class accent; it did not become standardized in cut or color until a generation later. Some matters followed individual conviction and were odd but not unusual, like Fox's leather breeches, so often later re-tailored. Fox and Nayler apparently also defied puritan custom in wearing their hair long as an imitation of Christ, and in the belief that, like

18. Nayler, *Works,* p. 91. On standards of dress under the Tudors see also Knappen, *Tudor Puritanism,* pp. 412, 437.

19. On the midwives of Barbados cf. *JFHS,* 37 (1940), 22. See also Bache, *Few Words,* p. 10; *FPT,* p. 240 n. Elizabeth Haddon's mother gave up domestic music and burned her embroidery. Bache gave up both his excise-collecting and, subsequently, a shop selling "Rings and Toyes to proud and vain people." On ribbons and laces, cf. Swarth. 1/373 (*EQL* 4) and many references listed by Nuttall in *EQL,* p. 82. On Quaker art and music see Tolles, *Atlantic Culture,* pp. 77–79, and his *Meeting-House and Counting House* (Chapel Hill, University of North Carolina Press, 1948), pp. 123 ff.

20. *An Epistle of Our Antient Friend George Fox . . . to Keep Out of the Vain Fashions of the World* (Dublin, Dublin Yearly Meeting, 1734).

21. Ellwood, *Life,* p. 41.

Samson and the Nazirites, they drew supernatural strength from it. At other points, Friends assumed that what was puritan bias was self-evident to all tender consciences:

> The Fool's py'd Coat, which all wise Men detest
> Is grown a Garment now in great Request.
> More Colours in one Wastcoat now they wear,
> Than in the Rain-bow ever did appear . . .
> The Women wear the Trowsies and the Vest,
> While Men in Muffs, Fans, Peticoats are drest:
> Some Women (Oh, the Shame!) like ramping Rigs,
> Ride flaunting in their Powder'd Perriwigs:
> Astride they sit (and not ashamed neither)
> Drest up like Men, in Jacket, Cap and Feather.[22]

Modern Quaker tastes in both poetry and feminism have come closer to Milton's ideals than to those in this tract by his secretary Ellwood. But seventeenth-century stage plays were often bawdy, May games revolved around love-making, football games were murderously violent, and puritan restraints therefore seemed godly. As to tobacco, it is interesting to find that the Quaker Thomas Curtis, who had only recently "ripped off his gold buttons, and his wife . . . stripped off all her jewels and rich attire," was shocked and upset to find Devonshire Baptists with pipes in their mouths.[23] On this issue, puritan opinion was divided, as it still is. Fox once put John Story's pipe into his mouth, "least his rude tongue shoulde say I had not unity with the creation." [24] Similarly, in refusing to drink any man's health, they carried puritan austerity a step further; they protested all drunkenness, yet they took beer drinking for granted.

Friends learned from many radical puritans to avoid the names of months and weekdays that stemmed from Janus, Thor, and other pagan gods. It is only recently that the use of "First Month" or "Fifth Day" has been peculiar to Quakers. Like puritans, they angrily ignored as papist relics Candlemas, Michaelmas, and Christmas. Going further, Fox teased the puritans by Old Testament arguments (picked up from Seventh-Day Baptist friends) that de-

22. Ibid., pp. 198–99. Cf. Fox, *Journal*, Camb., *1*, 176–77.
23. Swarth. 3/87 (*EQL* 470), Curtis to Fox. Cf. Alex. Parker, quoted in L. V. Hodgkin (Holdsworth), *Guilielma, Wife of William Penn* (London, 1947), p. 35.
24. Fox, *Journal*, Camb., *1*, 44.

nied the sanctity of even the puritans' own Holy Day. (Though Friends Meetings might be held on any day of the week, there is no evidence that they preferred Saturdays to Sundays.) Like many puritans, they refused the name of Saint to any but the Elect community they belonged to. They also refused to consider steeple houses or buildings holy, or to call stones and wood a church. Thus old place-names took strange forms in many Commonwealth writings—St. George's Churchyard becomes George's Yard, and Grace-Church Street is called Gracious Street.[25]

Quaker simplicity, however, involved also a direct protest against the crushing of the poor: this was one of the rare places they attacked injustice head on, without a call to submit totally to the Light. The radical puritan tradition caught fire here: "Is this the Saints' Practice . . . to live in the Lusts of the Flesh, Sporting and Gaming and calling it 'Recreation,' living in Excess of Aparel and Diet . . . when your Brethren want Food and Rayment." [26] This was the special message of Penn, when he became a Quaker with all the student-aristocrat's idealism:

> When people have first learned to . . . obey their Creator
> . . . to alleviate . . . their oppressed tenants . . . when the
> pale faces are more commiserated, the pinched bellies re-
> lieved, and naked backs clothed . . . then it will be early
> enough for you to plead the indifferency of your pleasure.
> But that the sweat and tedious labour of the husbandman
> early and late, cold and hot, wet and dry, should be converted
> into the pleasure . . . of a small number of men; that the
> cart, the plough, the thresh, should be . . . laid upon nine-
> teen parts of the land to feed the . . . delicious appetites of
> the twentieth is . . . horrible injustice.[27]

The puritan horror of waste had reinforced the concern for human need. Quakers warned landlords who "grind the faces of the poor,

25. The use of numbers instead of names to indicate weekdays and months was common among the Baptists: cf. *The Records of Churches of Christ Gathered at Fenstanton, Warboys and Hexham*, ed. E. B. Underhill (London, 1847), pp. 302, 306, 311, 317 ff. Seventeenth-century England lived under the old-style calendar whereby new years began in March, so that the months from September to December had numerical names already.

26. Nayler, *Works*, p. 46.

27. William Penn, *No Cross, No Crown* (14th ed. Dublin, 1797), pp. 280–81.

who rack and stretch out their Rents." [28] This echoes the Pilgrimage of Grace, as well as Old Testament prophets who had protested deceitful weights and measures. Individual Friends made specific proposals to Parliament for legal reforms to improve the conditions of tenants and beggars; they urged rebuilding the poor-relief system, since even the Elizabethan Poor Law had broken down during the civil wars. Of course, like most radical puritans, they wanted this welfare program endowed out of lands of the church and out of sequestered royalist estates. They urged that "all servile Tenures or Copyholds" and "all Fines that belong to Lords of Manors" be abolished, without facing the alternative dangers in unrestricted rentals. Unlike much legislation inspired by fear of vagabonds, the Quaker proposals at least always made their main aim the survival of men who, "being in poverty . . . ready to perish for want of the creatures, raise up thoughts in them to steale; which them that are rich . . . might take away the occasion, and prevent temptation." [29] But even concern for the suffering of the poor did not turn them for long from their attack on the pride of the rich, for their sermons still proclaimed: "Wo unto you that are called *Lords, Ladies, Knights, Gentlemen* . . . *Master* and *Sir* and *Mistris* . . . because of your much Earth, which by Fraud, Deceit and Oppression you have gotten together." [30] Friends at this time were scornful of the growing puritan idea that prosperity showed God's favor: Men claim as God's

28. William Tomlinson, *Seven Particulars,* quoted in Tindall, *Bunyan,* p. 103.

29. George Fox, *To the Protector and Parliament of England* (London, 1658), p. 12. See also Thomas Lawson, *An Appeal to the Parliament Concerning the Poor, That There May Not Be a Beggar in England* (London, 1660). In the North of England the Poor Law had never achieved the strength finally built up for it elsewhere under Charles I: cf. E. M. Leonard, *The Early History of English Poor Relief* (Cambridge, 1900). Lawson's title phrase on beggars (from Deuteronomy) had become a radical puritan battle cry. On the roots of these Quaker proposals in radical puritanism, see Margaret James, *Social Problems and Policy during the Puritan Revolution* (London, 1930), chap. 7. In *A Mite of Affection Maintained in 31 Proposals* (1659), Edward Billing proposed abolishing "Copyholds within the Common-wealth, being the badge of the Conquest"; the idea that the freeborn Saxons lost English liberty at the Norman Conquest, which Justice Coke had made into a weapon for Parliament against Charles I, had much justification in the northwest where the manorial system was only with difficulty imposed on free-owning homesteaders. Like the Pilgrimage of Grace, Fox merely suggested that "Fines that belong to the Lords of Manors be given to poor people, for the Lords have enough" (*To the Parliament . . . 59 Particulars* [London, 1659], No. 32).

30. Parnell, *Several Writings,* pp. 28–29.

gift what they have "stolen . . . in usury and oppression and deceit." [31]

Though they knew that wealth led to pride, Friends never despised the physical world. Fairs were vanity, but Quaker ethics was not founded upon the thrill of renunciation in worship of "the lean goddess Abstinence." [32] God had made the Creation good, and a man who was led by the Spirit of God would have unity with the Creation. In fact, as was shown above, Friends expected to control the physical world miraculously. Like the puritans, they regarded daily work as a calling from God which urged each member to govern and order all the men under him with God's wisdom. Quakers did not work out detailed codes of action for each vocation, as had the puritans Baxter and Perkins; nor did they simply assume, like the Lutherans, that faith and love will hallow any vocation. Friends put preaching first, but at home they knew no alternative to hard work, and, not surprisingly, they later became famous for building schools and factories, studying Botany, and devising new inventions.

Friends Meetings watched the business as well as the personal lives of their members, and the Testimony of honesty applied most of all to the marketplace. Their rejection of all oaths apparently came from radical puritan tradition, being also the stand of many Baptists. This may explain why, in arguing against oaths, Quakers always stood behind Matthew 5:33–37 and James 5:12, turning from the Bible to rational or historical arguments only when pressed.[33] But even about honesty, the heart of the matter for Friends was that all statements should be true: "Our yea is yea . . . and our nay is nay. . . . Let us suffer as much for breaking it as for breaking an oath." [34] Emotional reactions of Quakers must have been strengthened by the world's use of oaths in profanity and by the oaths of obligation forced upon unwilling farmers by

31. Francis Howgill, quoted in Hayes, *Gray Ridge*, p. 71.

32. Tawney, *Religion and Capitalism*, p. 249. Cf. Henry Hodgkin and W. C. Braithwaite, *Mission and Message of Quakerism* (London, 1912), p. 22.

33. Cf. Fisher in "Episkopos Aposkopos" p. 63, in *Works*. In every Testimony where Friends took a legalist or absolutist position, instead of linking the standard to obedience to the Spirit, the puritan background of Quakerism evidently survives almost unchanged.

34. George Fox's broadside *Our Covenant with God and with All Men Is Peace* (London, 1660). Cf. Crook, *Case of Swearing*, p. 12; anon., *The Case of the People Called Quakers Relating to Oathes* (1673), p. 26.

tenancy customs and later by both sides in the civil wars. We can notice, too, the traditional integrity of the North Countryman who "would not perjure himself for four of the best dukes' lands in France." [35]

Friends witnessed against the world's apostasy, from which all deceit came. In court, as they were bound by the truth within themselves, they saw no need for requiring oaths. When they later gave up hope of winning the world, they were willing to have affirmations legalized, accepting a separate Quaker standard; but under Cromwell and Charles II they suffered heavily rather than take oaths. Justices of the Peace discovered that, rather than trouble to prove other charges against Quakers, they needed only to tender some form of the oath of allegiance and then jail Friends as subversive when they refused.[36]

In buying and selling, Friends protested: "How is Trading become a Trap, to captivate Men into deceitful Dealing." [37] They advised each other and Londoners at large: "All ye who buy or sell . . . live in the fear of the Lord . . . and do not speak better or worse of the Creatures than you know them to be, thereby to get greater gain . . . Keep in the Light . . . and let that be your rule, and not the price of the Market." [38] One application of this was the "single price" set by a Quaker merchant according to the value of his wares in a day when bargaining was still usual. The Middle Ages had believed that a just price was attainable; the courts fixed prices, watched by the Church. As feudal society broke up, the puritans had made the fair price the responsibility of each individual merchant. Due to the complexities of trade, however, puritan standards were elastic, whereas a Quaker would not com-

---

35. Dodds and Dodds, *Pilgrimage of Grace, 1,* 60.

36. From the beginning, the oath of Praemunire (intended to ensure the loyalty of Englishmen to the king against the pope) was used against Quakers, even when under no suspicion whatever of popery. So were the Oath of Abjuration of 1655 and the oath of allegiance to the King required in 1660, both of which most men had signed even though they were contradictory. The oath required in the Quaker Act of 1662 was thus also framed to trap Friends, in the absence of any other charge against them.

37. Nayler, *Works,* p. 398.

38. George Fox the Younger, *A Collection of the Several Books and Writings* (London, 1662), pp. 42–43. Having the same name as the founder of Quakerism, to whom he was not related, the author always carried this nickname among Friends, although older than his namesake. On merchants see also Swarth ς /8

promise: once set by the merchant's own conscience, his price had to remain fixed. In time, of course, the single and honest price brought Quaker traders trust, and hence greater trade, honor, and wealth (as Fox noted without regret), but they were saved from these dangers for three decades by ruinous persecution. Before 1689, only three or four Quaker merchants were strong enough to employ two dozen workmen.[39]

The group life of early Friends was itself involved in their witness to the world, both by maintaining standards of private conduct and by the example of their mutual aid. The conflict between the Spirit and the world made the "camp of the Lord" aware of their role as a group. Individual Friends, being spokesmen for the Spirit, knew that they represented the Quakers as a whole. This explains their careful watch over each other's conduct—"so that all may see you to be Children of Light."[40] From this role later developed Elders and Overseers, whose duties included discipline, and, if necessary, the disowning of ex- or would-be Quakers of whom the group was ashamed.

Friends did not, however, think of themselves as a sect. They did not, like most sects, consider themselves a permanent minority that must live as a tight city set upon a hill, not involved with mankind, except as individuals sought refuge with them. Quakerism, on the contrary, expected to sweep the world. As the true Church, they had for a long time no special title or name for themselves: "I am not one of them [wrote Fox], which calls them selves papists, common prayer men, nor presbiterians, independants, anabaptists, puritans, nor heathens, which be out of the life of God; but that which God has caled me to . . . the elect before the world began."[41] Since the Spirit was primary and not the group, Friends disowned a renegade, but there were no steps for giving him over to Satan, as was standard among Baptists of those decades. Neither were there ceremonies for entrance into Quaker membership. London Meetings listed members to define the group

39. Cf. Isabel Grubb, *Quakerism and Industry before 1800* (London, 1930); also Fox, *Journal*, Nickalls, pp. 169–70, where Fox ends on a worldly note: the Friends attracted as much trade as anyone, "insomuch that then the cry of all the professors was, 'if we let these people alone, they will take the trading of the nation out of our hands.' And this hath been the Lord's doing to his people."

40. Nayler, *Works*, p. 34.

41. Fox, *Journal*, Camb., *1*, 333.

for whom a Meeting was responsible in giving assistance in case of hardship or persecution, and for supervision of marriages and publications. Friends' strong informal loyalty achieved at least as much as enforced unity could have. The "sense of the Meeting" and the leadings of "weighty Friends" made individualists restrain their own impulses and urged ahead the hesitant. Thousands of women circulated and signed petitions about tithes, and little books survive in which all the women of a local or a regional Meeting set down each in her own words her refusal to pay tithes.[42]

The unity within their group was precious to Friends, and they pointed to it as the work of the Spirit. Thus their mutual care was also a witness to the world. Their offers to take the places of other Quakers in prison were noticed even by Oliver Cromwell.[43] Funds were raised from 1653 onward for Friends who had been thrown into prison and had no other means of support. By the 1670s, when a Friend who disgraced the group by bankruptcy would face disownment, careful machinery in each Meeting provided loans to the hard-pressed, and fire collections and flood relief were usual after sudden disasters. Meetings saw to it that a boy needing work was apprenticed to another Friend. Nailsworth Meeting recorded: "Friends do approve that James Collins of Luckinton may goe to Nicholas Wastfeild on tryall and if they like and approve of Each Other, friends do conclude to add their assistance towards the binding him an apprentice."[44] All the provisions of the halting Elizabethan Poor Law system were supplied fully by Friends within their own fellowship. The effectiveness of their care became in itself a testimony that their group life was the work not merely of men but of Christ.[45]

The early establishment of Quaker schools has been the cause

42. See Kendal MS No. 3; also Douglas in *JFHS*, *48* (1956), 31. Later Quaker generations simply disowned tithe payers out of hand.

43. Fox, *Journal*, *1*, 245. In addition to three notable occasions in London when Friends offered to replace prisoners, in 1656, 1658, and 1659, Daniel Baker offered his life to the Inquisition at Malta for the freeing of Katharine Evans and Sarah Chevers: all three were almost executed but were finally released (see Braithwaite, *Beginnings*, pp. 431–32).

44. *JFHS*, *37* (1940), 36. Cf. Kendal MS. No. 103, "Minutes of General Meeting of 1671;" ibid., Minutes of Skipton General Meeting, 1659; Arnold Lloyd, *Quaker Social History*, *1669–1738* (London, Longmans, Green, 1950), chaps. 12 and 13, a detailed description.

45. Robert Barclay, *The Anarchy of the Ranters* (London, 1676), p. 39.

of praise and surprise. But the kind of informal schoolteaching that had been carried on by John Banks was standard in rural parishes and could easily be transferred to Quaker auspices. Friends like Thomas Lawson who had been parish ministers found teaching their most obvious way to make a living. Conflicts over the salary of the teacher or his assistant appear in local Meeting records along with certificates accrediting teachers who moved to America.[46] First-day schools or Sunday schools in the modern sense did not yet exist, but George Fox turned as early as 1657 to the publishing of "A Catechisme for Children, that They May Come to Learn of Christ, the Light, the Truth." There was no sharp line between religious and ordinary learning, and both Fox's Primer and Catechism of 1670 and a similar book ten years later by Crisp and Fox the Younger served double duty. Along with the alphabet, primers taught the Light within: "Q: Father, how may I know a thought and an imagination from the Light? A: Child, the Light discovers them and makes them manifest, which cometh from Him by whom the World was made, which Light was before the thoughts were, and if the Light be hearkened to, the thoughts and imaginations shall not lodge within thee. Heb. *1:2*." [47]

Many provisions for early Meetings were substitutes for ceremonies that, until the Cromwellian regime, had been carried out only in parish churches, notably baptism, marriage, and burials. Friends rejected baptism, of course, and no equivalent was needed in an era before birth certificates; the recording in Meeting minutes of "birth-right members" was standardized only in 1737. For funerals, Friends developed a simple form of memorial meeting based on silence like ordinary worship, with spontaneous speaking when the Spirit led. Friends had their own burial grounds by 1660 and stressed the simplicity of the coffin and of the interment, which they later made uniform.[48]

46. See Irene L. Edwards, "Early Discipline in Southwark," *JFHS, 31* (1934), 77 f., for the conflict of Francis Lea and Richard Scoryer. Cf. *JFHS, 35* (1938), 31, for the certificate for schoolteacher Christopher Taylor on his moving from Waltham Abbey School to Pennsylvania.

47. George Fox, *A Catechisme* . . . , quoted in *JFHS, 35* (1938), 4–5. Cf. William Fryer Harvey, "Guidance for Young Quakers in the Use of Silence, 1657–1847" in the same issue.

48. Cf. Penn, preface to Fox, *Journal*, 1694; Tolles, *Meeting-House*, p. 120.

Quaker weddings had their own established customs by 1660. While legal marriages before the Commonwealth were always performed by authorized clergy and entered into the parish registers along with christenings and burials, the custom of "handfast marriages" before lay witnesses was already known in the North, where parishes were large and parsons few. The Westminster Assembly in 1645 replaced the Prayer-Book ceremony with a simple marriage service in the new Directory of Worship, and the direct vows of man and wife which were the center of this were used with little change among Friends.[49] Not only had the puritan victory broken the uniformity of the old rituals so that variety and confusion might often result, but the changes in the parish church organization had left many Independent and separatist churches actually in charge of their own weddings. Cromwell's hope was a civil marriage register alongside the parish rolls, but there is little evidence that Friends used this way out. Despite the much more urgent matters over which Quakers were permanently afoul of the law, there remained legal as well as moral reasons for insisting that Quakers must be married in the presence of their local Meeting and with its blessing, as Fox advised in 1653. In 1655 the marriage of Agnes Ayrey and John Spooner came under George Taylor's criticsm, as had that of Thomas Holme and Elizabeth Leavens the year before, because of its informality: "It were well if it had beene done in the light, our spirits Cannot relish it, only wee Leave it in silence, for feare of giving offence, but it were well if less of that were practised amongst Friends." [50] But within a year and a half of Cromwell's ordinance on civil registry of marriages, Richard Hunter and Elizabeth Atherton were in trouble for maintaining the Quaker wedding as valid by itself.[51] In this same year of 1656 Margaret Fell recommended in a general epistle that Friends draw up a formal certificate of marriage to be signed as witnesses by all Quakers present. Many early certificates have been found, showing how they were gradually shaped into a standard form. The couple themselves, having repeated their vows to each other in a silent meeting called for their wedding, then set their own hands to a certificate which was read

---

49. Ruth G. Burtt, "The Quaker Marriage Declaration," *JFHS*, *46* (1954), 53–59.
50. Swarth. 1/214 (*EQL* 126), Geo. Taylor to M. Fell (February 26, 1654/55).
51. Swarth. 1/357 and 358 (*EQL* 338–39), Richard Hunter to M. Fell (1656).

aloud and signed after the meeting ended. When George Fox married Margaret Fell in Bristol Meeting in 1669, eleven years after Judge Fell's death, her daughters and their husbands gathered and "not onely declared their free assent to said intended marriage butt also . . . signifyed that they had a sence that the thinge . . . doth stand in the Covenant of light and life & therefore doe rejoice." [52]

Quakers increasingly demanded the approval of all living parents or guardians, a personal interview of the engaged couple before the Men's Meeting or Monthly Meeting, and the announcement of the wedding two weeks beforehand. The feared dangers sometimes materialized and led to postponed weddings—previous commitments, unworthy past conduct, and, most often, the inadequate background of either bride or groom in Quakerism. Couples who in impatience went off to be married by parish ministers or by a gathering of Quaker friends not authorized by the Meeting faced more severe discipline. Those who rejected it, or who married non-Quakers, were inevitably disowned. The later strictness of this pattern was tragic, and some 50,000 Friends were disowned in the eighteenth and nineteenth centuries for marrying "out of Meeting." [53] But in the days of the Lamb's War tolerance was not simple: "All such as marry by the preists of Baall . . . who have had their hands in the blood of our Bretheren . . . must come to judgment." [54] The need for strictness was demonstrated by a messy episode in which a supposedly Quaker Londoner, who had been married out of Meeting, turned Baptist and was told by the Baptist elders that his previous marriage had no standing and that he was free to marry a Baptist girl, which he then did. [55]

Married life in Quaker circles was seldom easy. Other Friends usually watched over the needs of a traveling preacher's family or the children of Quakers in prison. But some wives, like Crisp's, opposed their husbands' preaching plans, and the silence of many wives represented grim resignation. But letters home from preach-

52. Bristol Men's Meeting Minutes, August 18, 1669, quoted in R. S. Mortimer, "Marriage Discipline of Early Friends," *JFHS*, *48* (1957), 185.

53. Tolles, *Meeting-House*, p. 120.

54. Letter of George Fox, quoted in Kendal MS. No. 103, p. 29. Cf. Mortimer in *JFHS*, *48*, 175–95.

55. I. Edwards, "Early Discipline," *JFHS*, *31* (1934), 72–76.

ing Friends, like John Banks' to his doubly hard-working wife, show a real sense of comradeship in the mission. Some statements became classics:

The testemony of William Edmondson for my dear wife Margrett . . . We were married in the year 1652, she willingly left her relations & country, and came with me to live in Ireland, and when I was convinced of gods blessed truth [on a visit to England in 1653] she never reflected or opposed me as touching religion, nor in my testemony against tithes . . . and in all my imprissonments for truths testemony she bore it cheerfully. . . . When I was called to travell in the service and labour of the gospell . . . She tooke the charge of our outward concerns & famely upon her in my absence . . . and I doe not remember if ever she was terrefyed . . . but often . . . would tell me she was not afraid. . . . When the cruell & bloody rapperies besett our house & poured in shott on both sides in at the windows with many oathes threatning our destruction setting the house on fire, we being in it till about two parts of it was consumed, I did not hear her complain or show fear of death but attended me to know my mind, and when I opened the doors & they tooke me and my two sons from her barelegged and bare [headed] and left her striped into her shift . . . all this she bore. . . . Though they destroyed our house & all that was in it . . . when it pleased god miraculously to restore me and my [sons] to her she was well content.[56]

Howgill, dying in Appleby jail, wrote gently to his daughter Abigail to commend her to her mother's care and, as they should grow older, to cherish her and bring her comfort. When Ann Dewsbury died before her husband, Margaret Fell wrote to him "as A testemony of my deare Love and unyty . . . not knowing whether thy wife be yett in the Earthly Tabernacle; but a member of the boddy of Christ I know she is, which boddy is made perfect Thorow Tryels and Sufferings and he a man A Sorows for the boddys sake." [57]

---

56. Book of Record of Mountmellick Meeting, quoted in *JFHS, 33* (1936), 32–33.
57. Dews./25, Margaret Fell to Dewsbury (May 8, 1659). Cf. Howgill, *Works,* h2, "Testament to his daughter Abigail."

Meetings had sometimes the less happy lot of settling quarrels between Friends. Fox reconciled Edward Billing's broken marriage at Leith in 1657. The great breach between Nayler and Fox took the best efforts of all the leading Friends three years to heal, and some conflicts after the Restoration were insoluble and led to small schisms in Quakerism. During the summer and fall of 1656 an argument over financial matters between Anthony Pearson and Lancelot Wardell aligned both George Taylor and Margaret Fell on Pearson's side, but it may have started the drift that took Pearson out of Quakerism and by 1661 swung him back into the respectability of the established church.[58] Most disputes, however, had the innocence and directness of the charge that John Scafe had stolen Thomas Wilson's mare.[59] Considering the emotional intensity of Quakerism, it is surprising that quarrels were so rare, and no formal machinery seems to have been needed to heal them in the early years. A Friend could write to another with honesty: "wordes cannot express my love to thee. I am satisfied in that I love thee." [60] Quakers spent their energy fighting the world rather than each other.

58. On Billing's wife cf. Fox, *Journal,* Nickalls, p. 320. On Nayler see above, p. 65; on Pearson and Wardell, Swarth, 1/278 (*EQL* 290); 1/282 (*EQL* 298), 1/283 (*EQL* 313), 1/284 (*EQL* 318).

59. Swarth. 1/32 (*EQL* 102), John Wilkinson to M. Fell.

60. ARBarc./120, Thomas Stacey to Fox.

7

The Kingdom of This World

LET the saints be joyful in glory: let them sing aloud upon
their beds.

Let the high praises of God be in their mouth, and a twoedged
sword in their hand;

To execute vengeance upon the heathen, and punishments
upon the people;

To bind their kings with chains, and their nobles with fetters
of iron;

To execute upon them the judgment written: this honour
have all his saints. Praise ye the LORD.—Psalm 149

IN THE NAME of the Lord and His rule on earth, the puritans had
killed a king and fettered their noblemen. Every victory increased
their awe of God's power to use His humblest saints in bringing
forth His kingdom. With precisely the same attitude, the Quakers watched the power of the Spirit spread its inward conquest
throughout the world. The struggle of the Lamb's War still continued, inwardly against the "old Adam" and Satan himself, and
outwardly against the pride of the mighty. But Friends pointed
to victory over sin within their own lives and passed beyond
judgment and anguish. Outwardly, the number of Quakers grew
geometrically between 1652 and 1657. As new men in each region
of England and America were conquered, they took up the campaign: Christ had not saved "a few raging quakers only, but with
ten thousand of his saints is he come." [1] There were about 500

1. Nayler, *Answer to Baxter*, p. 58.

Friends convinced before 1652, 5,000 by 1654, and at least 20,000 by 1657. Had the pace been maintained, the world would have turned Quaker within a generation. It was a glorious vision for which to live.

Early Quaker thought was apocalyptic, viewing the era as the climax of history. Like the puritans, the Quakers linked their victories with the final crisis in which God would judge and transform the world. They formulated no political doctrines, for the whole world was being brought out of darkness into light by the Spirit's power, and the future of governments was simply a part of this process. The kingdom of this world would become the kingdom of our God and of His Christ. Friends and puritans were as familiar with the visions of Daniel and the Book of Revelation as they were with the Sermon on the Mount. "Christ hath all power in heaven and earth given to him. . . . That which slays mysticall Babylon is not the kings of the earth," wrote a Friend, "and the saints slay not . . . with the carnal sword. . . . Their weapons are not carnal but spiritual. . . . The beast hath been long up . . . but the Lamb and the Saints are trampling him to pieces . . . and getting the victory over him. And the everlasting gospel is preaching." [2] The Great Beast, the Whore of Babylon, Cain, Balaam, and Antichrist were useful biblical names for any enemy of Quakerism and the Spirit, until these epithets lost all clarity by repetition in hundreds of Quaker tracts and sermons. However, they were rightly understood as labels for the demonic pride that makes men claim to be independent of God or try to act without him. The Friends insisted that only Spirit-led actions could escape judgment, and they set the Spirit's leading in stark contrast to all human wills and choices. They were thus quite at ease within the supernatural and miraculous outlook of the Apocalypse, and could apply these lurid symbols quite matter-of-factly to the well-fed squires and well-meaning parsons of puritan England. They could claim to see some elements of the Christian apocalyptic hope, such as the outpouring of the Spirit and the Second Coming of Christ, fulfilled in their own lives.

Because Quaker beliefs were deeply apocalyptic, three further points need to be made before linking them to the world of

2. Nayler, *Man of Sin*, epistle to reader; cf. Thomas Salthouse, *A Candle Lighted at a Coal from the Altar* (London, 1669), p. 4.

politics. First, Friends knew they lived in time and space. Though the spiritual enemy, and even the battle and the bloodshed, were described symbolically, the Lamb's victory was an event expected within English history. Quakers spoke constantly of the "Day of the Lord" even when they did not explain what they meant in detail, and "sounded forth the Day of the Lord" not only in marketplaces but on the empty mountain-tops of Pendle Hill and Cadr Idris:

> After this wee past away & came to another great tounde on a markett day: & John app Johns declared the everlastinge truth through the streets & declared the day of the Lord amongst them & many people in the evenings gathered about the Inn. . . . And soe some service for the Lord wee had with the people both over night & in the morninge. . . . And then wee came to a hill which they say was 2 or 3 miles high: & on this hill syde I could see a great way: & I was moved to sounde the day of the Lord there . . . & tolde John app Jhons . . . in what places god would raise upp a people.[3]

By contrast, the "spiritual puritans" of that time, like existentialists today, understood most biblical symbols about war, judgment, and God's kingdom to be images of timeless reality. Judgment occurs now, they said, for each man in each new moment of decision. God is ever-present and continually confronting men. His "victory" is the invisible focus and end of our actions. But though early Friends looked for God's kingdom and victory within men and not in physical catastrophes, for them it was to be a real event, the actual climax of sacred history: "The mighty day of the Lord is come and coming, that . . . the secrets of every ones hearts shall bee revealed with the light of Jesus. . . . If you hate that light & goe on in the evill, this will bee the Condemnation. . . . Therefore, now you have time, prize it; this is the day of your vissitation & salvation proferred to you." [4] Thus, as Chapter 5 described, the Quaker prophet brought not merely a way to knowledge of the Lord but God's message as an ultimate chal-

---

3. Fox, *Journal*, Camb., *1*, 280–81. Cf. Camm and Audland, *Works*, pp. 66–68; Fox, *Journal*, Camb., *1*, pp. 40, 52, 53, 278, 305–06.

4. Fox, *Journal*, Camb., *1*, 206, 54. On spiritual puritans see Sippell, *Werdendes Quäkertum*, pp. 106–08.

lenge: "experience was one thinge, but to goe with a message & a worde from the Lord as the prophetts and the Apostles had . . . this was another thinge." [5] To reject a Quaker's warning was to reject God, perhaps forever. The Light itself was not a timeless guide but the inward power of Christ, who was marching on His way.

As a second part of their apocalyptic belief, Quakers expected the Lamb's victory not only in history but within the human community. The convinced Quaker was not saved individually but as a member of the Camp of the Lord whose mission was to all men: "All in whom [he] Reigns . . . are at Wars with all the World, and the World with them. . . . If you be in his Kingdom . . . then are you at work with him in his Day, wherein he is coming *in Thousands of his Saints to take Vengeance* . . . upon his Enemies. Now you who are asleep, and at ease in the flesh, are not of his Kingdom." [6]

The Day of the Lord was preached as "a day of wrath, a day of trouble," but the Friends' own experiences had shown judgment to be the first stage of deliverance. It should thus be obvious as a third point that Quaker apocalypticism was not a mere negative reaction against evil. Here, probably, positive and negative aspects of all apocalyptic thought should be distinguished. Negative apocalypticism has often emerged in grim times like the Greek or Roman rule of Judea, which seemed so overwhelmingly evil that men who believed in God's justice could not conceive of His accepting such cruelty. It requires that something must break, that God must act to turn the world right-side-up. The revolution seems inevitable, when the mighty will be put down and the wicked punished. If the miracle is to come from God's power (or even from the dialectic of history), it may appear darkest before the dawn. Negative apocalyptic outlooks include positive faith in God and give courage under crushing persecution like that of Daniel or in the Warsaw ghetto, but man's chief part is to endure. Positive apocalyptic faith, on the other hand, springs from the awareness of a power already at work in the world. Though it may seem only a tiny mustard seed, it has the strength to push all before it, and emphasis is put on joyful wonder rather than on

5. Fox, *Journal*, Camb., *1*, 54.
6. Nayler, *Works*, p. 392.

desperate hope; man's call is to awaken and commit himself in time rather than merely to endure. The righteous will not live by their faith alone through the time of crises. The positive apocalyptic message calls even the most righteous to open themselves still more to God's present power. Many great movements of religious awakening have been apocalyptic in this form: Jonathan Edwards and the early Franciscans alike expected the wonderful outburst of faith they saw around them to sweep on to the end of the world, and even Luther at first had hoped for the return of Christ within decades.

When the positive and negative visions are combined, emotional intensity is doubled. Horror at evil and rejoicing in the Spirit's power tend to reinforce each other in any case, as do positive and negative electrical charges in a condenser. Like Saint Paul and the Gospel writers, Quakers felt strongly in themselves the powers of both darkness and light. The transforming power was already at work; but the world it was to conquer remained actively hostile: "Principalities and powers" of evil were ruling nations of men. The Gospel was both good news and judgment, though the power of the Spirit could make even judgment itself ultimately redemptive.[7]

The combination of positive and negative apocalypticism underlay the early Friends' belief that the Lamb's War was simultaneously the Day of the Lord's Judgment. Much Quaker preaching seemed merely to announce a future Day of Judgment soon to come: "the Day of the Lord is . . . nigh at hand, a day of wrath . . . a day of darkness and gloominess . . . for all the Earth shall be devoured. Who waits upon the Lord in his Light . . . shall see this fulfilled and shall be preserved."[8] They often described the coming judgment quite physically, accompanied by fire and brimstone as tangible as those in the Book of Revelation. "Oh, England . . . thus hath the Lord spoken: 'The People are too many, the People are too many; I will thin them, I will thin them. . . . An Overflowing Scourge, even an exceeding great and terrible Judgment is to come upon thee. . . . The Remnant of my Holy

---

7. See above, p. 128. Note similarities to these doctrines in the Marxist view of history.

8. M. Fell, p. 183: "A Loving Salutation to the Seed of Abraham" (1657). Cf. Camm and Audland, *Works*, pp. 66–68; Fisher, *Works*, p. 780.

Seed, which shall be preserved . . . shall rule the Earth . . . and they shall forgive and love their Enemies.' " [9] More significant, however, are the sermons identifying the divine Judgment with the inward anguish and suffering of condemnation which immediate response to the Light required: "For now the day of their Torment is begun . . . Terrour, Wo and Misery is coming upon all the Inhabitants of the Earth; let all Flesh bow and tremble before the Lord; his Fire is kindled, and his Sword shall be made . . . drunk with the Blood of his Enemies . . . and the Vials, Wrath, Judgment, Vengeance and the Mighty Storm of Hail shall be poured upon the Heathen." [10] The inward judgment which they called all men to face would replace in full whatever physical hell-fire or other punishment the unrepentant might face in the future. Whether now or later, inwardly or outwardly (and Friends seldom made this clear), the same evils were to be condemned and destroyed by the same Spirit. Moreover, the Lamb's War ended in peace. Thus, though the Day of Judgment was still ahead for most men, Friends could regard it as already past for themselves: "The good and blessed Day of the Lord is come . . . for when the acceptable Year of the Lord came unto us, Judgment was laid to the Line, and the Lord did arise to shake terribly the Earth, the loftiness of Man was bowed down . . . and many Faces gathered paleness . . . because of the mighty Power of the Lord which was made manifest." [11]

The similarity between inward and outward judgment, and between present and future victory for Christ, made Quaker ideas of both heaven and hell double-edged. Fox himself could speak as if eternal life and the New Jerusalem were wholly present and inward now for the believer (and would hence seem to abandon apocalyptic hope and speak as a spiritual puritan would do): "All within the light of Christ . . . and within the power of God . . . which was the walls of the Citty, such were within the Citty . . .

9. George Fox the Younger, *England's Sad Estate* (London, 1661), pp. 7–8. Cf. his *Noble Salutation to Thee, Charles Stuart* (London, 1660), p. 21.

10. Camm and Audland, *Works,* pp. 81–82. Cf. Burrough, *Antichrist's Government* (London, 1661), chap. 3.

11. Camm and Audland, *Works,* pp. 184–86. Cf. Burrough, *Works,* p. 518; Fox, *Great Mistery,* pp. 26, 211; William Dewsbury, *Works, The Faithful Testimony of that Antient Servant of the Lord* . . . (London, 1689), p. 181. See also Bohn, "Puritans and Quakers," pp. 215–17.

and such as resiste the holy ghoast quencht & vext & grievd the spiritt of God . . . such were the doggs & unbeleivers without the Citty & made upp the great citty Babilon . . . and over such the second death has power." [12] But the theologically more alert Fisher was also more frank to say that he expected heaven and hell both in the timeless present and in future time: "Heaven is . . . in very deed in his Peoples Hearts . . . but . . . shall be manifest and known not only inwardly, in their Hearts who wait for it, but outwardly also, to such as wait not . . . who shall see themselves shut out Everlastingly from sharing in it. . . . Hell is the . . . Lord's Judgment . . . of which, (while not denying it to be also a certain *Local Place*), we affirm that it is within in the Conscience of every Malefactor." [13] The emphasis on heaven and hell was generally upon the present, not the future.

When they considered the coming of God's kingdom, however, their stress was upon the future. Christian tradition has always expected the Second Coming, or return of Christ, and the millennium, or rule of Christ on earth. The puritans spoke often of Christ coming as Judge and King—some expecting a physical return, and others meaning that Christ would rule through his saints. Radical puritan hopes were strong enough to prevent Cromwell from accepting for himself the crown of England. The return of Christ was indeed already present for Friends: He was come through His inward Light to teach His people Himself. The temporal reality of the kingdom had begun. But this was a recent event, and God's power, though it had always ruled the physical earth, had not yet conquered the hearts of all mankind. A time was therefore still to come when Christ would rule as King over all men.

The Friends rarely specified how this would come about politically. When Quakers foretold the rule of the Saints, they meant the power of their own company, but they appealed to all men to join them before that day came. What would become of the rebellious in the day of glory, whether the "chains and fetters of iron" were to be literal or symbolic—of this the Quakers' opponents were never quite sure, despite constant Quaker assertions that their weapons were spiritual, not carnal: "There's no ques-

12. Fox, *Journal*, Camb., *I*, 173–74. Cf. Fox, *Great Mistery*, p. 131.
13. Fisher, pp. 851–52.

tion if the spirit (that is, Advantage or Opportunity) did but move, they themselves would be the inflictors of all the punishments in that Sacred Book." [14] The Friends expected the coming of peace, social justice, and equality, in the reign of the Spirit. Yet within the Quaker Camp of the Lord, the kingdom had in a real sense already begun. Perhaps the immediate and self-evident presence of the kingdom, rather than hesitation to prophesy, explains the Friends' lack of speculation about its future form. Quakers did claim supernatural foreknowledge of judgments to come upon men and cities they knew well: Cromwell and Charles II, Bristol and London.

An interesting side light upon Quaker millennial hopes was their mission to the Jews. Reading St. Paul's Epistle to the Romans convinced them that the Jews would come to Christ's Light now that the kingdom was consummated. Thomas Lawson hunted down a Hebrew lexicon; Fox, Stubbs, and others learned a little Hebrew; Friends in Amsterdam made contact with the scholarly Rabbi Manasseh ben-Israel. In the same period, and for similar reasons, Cromwell's council was negotiating with the Rabbi for the return of Jews to England, from which they had been banned for four centuries. Margaret Fell wrote two tracts for the Jews, which were published in Holland despite translation problems. Her open letter to Manasseh himself was a chain of the Old Testament quotations best loved by Christians and unlikely to convince a Jew. Her "Loving Salutation to the Seed of Abraham" the next year (1657) was more tender in tone and assumed that the Jews already knew the Light and could trust it to fulfill Jeremiah's "new covenant," the hope of Israel.[15]

Moreover, the role of the Quakers in apocalyptic history gave them a keen though polarized sense of the past. Friends spoke of all Christian history since the Apostles as apostasy. Even the mild Anglicans had declared that the Church of Rome had been corrupt since the Dark Ages; the puritans had pushed back further

14. *Tracts of the Congregational Historical Society, 3,* 201–02, quoted in Armsby, "Quaker View of the State," p. 18. Cf. Nayler, *Works,* pp. 381–82; Fox, *Journal,* Camb., *2,* 12–13. The complex pattern by which a second day of judgment would follow the millennial era of the return of Christ, which the Book of Revelation made traditional, would have fitted the Quaker ideas well, but it is not explicit in most of their writings.

15. Cf. M. Fell, pp. 101 ff., 152 ff.; *JFHS, 28* (1931), p. 13.

the date and depth of the fall from grace of the Roman church, identifying all bishops, vestments, and liturgies as products of the Antichrist. Now Quakers included the orthodox puritans among the members of the "Synagogue of Satan," together with their Presbyterian prototypes in the church of New Testament times.

> It was the generall talke of the preists and professors & other sectary preachers that the false prophetts & the Antichrists shoulde come in the "last days" & that wee were they. And I was moved to open this through the nation howe that . . . it was themselves. . . . For as Christ saide . . . by the fruites yee shall know them. . . . Before the disciples deceased, the antichrists false prophetts & deceivers did come . . . and this "last time" was above 1600 yeeres since. . . . And since has the Apostacy gonne over all nations . . . since the Apostles days.[16]

The Friends regarded themselves as "primitive Christianity revived" in the "last days." They spoke and thought of themselves as the "true church." They rejected the sacraments and ordinances of all other churches throughout history, not simply because the forms were unbiblical or contrary to the "gospel order" but because these groups were not true churches. The true church was not linked to buildings or to the historic succession from the Apostles, or even to the Covenant of the Elect; the true church was known by the power of God's Spirit within it. On this point the Quakers were heirs of the Seekers.

On such a basis the Friends recognized only some individuals and a few small groups to have been truly Christian before them: "A few Hereticks . . . were our Predecessors of old . . . though we go under the name of Hereticks with them." [17] Their confidence in the now visible power of God made them able to accept quietly the upsetting belief that for centuries the vast majority of Christendom had died in apostasy as reprobates. After all, the biblical Israel had at times fallen away, except for a few despised prophets, but God's mercy and power had not failed. And "so if

16. Fox, *Journal*, Camb., *1*, 246–47, 249.
17. Nayler, *Answer to Baxter*, p. 12. Lewis Benson has discussed the basic apostasy of all formal churches as disobedience to the Spirit in "The Early Quaker Vision of the Church," *Quaker Religious Thought*, 2 (1960), 1 ff.

it be but a few Years in comparison, since we, or any of us, were changed and turned to the Lord, yet it was at the time when the Lord . . . saw good to visit us, and we can truly say it was an acceptable day." [18] This was not the Anabaptist vision of the church, however, a church Roger Williams and the Mennonites saw as forever only "a garden in the wilderness," a persecuted minority in an unchristian world. Early Friends, though they shared the Anabaptists' radical attack on the established church and state, shared the puritan belief in God's dominion over history.

The Quakers were thus able to adopt the puritans' vision of England and English history even while rejecting their churchmanship. They took as their own heroes the Protestant martyrs under Mary Tudor and acclaimed the early reformers to whom puritans had looked back: "the Waldenses, Lollards, Hussites, Lutherans and our own noble martyrs who . . . confirmed their religion with their own blood." [19] The puritan doctrine of providence had been applied not only to history in general but to contemporary events (not without occasional personal slant or partisanship). Even Baxter affirmed, with some malice toward the Baptists:

> I am not of their minde that make light of the strange Providences in our military affairs and changes of State, though I think every carnal admirer of them doth not understand them. . . . The more remarkable Providences of our heavy spiritual judgments [show that] the hand of God is apparently gone out against your waies of Separation and Anabaptism. . . . You do but prepare too many for the further downward progresse: Seekers, Ranters, Familists and now Quakers.[20]

Friends shared with all these groups the faith that the English Commonwealth was part of God's unfolding plan of history, so that "in all these overturnings" nothing came to pass "without the knowledge of the Lord." [21] Like the puritans, they interpreted

18. Camm and Audland, *Works*, pp. 225–26. Cf. Fisher, p. 636.

19. Penn, *Witness*, p. 72, from "the Great Case of Liberty." Cf. M. Fell, p. 42; Nayler, *Answer to Baxter*, p. 40.

20. Baxter, *Quakers Catechism*, p. B-1.

21. Alexander Parker, in *Letters of Early Friends*, p. 368, quoted in Armsby, "Quaker View of the State," p. 21. Even Roger Williams, who strongly disagreed about Massachusetts' divine right to dispossess the Indians, saw its founding and Rhode Island's as acts of providence in relation to English Christianity.

current history as a succession of steps by which God's providence moved to complete the unfinished Reformation: "the old monastical, massy ministry and their . . . foggy forms of . . . Holy Water, Latine Letanies, Ave Mari's . . . and such like were sent packing first, and after them the Protestant imitations, (viz.) . . . Easter-Reckonings, . . . Midsummer-Dues, Christening with Crosses, marrying with the ring . . . High-Altar Service, Rayls, costly Windows, together with the large Popish pay of Fat Parsonages . . . Tythes, etc." William Penn long afterward summarized the history of the branches of puritanism in this light (reversing, of course, Baxter's opinion of it):

> The children of the Reformers, if not the Reformers themselves, betook themselves very early to earthly policy and power to uphold and carry on their Reformation. . . . And for worship, there was, for the generality, more of man in it than of God. . . . God was therefore pleased in England to shift us from vessel to vessel. And the next remove [from Anglican to puritan] humbled the ministry, so that they were more strict in preaching, devout in praying, and zealous for keeping the Lord's Day. . . . But even . . . they appeared rigid in their spirits rather than severe in their lives . . . which brought forth another people that were yet more retired and select . . . and under mutual agreements and covenants of fellowship they kept together. . . . They admitted any member to speak or pray as well as their pastor, whom they always chose and not the civil magistrate. . . . Which drove many a step further, and that was into the water, another baptism. . . . It was about that very time . . . that the eternal, wise and good God was pleased to honor and visit this benighted and bewildered nation with His glorious dayspring from on high.[22]

Success was not the ultimate criterion in history, however. Political events were measured by their religious results; so Friends wrote to Cromwell much as he had himself spoken to Parliament: "If ye will not own the Lord in his own work, he will do it another

22. Fisher, pp. 590–91; Penn, *Witness*, pp. 12–16. Cf. Salthouse, *Candle Lighted,* p. 9; Burrough, preface to Fox, *Great Mistery*, and Fox, ibid., 44; Nayler, *Man of Sin*, p. 5. Fox ascribed all of England's woes in religion to Augustine of Canterbury, "Austin the monk and his snap-sack of ceremonies."

way, and you shall be cast by as not worthy, with the rest that were cast out before you." [23]

Friends reacted in two ways toward the actual government of England—as puritans and as obeying only the Spirit. Their national pride in England, "the garden of god, although many wild beastes be In It," [24] was intensified by the fact that God had chosen to begin there His transforming of the world. But English rulers were judged only by their response to the Light and to the Quaker ministry. Nayler wrote encouragingly to the 1653 Parliament of Saints but warned them that God's promise of the rule of the Saints held only while they obeyed the Spirit's guidance. The leading Friends absorbed strongly puritan political attitudes from the Parliamentary armies in which many had fought, and from all the debates, tracts, and hopes of the time. Fox himself wrote to the King of Spain: "Friend, thy Cruelty is come up into remembrance with the Lord . . . in this day of the Lamb wilt thou be recompensed, and thy Inquisitions, thy Fires, thy Swords, thy Torturings, shall not secure thee. . . . Now shall the Lamb and the Saints have the Victory . . . which shall rule all nations with a Rod of Iron . . . as you have killed . . . so shall you perish by the Sword." [25]

Personal friendships with puritans in politics were maintained by many Quakers. In 1656 non-Friends close to Walter Clement asked his release from prison, reminding Major-General Desborough that "at the election here for parliamt men" they had "stood very fast to him and his partie." [26] Gervase Benson and Anthony Pearson, Quakers who served Cromwell as justices of the peace and in various county offices, addressed the Protector and other officials as if they were old colleagues. Pearson had been secretary to Heselrige, one of the "five members" who had led the revolt of Parliament in 1642. George Bishop, who had taken part in the Putney debates while a puritan soldier, remained active in radical politics in Bristol even after becoming a Quaker, as did Dennis Hollister. James Nayler seems to have known of an army petition

23. Camm and Audland, *Works*, pp. 312–13. Cf. Fisher's own address to Parliament in *Works*, pp. 7–8.

24. ARBarc./61, Howgill to Fox from Ireland.

25. Fox, *Doctrinals*, pp. 195–97.

26. Swarth. 1/181 (*EQL* 321), Walter Clement to M. Fell, Olveston, October 4, 1656.

to Parliament in 1653, three months before it was openly presented. In London he held meetings at "Lady Darcy's," attended by many ladies of Cromwell's court, as well as lords, army officers, Sir Harry Vane, and "some of the hyest priests in the cittie." [27] The younger generation of Quakers around London—William Penn, Thomas Ellwood, and William Mead—were still more deeply involved in puritan politics. Isaac Penington was already a well-known writer of puritan tracts, and George Fox the Younger wrote, as a Friend, many tracts echoing the Leveller platform. In addition to the fruits of these friendships in direct Quaker political action, a network of personal contacts paved the way for broader Quaker outlooks and made possible their direct appeals to the governments. Friends denied that they were Levellers, as their opponents frequently claimed; their "conspicuous lack of interest in the contemporary fashion for Constitution-making" [28] came less from putting men above platforms than from putting the Spirit above either.

The printing of Quaker tracts is a good example. Most tracts, though written in prison or following a debate, came from a sense of immediate "leading" from God. But after the manuscripts were approved at Swarthmore Hall (if Fox's wishes were followed), they were delivered by a traveling Friend to the London homes of Amor Stoddard or Gerrard Roberts, who arranged for printing. Swarthmore guaranteed to take several hundred copies each of such tracts, advancing money to cover the costs. The printers, however (especially Thomas Simmonds and Giles Calvert), also handled the largest proportion of tracts from the Levellers, Winstanley's Diggers, Jakob Boehme, and the Family of Love, as well as the Quakers. Calvert's sister Martha, wife of Simmonds, was a leading supporter of James Nayler, and Calvert himself was warmly greeted by Fox, Nayler, and Alexander Parker at a London Friends Meeting in 1655, although neither printer was a Quaker. A year later Calvert was prosecuted by Cromwell's Coun-

27. Swarth. 3/80 (*EQL* 195), Nayler to M. Fell, November 3, 1655. Cf. 3/66 (*EQL* 21) and notes in Nuttall, *EQL*, pp. 88–89, 197; Cole, "Quakers and Politics," pp. 7, 27, 173.

28. Cf. Cole, "Quakers and Politics," p. 127. Friends did not mean to subject rulers to laws of any type as did Overton, Coke, Henry Parker, or the Fifth Monarchy biblicists, each in his special way. The Spirit was always judge of laws as well as of men.

cil for having printed Edward Burrough's tract "A Trumpet of the Lord Sounded." In 1661 Calvert's license to print was again suspended, this time by the antipuritan Royalists, though his wife and a former colleague continued to print under his old insignia of the Black-Spread-Eagle.[29]

The tension between Friends' familiarity with puritans and rigorous dualism about obedience to the Spirit is shown in their attitudes to Oliver Cromwell himself. The Protector was a radical puritan in outlook, and he listened humbly to other men who also sought God's guidance. He was, moreover, committed to freedom of worship for all groups, and even intervened, late in 1655 and throughout 1656, with local justices who had imprisoned Quakers. Characteristically, he defended Friends most strongly during the Nayler crisis, and at quieter times restrained them from interruptions of the parish ministers. Thus Friends approached the Protector very hopefully in their first interviews in 1654. In March, Francis Howgill and John Camm, after eleven days of waiting, were given an hour with Cromwell and found him friendly, but in a later visit they became alarmed because he refused to condemn the parish ministers. Anthony Pearson saw him in July, after ten days of asking through friends at court, but gave him a characteristic message while "walking on the leads on the house topp":

> I showed him what great thinges the lord had done in the north wch was goeing over England & should passe over the whole Earth . . . & now was the lord comeing to establise his owne law & to sett upp righteousness in the earth & to throw downe all oppressors, & I showed him that now . . . should be . . . noe more . . . warrs & fightings without, for the seed was redeemed out of all earthly thinges & that nature whence warrs arise, wch are from the lust . . . & then I showed him the way how the lord had raised upp the seed . . . & then declared to him the cruell persecutions . . . & lett him see how the guilt fell upon his head . . . & the injustice of Q. Maryes Law; there he stopped me & began

---

29. See Altha E. Terry, "Giles Calvert, Mid-Seventeenth Century English Bookseller and Publisher" (Columbia University, 1937) and its summary in *JFHS*, 35 (1938), 45–49. Also Swarth. 1/162 (*EQL* 167), 1/272 (*EQL* 262). On press censorship see Haller, *Liberty*, chap. 5; Lloyd, *Social History*, chap. 11.

a long discourse to justify that law . . . & in his witt laboured to perswade [the bystanders] against what I sayd, & told them the Light of Christ was naturall, & that the light within had ledd the Ranters & all that followed it into all manner of wildnesses . . . & [he] justified the preists.[30]

When Pearson began to attack the courtiers again, Cromwell finally had him escorted out, leaving Pearson convinced—until their next interview—that the Protector was wholly hardened against God.

From this time on, Quaker appeals to Cromwell, whether in print or in person, usually concerned tithes or persecution. On some occasions Friends implied that it was enough to hope that the government would allow greater freedom for the Spirit to work through the Quakers, but the shift in outlook was not basic. The very warning that Dewsbury wrote to Cromwell, causing his arrest for sedition in 1655, reaffirmed the hope of converting the state, which was implied in the apocalyptic challenge of the Lamb's War:

> Thus saith the Lord God of Heaven and Earth to thee, Oliver Cromwell, Why does thou slight my Counsel, and harden thy Heart against it, which I declare to thee by my Sons and Daughters, and is witnessed in thy Conscience by my Word in thee, which called on thee to trust no longer in the Arm of Flesh, nor seek great things for thy self, as those did [whom] I drove out before Thee in my Wrath . . . and hath given thee power into thy Hand who promised me in the day of thy Distress . . . thou wouldest take away all these Unrighteous Laws. . . . If thou wilt not hearken to my Counsel . . . I will hasten the day of my Righteous Judgments upon thee.[31]

The tract for which Burrough and Calvert were indicted was even more boldly theocratic: God would overthrow Cromwell unless

---

30. Swarth. 3/34 (*EQL* 70), Anthony Pearson to Fox. At Pearson's next interview, he persuaded Cromwell to order the freeing of Aldam from York, and was much more cordial: cf. Swarth. 1/216 (*EQL* 95), and Braithwaite, *Beginnings*, p. 436.
31. Dewsbury, *Works*, pp. 4, 7. Cf. Caton Manuscript No. 1 as quoted in Cole, "Quakers and Politics," p. 38; William Dewsbury, *A Discovery of the Ground Whence the Persecution Did Arise* (London, 1655); Nuttall, *EQL*, p. 111 nn.

he repented.[32] George Fox expressed the puritan idea of a Holy War against popery in sanguine terms: "Invite all them that professe against the Pope, in all Nations, [to] joyn with thee against him, & do not loose thy Dominion nor authority . . . and let thy souldiers go forth with a free willing heart, that thou may rock Nations as a cradle."[33] Fox was not consistent: like Pearson, he had already spoken decisively against "the arm of flesh," though the Quaker "peace testimony" was not yet clearly worked out. Yet the basic protest of Friends against war was still against the lust and lordship from which wars spring. Fox made it clear to Cromwell that only if he were absolutely disinterested and "thundered down . . . deceit" could God grant that "the King of France should have bowed his neck under thee, the Pope should have withered as in winter, the Turk in all his fatness should have smoked."[34] It was quite fitting that Fox and Morford in their last interviews with Cromwell should have warned Cromwell primarily against assuming the crown, lest he lose "the power of God."[35] Pyott, Halhead, Salthouse, and others in tracts of this year 1657-58 gave the same warning.

Cromwell had now committed his authority in support of tithes for the parish ministers, so that from 1656 onward many Quakers were imprisoned for failure to pay tithes alone. He allowed Benson, Pearson, and John Crook to lose their commissions as justices, and other Friends to be dismissed from the army, yet he kept Quakers in his household retinue (probably Mary Saunders, Lettice Shaine, and Charles Harvey). He had ordered Thomas Aldam's release from prison and received Aldam and Fox cordially and at length in 1655. In the years of sharper conflict after Nayler's trial in 1656, Cromwell still received Friends: Fox and Morford, Thomas Rawlinson, Mary Howgill, Ann Blaykling, Edward Pyott, and perhaps George Bishop.[36] When he died in 1658, his effigy was carried in a state funeral, and Edward Burrough took it as a symbol "that all men might see the first cause is lost, and that zeale which his Kindred and Army had once in their hearts against

32. Burrough, *Trumpet of the Lord*, pp. 2–3.

33. MS Letter (1654) quoted in Cole, "Quakers and Politics," p. 67.

34. Devonshire House Portfolio 9/79, quoted in Braithwaite, *Beginnings*, p. 440.

35. Fox, *To the Protector and Parliament*, p. 62. Cf. *Journal*, Camb., *1*, 260.

36. *ESP*, pp. 6–10, 14–19; Swarth. 3/11 (*EQL* 374), Thomas Rawlinson to M. Fell, March 26, 1657.

Popery is extinguished, & people turned again to gaze after Images.
. . . A pitty struck through me for once noble *Oliver* that is now
dead, and then I said . . . is it ended all in this, all his former
good Service for God & the Nations, all his victories . . . and his
beating down Superstition." [37]

The Quakers never formulated a systematic theory of the state
until the 1680s when Penn, in writing constitutions, blended
Quakerism and Whig liberalism. But clearly they did not consider
the state as in essence anti-Christian, for they regarded all rulers
as under the government of Christ and as magistrates for him.
Some writers, especially in later periods of persecution, began to
speak more often of the state as a policeman, merely intended to
punish evildoers. An Anabaptist would have preferred that the
unhappy lot of the policeman be given to non-Christians; but
Quakers said that if God's justice were to be enforced, it could and
must be by men under the Spirit: "As Government came from
God, so the righteous execution of it depends upon God. Every
man needs God's help daily, else he may easily err in his course;
and governments and governors need God's help much more, in
the many intricacies and perplexities which they often meet
with." [38] Any non-Christian magistrate who refused the Spirit's
leading was in fact rebuked by Friends. On this basis they interpreted Paul's phrase "be subject unto the higher powers" as "a
power which is of God, a power they are still subject to for conscience sake, whether there be any Persons to execute that Power
or no . . . and is one with that in the conscience." [39] A similar
doctrine was used by John Knox, Buchanan, and many other Calvinists to justify godly resistance to tyrants, and notably by Parliament in the revolution against Charles I. Yet Friends did not like
the Calvinist's appeal to natural law or the Bible, much less to the
lesser magistrates and lower authorities in society, for an authority
above kings: they looked only to the Spirit.

Early Friends believed that the Lord would entrust the estab-

37. Edward Burrough, *Works*, pp. 457–61. Cf. Cole, "Quaker and Politics," pp.
46 ff., 76–77; Braithwaite, *Beginnings*, chap. 17; ARBarc./24.

38. Penington, as quoted in Robert Leach, *The Inward Journey of Isaac Penington* (Wallingford, Penn., Pendle Hill, 1943), p. 35. Cf. Fox, *Journal*, Camb., *1*, 83.
Fox, *Saul's Errand*, p. 18; Nayler, *Works*, pp. 300–01; Burrough, *Works*, pp. 598–606.

39. Nayler, *Man of Sin*, p. 43. Cf. Fox, *Journal*, Camb., *1*, 131–34; Camm and
Audland, *Works*, p. 109.

lishment and enforcement of the law to faithful and just men. They rarely defined in detail how such godly rulers were to receive power, but the rule of the Saints did not mean equalitarian democracy:

> Many who are not Free-men of some Corporations or have not Free-land are not permitted to chuse Parliament men . . . though they be far more honest and understanding than men that . . . have such Land. But it hath been the complaint of the soberest . . . men in several Counties, when they should have chosen Parliament men that they could not chuse such a man as . . . would act singly for the good of the People of God . . . because they were over-voted by the wild, disaffected People . . . stirred up by their Priests. . . . The flock of Christ is a little flock . . . a Parliament that is chosen by the most voices are not like to act for God.[40]

This was the spirit of the Parliament of Saints. Early Friends, having been socially disinherited, had no sense of the nation as a social organism from which to draw a constitution, nor any concept of uniform natural law to supplement daily direct dependence on the Spirit. They did not, even in theory, ultimately separate the state from the true church: "The Magistrate that is in the power of Christ . . . is a member of the church, and knows who worships God and who worships Idols." [41] Like the Massachusetts puritans, Friends wanted pure worship alone to be protected by the ruler.

Direct political action of Friends—though "often in spirit . . . att the dores of Oliver's . . . house"—was in practice largely limited before 1658 to appeals against persecution and tithes. The Lamb's War was for the most part a preaching campaign. Fox and others had sometimes addressed assize judges personally to protest against unfair price or wage laws, complex legal entanglements, and capital punishment. Robert Barwicke and Aldam at York had been excluded from serving on juries only because they refused oaths and hat honor in court.[42] Gervase Benson urged Friends to

---

40. G. Fox the Younger, *A Collection*, pp. 89–90. Cf. Edward Burrough, *To the Parliament of the Commonwealth* (London, 1659).

41. Fox, *Great Mistery*, p. 96.

42. See Aldam's letter, ARBarc./122 (1654); Aldam's letter to the judge, ARBarc./72; the York Assizes engrossment for Fox, ARBarc./128; and Fox, *Journal*, Nickalls, p. 65; also Nayler, *Works*, pp. 136–37, on lawyers.

vote in the York election of 1656, and Bishop was active at Bristol, but Quakers usually expected more from Cromwell than from local politics. Events in London were more closely reflected in Quaker appeals and petitions than their lofty language indicates,[43] but the stability of the Protectorate is demonstrated by the indifference of Friends to the Fifth Monarchist plots or any other proposals for replacing Cromwell. In September 1658, however, Cromwell died, and within a month a group of twenty prominent Friends (among them Pearson, Crook, Fisher, Billing, Curtis, Stoddard, and Gerrard Roberts) presented a long petition to the Council of State and the new Protector, Richard Cromwell. A list of 115 Friends then in prison was enclosed, concerning whom the Council requested and received in due course detailed statements from their judges and jailers. (Sixty had been arrested over tithes, forty-two for interrupting ministers, five for refusing hat honor, three as vagabonds, two each over oaths and illegal meetings, and three for other charges). The petition itself summarized the issues on which Quaker consciences conflicted with the laws. It included an appeal against the long delays in court, the high fees of officials, and the greed of lawyers, but ended on a note still apocalyptic:

> Now is the lambe risen & riseing to make warr with the great dragon, the beast, & false prophetts . . . & the saintes shall have the victory. Therefore lett all Kings, Princes, Rulers, Magistrates be warned not to take part with the beast, nor to vphold with their power the false prophetts [i.e. the parish ministers]. But leaue Christ Jesus in his saintes to manage the warre, whose warrfarr is not carnall . . . yett are they mighty through God to the pulling downe of strongholds. . . . that way may be made for the lord Jesus Christ who is comeing to reign . . . himself. . . . And we leaue it to that of god in you all to weigh & Consider, whether it be not tyme to reforme both Lawes, Courts & officers.[44]

The political crisis continued to present new challenges, however. With poor foresight, Friends approved when the army was suspicious of the mainly presbyterian Parliament and forced Rich-

---

43. See Nuttall's introduction, *EQL*, pp. 14–16.
44. *ESP*, pp. 43–44.

ard Cromwell to dismiss it.[45] The army leaders then recalled the
Rump Parliament, which had first established Oliver Cromwell's
power, and forced Richard to abdicate. Radical puritans and re-
publicans were dominant for the moment under the leadership
of Sir Harry Vane. George Bishop, who had already written to the
generals in support of the Rump's recall, rejoiced. By quick
Quaker action, within six weeks a massive deputation was organized to protest imprisonments, it submitted two petitions, with
15,000 and 7,000 signatures respectively (the latter entirely of
women) to urge the abolition of tithes. During this same year,
1659–60, there were published the three tracts most carefully listing the legal reforms Quakers wanted: Edward Billing's *Mite of
Affection . . . in 31 Proposals,* Thomas Lawson's *Appeal to the
Parliament Concerning the Poor, that There May Not Be a
Beggar in England,* and George Fox's own *59 Proposals.*[46] The
main legal reforms suggested were to publish all statutes in English, to decentralize and shorten law procedures for the sake of
poor plaintiffs, and to end capital punishment for theft. Quakers
could list in bitter detail the needed improvements in jails and
jailers. Tithes and the parish ministry were to be abolished, and
imprisonment ended for refusing oaths and hat honor and for
vagrancy charges against traveling preachers or those proclaiming
judgment in fairs and markets. These issues were interpreted only
from the Quaker viewpoint. The puritan concept of the state as
moral supervisor was upheld, however, in Quaker demands for
the abolition of images, cards, and dice, "Gameing-houses, Musick-
houses, bowls, Shoffel-board, and Fidlings," actors, May-day games,
and any sport "that pleases the fleshly mind": "Let all this wearing
of gold Lace and costly attire . . . be ended, and cloath the naked,
and feed the hungry with the superfluity." [47] Billing wanted pen-
sions for disabled Cromwellian soldiers or their families and rein-
statement of the radicals whom Cromwell had dismissed. All three

45. Elizabeth Adams had broken a jar at Parliament's door as a Jeremianic
protest, which showed where Quaker sympathies lay. A group of prominent Friends,
offering to lie in prisons so that Quaker prisoners could be released, came to the
bar of Parliament and were rejected.

46. On economic proposals in these tracts see above, p. 171.

47. Fox, *59 Particulars,* pp. 12–13. There was also a marked rise in general
Quaker tract-writing, from 75 tracts in 1658 to 180 in 1659 (Joseph Smith, *Descrip-
tive Catalogue of Friends Books,* 4 vols. London, 1867, cited by Cole, "Quakers and
Politics," p. 90 n.).

Quaker tracts urged restraint of rents and relief for the poor, the old, the blind, and the lame. Billing also proposed annual parliaments chosen from all religious sects, or from redrawn voting districts, in accordance with Leveller and Fifth Monarchist ideas.

Vane and the puritan radicals in power desired or discussed most of these political reforms, but before enacting them, they found they needed desperately to secure their own position against the royalist rising of Sir George Booth, against the mass of orthodox puritans, and in the end against the puritan army itself. "They searcht many houses last first day at night for caveleres & papists," wrote Rawlinson from London in May.[48] In this crisis, when all the gains of the twenty-year revolution were at stake, the radical puritans turned for support even to the Quakers. Tracts by Fuce, George Fox the Younger, and Humphrey Bache show the intensity of Quaker sympathy; the millennium had never seemed nearer, or more in danger. Penington, Burrough, and Fox were cautious about Vane, but equally hopeful. Alexander Parker wrote in June, when Vane's committee had begun to consider the imprisoned Quakers:

> the Comittee of Parliament . . . examine things very fully, and whether they doe anything or nothing as to the enlargemt of friends its serviceable that the wickednesse of greedy and covetous men are brought to Light; much cannot be expected from men in that nature, for though there be a change of names, yet the old nature is still standing. . . . But whatever the Consequence be, this I know and feele, that Truth hath great advantage and an open dore is further made for spreading the truth abroad. The Lord prosper his work.[49]

Gerrard Roberts and some leading London Friends asked the Quaker meetings of every county to send up lists of men who would be acceptable as justices of the peace, and of others who were known persecutors. Many answers were sent, some lengthy and explicit.

The crucial decision came in August, when Anthony Pearson and George Fell (like his father, a non-Friend) raised a force of

48. Swarth. 3/10 (*EQL* 478), T. Rawlinson to M. Fell, London, May 1659.
49. Swarth. 1/84 (*EQL* 485), Alex. Parker to M. Fell, London, June 22, 1659. Cf. 1/145 (*EQL* 484) from Robert Benbricke.

militia to meet Booth's royalist revolt, and the government named
among the national Commissioners of Militia seven Bristol Quakers and apparently fourteen others in London and elsewhere.
Parker wrote to Fox that he "left friends att Bristoll pretty well,
onely in some litle straite about their acting as Commissioners.
. . . I can neither persuade them to it nor dissuade them from it; I
desire to have a word from thee." [50] Fox, however, was entering a
ten-week period of great darkness and depression, partly due to
the pressure of these decisions and the disintegration of the radical
puritan movement, and partly due to physical exhaustion. He
wrote to Friends at Bristol a very confused letter urging that those
enrolled as militia commissioners "get amongst them & . . . in-
forme them in the things that is good . . . & torments the contrary. . . . [But] keep free to beare testimony to the good & agst
the evill & keep Authority over the unjust, Answering the Just in
every one." [51] By January of 1660, Fox had recovered himself and
spoke for a clear policy of disinvolvement and the use of purely
spiritual weapons, but by then events had outrun him. Other
radical puritans were drifting and dividing even more than the
Friends. When the army suspended the Rump Parliament in October, many Friends, such as Howgill, approved, since the Parliament had not yet abolished tithes. Parker found men hungrier
than ever for his preaching, and he clung to the providence which
would make "all these overturneings work for good unto the people of God." [52] The army leaders, however, and especially the garrisons under Monck in Scotland, were in fact arranging to restore
a king and were negotiating with the son of Charles I.

The radical puritans resigned from Monck's army, and presently
from the government, in despair. Despite all Cromwell's efforts to
balance and combine them, the radical and the orthodox puritans
had defeated each other; in 1660, as during most of the preceding

50. Swarth. 3/143 (*EQL* 488), Alex. Parker to Fox, August 7, 1659. On the events
of this crucial summer see Cole, "Quakers and Politics," pp. 142–46; James Maclear,
"Quakerism and the End of the Interregnum; a Chapter in the Domestication of
Radical Puritanism," *Church History*, 19, 240–71; Tolles, *Atlantic Culture*, chap. 3.
The Quaker militia commissioners included Pearson, Stoddard, Pyott, Thomas
Curtis, and Dennis Hollister. George Bishop's name was vetoed by Parliament. A
lesser Friend, John Hodgson, apparently re-enlisted in the army.

51. For Fox's answer, dictated and far from clear, see Swarth. 7/157.

52. Swarth. 1/168 (*EQL* 496), Alex. Parker to M. Fell, Chalfont, November 8,
1659. Cf. 4/268 (*EQL* 503), Will Caton to Fox, December 20, 1659.

half-century, the balance of power was held by Presbyterians who ultimately hated "the sectaries" even more than they hated bishops or the King. As the Anglicans and Royalists re-emerged, popular impatience broke out against Puritanism in general. Quakers found mobs hostile, and spoke more and more often of "the rude people," especially apprentices, "some beatinge there masters & not sufferinge the shops to be opened, threatninge friends who opened theres." [53] Army units themselves kicked and beat Quakers at Meetings. When the King was finally installed in May, Friends were "pulled out of theire meetings & imprisoned, others thereabout have had halters putt about their necks . . . for not drinkeinge the Kings health (as they call it); another at Gloust., his beare thrown in his face . . . & lipps cutt with the glasse for the same cause." [54] The old Cromwellian soldier, George Fox the Younger, wrote directly to King Charles himself in fury against so much drink in such a cause: "How much Wine and Strong Drink hath bin devoured in waste by peoples drinking of healths unto thee . . . and what abundance of wood hath bin wasted and devoured in makeing of great Bone-fires . . . to rejoyce because of Thy coming . . . and such noises . . . by Shooting of Guns . . . by ringing of Bells, and by . . . shouting like riotous mad men." [55]

The Friends were nevertheless as confident as ever that God's power and the apocalyptic kingdom were not set back but indeed advanced by Charles' coming. As God had used the kings of Assyria and Babylon, so He was using Charles Stuart—as they told him to his face. He had claimed the throne as Charles II from the moment of his father's death, but Burrough, Nayler, Salthouse, and George Fox the Younger explicitly ignored this in explaining to the King the lesson of recent history:

> Concerning thy Father, and those that took His Part, there was an eminent hand of God in breaking them down. . . . [God] saw that those that took part with thy Father did glory in their Wisdom, Riches, Nobility, stoutness and strength, and vaunted themselves over them that were made of the same blood. He . . . did then appear in contemptible Instru-

53. Swarth. 4/134 (*EQL* 517), Dewsbury to M. Fell, March 1660.
54. Swarth. 1/321 (*EQL* 529), Clement to M. Fell, June 10, 1660.
55. G. Fox the Younger, *Noble Salutation*, pp. 13–14.

ments . . . Tradesmen, Ploughmen, Servants and the like
. . . And in several of them there was once a tender honest
good Principle, in the day when they were low . . . and true
Desires . . . after a just Liberty. But . . . when they had
Rest and Fulnesse, they forgot the Lord . . . and they forgot
the Oppression of their Brethren also . . .

Then the Lord raised up many Prophets and Servants, and
sent [these Quakers] . . . and plainly showed unto them
what the Lord required at their hands . . . but they would
not hearken . . . so that then the Anger of the Lord was
kindled against them . . . and then they began to Divide and
Split amongst themselves, and . . . their Courage began to
fail . . . and they wrought their own destruction. . . . And
if thou dost not speedily seek to stop this abounding ungodliness which flowes in this Nation . . . verily an evident hand
of God shall come upon thee. . . . Let no man deceive thee,
by perswading thee that . . . the Kingdom was thy own
proper right . . . for all the Kingdoms of the Earth are
properly the Lords.

Charles Stuart must either be converted to God and ruled
by him, or he cannot rightly rule for God in this nation.[56]

For the first months of the Restoration there was firm ground
for the Quaker hope that Charles' government might be more
tolerant than the last days of Cromwell's. Monck intended toleration to reconcile the Baptists to the return of bishops and Presbyterian rule. Charles himself was a skeptic, quietly moving toward
Catholicism; he genuinely disliked persecution. His Declaration
of Breda in April 1660 had placed on record his promise of freedom to worship for all men, should Parliament approve. The rest
of the year was an easier time for Friends. The Presbyterians in
Parliament, however, even while negotiating for an inclusive national church, rejected the King's proposal for a system combining
presbyteries and bishops, for the very reason that it allowed free
sectarian worship alongside the Establishment. Within a year the
Calvinists found they had destroyed themselves by their refusal,
for by then the new Cavalier Parliament and the bishops at the

56. Ibid., pp. 5–10. Cf. Edward Burrough, *A Presentation of Wholesome Informa-
tion unto the King of England* (London, 1660); Burrough, *Works*, pp. 702–08;
Salthouse, *Candle Lighted*.

Savoy Conference earlier in 1661 would make no compromises
even with Presbyterians. Francis Howgill had already seen what
the trend would mean:

> Oh *England!* . . . Consider in what State thou wast twenty
> Years ago, and what Complaints filled every Corner of the
> Land . . . by Reason of many wicked Laws . . . and what
> Innovations and Impositions were made upon tender Con-
> sciences by those called Bishops . . . who were but a Stem
> sprung from that corrupt Root of Rome. . . . The Lord
> heard the Cry of the Oppressed . . . and many precious Men
> ventured their Lives and lost their Blood. . . . Oh People
> of *England!* Was it only a Form of Government . . . that ye
> pursued after? or was it not . . . Freedom it self . . . Right-
> eousness itself, that the heavy Yoak might be done away?
> . . . Oh People! will nothing satisfie you but *Egypt* again? [57]

The puritans were not under strong pressure until the Act of
Uniformity and other parts of the Clarendon Code of 1661–62
and did not face outright persecution until the Conventicle Act
two years later. In the meantime, the Friends were in more immediate danger and were jailed by the hundreds under a specially
written Quaker Act prompted by a suspicion that they had been
involved in a frantic little plot of the Fifth Monarchist Baptists
early in 1661. The leading radical puritans had already been executed for the death of Charles I, and the Quakers refused the
oaths of allegiance and supremacy, which would have turned away
the worst suspicions.

In three tracts written during the months when they still hoped
for toleration, and in a formal declaration to the King written by
Fox and the other leading Quakers two days after the Fifth Monarchists were hanged, Friends analyzed and spelled out clearly
their most distinctive doctrine about the Christian and the state:
their Testimony against war and fighting. The Quaker Peace
Testimony was announced through the streets at a time when they
needed to prove that they could be trusted not to revolt:

> We know that wars and fightings proceed from the lusts of
> men . . . out of which lusts the Lord hath redeemed us.

57. Howgill, *Works,* pp. 333–38.

> . . . We do utterly deny . . . all outward war & strife. . . .
> That Spirit of Christ by which we are guided is not change-
> able, so as to command us from a thing as evil, and again to
> move to do it. . . . The Spirit of Christ will never move us
> to fight and war against any man with outward weapons,
> neither for the Kingdom of Christ nor for the Kingdoms of
> this World.[58]

This was not a new Quaker teaching. Yet a few Friends had, until
then, been soldiers, and the Quaker faith in the kingdom of Christ
and the coming rule of the Saints had not been weakened. Before
the Peace Testimony can be fully understood, it is necessary to
consider the issues that Friends raised as to persecution, toleration,
and the relation of church and state.

58. Fox's declaration (1684 edition), quoted in Braithwaite, *Second Period,*
pp. 12–13. Cf. Richard Hubberthorne, *Something That Lately Passed in Discourse
between the King and Richard Hubberthorne* (London, 1660).

8

Persecution, Toleration, and the Peace Testimony

Though we walk in the flesh, we do not war after the flesh:
(For the weapons of our warfare are not carnal, but mighty through God to the pulling down of strong holds;)
Casting down imaginations, and every high thing that exalteth itself against the knowledge of God . . .
And he said unto me, My grace is sufficient for thee: for my strength is made perfect in weakness. Most gladly therefore will I rather glory in my infirmities, that the power of Christ may rest upon me. II Cor. 10:3–5, 12:9

FROM the outset, Friends expected persecution and hostility. Even under the Commonwealth they had been in prison in at least 2,100 cases, whether for contempt of court, disturbance of the peace, or refusal of tithes. In the sunniest year, 1654, the Swarthmore letters themselves report at least twenty-two new imprisonments; no foreign country, even Holland, had a clear record. In principle, persecution seemed inevitable, since the Lamb's War itself required struggle and suffering: "that spiritt which makes the Just & the good & seede of God to suffer within is the same that makes to suffer without when it is cast out within . . . and all the suffringes without is nothing to the suffringes within." [1] Judgment was the sign of the Spirit's activity and the only way to peace. They recognized the anger they aroused in proud and powerful hearers as the same resistance that they had fought within themselves. It

---

1. Fox, *Journal*, Camb., *1*, 288. Cf. Penington, *Works*, *1*, 463, 467. Fox said (*Journal*, Camb., *1*, 522) that 3,170 Friends had suffered before the Restoration. A petition to Parliament in 1659 named 1,860 cases during 1653–59 besides 144 still in prison (Braithwaite, *Beginnings*, p. 454). Even in Holland, Birkhead spent two years in prison (Swarth. 4/256, *EQL* 507).

was an inborn part of the "natural man": the "Word of God . . . ever comes at his own Will, and not at the Will of Man, but in a Cross to it." [2]

Violence was thus only the devil's method of hiding the real location of evil so as to turn men away from the warning within and without: "The Enemy . . . will set them to war against the Creature, and destroy the Creation, rather than that of his which defiles the Creature. And this cannot be avoided any other way but by minding the Light of Christ." [3] This insight about the projection of men's guilt and hostility underlay Quaker ideas on both war and persecution. Ultimately, outward war against evil would be futile because "the *government* of *Antichrist* is *in the heart,* not *onely* of *one* man in *some Nations,* but *in the hearts* of *all* such men." [4]

We may suggest, since the opponents of early Friends did so, that the Quakers' hatred of the world and their love of combat, however nonviolent, was partly a projection of self-hatred. Friends saw their outward cleavage from society as the by-product of their own inward separation from evil, but the world still represented temptation; thus the old Adam was perhaps not as dead as they believed. A change as drastic as that in the outward lives of early Friends could indeed hardly have been made without struggle. Self-will was the basic evil they fought, both in other men and in themselves, and not a mere scapegoat; yet the warmth and unity within their groups may have required this heightened hatred of the world. Small sects often seem to achieve remarkable sweetness, love, and mutual acceptance within their fellowship, along with a spectacular bitterness against nonmembers and backsliders. Perhaps resentments are thus transferred; this may be the price human nature must pay, since few men can avoid hating somewhat.

Friends expected to suffer as they shared in the Lamb's War; they also expected to win. Victory would come partly in spite of suffering and partly because of it, whenever their own pride and their antagonists' was thereby broken: "Dear Friends, let none suffer that to have Place in your Hearts, which would say, why is it thus . . . the Trial must yet be great, before the Dross be

2. Fisher, p. 3.
3. Nayler, *Works,* p. 364.
4. Burrough, *Antichrist's Government,* p. 45. Cf. Fox, *Journal,* Camb., *1,* 305.

separated from the pure Gold; for the Lord our God is about to work a thorow Work in the Earth." [5] Their suffering was deliberately brought to bear upon the consciences of their opponents. Only by wounding the conscience could the Spirit free the Seed within any man. Friends investigated cases of persecutors who had consequently been convinced: Cheshire reported that "Richard Sale, who was a constable to convay Richd Hubberthorne as a vagabond, was after convinced, then persecuted alsoe, & put in Litle Ease, the hole in the Rock" at Chester.[6] Although many sects have considered suffering a mark of the true church, it represents a negative part of their apocalyptic outlook, a sign of the increasing power of Antichrist and the nearness of deliverance. Friends, however, saw it as a positive setting for the Lamb's victories, and they went out of their way to seek out and confront their persecutors. In 1663 Fox said:

> they tolde mee that Coll. Kirby had sent his leifetenant there to search for mee, whoe had searched both boxes and trunkes for mee at Swarthmore. And as I was lyinge in bed, I was moved of the Lord to goe the next day to Coll. Kirbey's house . . . and soe I tolde him I came to visitt him, understandinge that hee would have seene mee . . . & he said . . . hee had nothinge against mee, but saide that M: ffell must not keepe great meetinges att her house, for . . . they met contrary to the act [of Uniformity].[7]

Friends responded to persecution as to a battle cry, and, at Launceston in 1656 and in Boston in the five years following, this converging attack of Quaker itinerants broke the back of the resistance. In the literature written from prison in the 1660s, when all the puritan groups were harshly persecuted, there is a marked contrast between the spirit with which Friends and others met it. The orthodox puritans stressed humility under arrest, sought to overcome their own impatience and bitterness, and warned each

5. Banks, pp. 173–74.
6. *FPT*, p. 18.
7. Fox, *Journal*, Camb., 2, 38. Cf. Bunyan, *Grace Abounding*, pp. 79–95; *George Fox, An Epistle to All My Dear Friends in America* (Swarthmore, Lancs., 1675); "Testimony of Irish Friends" in Burnyeat, *Truth Exalted;* George Bishop, *The Warnings of the Lord to the Men of This Generation* (London, 1660), p. 41; Burrough, *Trumpet of the Lord*, p. 53.

other against hating their persecutors (though, like the Friends, they noted some catastrophes that had fallen on their worst foes). Friends, however, wrote fiery tracts and letters to and about their tormentors and made persecution a contest, and a means for growth in power. "There is a summer religion," wrote Fox, "that is up and flourisheth while the sun shineth. . . . But this is not the nature of the sheep of Christ . . . but the sheep wil get atop of the highest hil, and mountain, and set their backs and tails against the storme and tempests, and bleat for one another; and when the dogs are abroad among the sheep, they wil run together . . . and so Christs sheep beareth fruite in the winter stormes." [8] Amid pain and injustice, Quakers did learn the spirit of patience, but persecution itself was a mark of the Antichrist they had enlisted to conquer.

In tracts for religious liberty, therefore, Friends drew no line between pleas for toleration and basic appeals demanding the hearer's total conversion. Persecution or conversion were the only responses that Quakers expected in the Lamb's War. Toleration was indeed the subject of more tracts than any other public issue in seventeenth-century England, especially among the Baptists, but between 1650 and 1670 Friends wrote more such pamphlets than any other group. Modern scholars have carefully studied several churches' arguments for toleration as used in different periods and places.[9] A similar study in detail of the early Quaker tracts is enlightening.

Religious liberty is basically each man's freedom to tell and respond to God's truth. It is quite distinct from freedom of thought about religion. Friends, in demanding religious liberty, were in no more doubt than were the Catholics and Presbyterians

8. Notes (evidently on a sermon by Fox) by Thomas Thompson, quoted in _JFHS,_ 28 (1931), 50. On attitudes in facing persecution see Gerald R. Cragg, _Puritanism in the Period of the Great Persecution_ (Cambridge, Cambridge University Press, 1957), pp. 67–76, 82–84, 119; Fox, _Doctrinals,_ pp. 222, 308; Camm and Audland, _Works,_ p. 203.

9. Cf. Freund, _Die Idee de Toleranz;_ Jordan, _Development of Toleration;_ Kühn, _Toleranz und Offenbarung;_ Nuttall, _Visible Saints,_ chap. 5. In general, the Baptists and Congregationalists argued from the free and uncoerced nature of conscience, with rationalistic and humanistic arguments already added by the Baptists before 1640. These had been used by Acontius and Chillingworth earlier and were taken up by Milton, Walwyn, and Overton (cf. Haller, _Liberty,_ chap. 5). Outright skepticism was used in argument mainly by Hales.

in their day as to where truth lay and what response God demanded. His own Spirit was at work: "Alas, poor Mortals! Think you to limit that which is Eternal? . . . If you can . . . dry up the vast Ocean with your breath . . . then may you limit the Holy One, and drown his Israel in the sea." [10] Therefore, the demand for liberty was always presented as a warning to those who stood in God's way: Beware lest "you be found fighters against God, you having seen what he hath done to those who withstood him before you. . . . Now this God requires it at your Hands, that you stop not his work, nor hinder his Spiritual Kingdom." [11] This "argument of Gamaliel" (cf. Acts 5:39) was a favorite among Commonwealth tract-writers. From some it showed real humility or skepticism about man's ability to know absolute religious truth, but Quakers never meant it to imply relativism about the Spirit's infallibility.[12]

Another form of relativism was used by many non-Quakers to distinguish the essentials of faith from the adiaphora, which were indifferent to salvation. A broad, comprehensive national church might tolerate variation in nonessentials, as Cromwell hoped to do, or, conversely, this distinction could be used by men like Bishop Laud to enforce a uniform liturgy precisely because no souls were endangered by unessential details. But Quakers could not speak this way. The Spirit led to truth in every area: "There is such a thing as heresie in itself," conceded Burrough. "Heresie is somewhat in Practice of Worship and in point of Faith and Doctrine that is either contrary to or different from the perfect Truth of the Gospel of Christ." [13] In worship it is wholly "his own . . . that the Lord accepts . . . and so here all Indifferency hath an end." [14]

Rationalism, like relativism, was never a starting point in the Quakers' arguments, though they sometimes appealed to reason when opponents were inconsistent. John Milton's argument in support of free speech—that truth has an innate power which can be trusted to overcome evil—is really based on faith in the power

10. Martin Mason's broadside *To the Parliament* (n.p., n.d.). Cf. Fox, *Journal*, Camb., *1*, 235.

11. Nayler, *Works*, pp. 188–89.

12. Cf. Fisher, pp. 59, 742, etc.

13. Burrough, *Antichrist's Government*, pp. 16–17.

14. George Bishop, *A Little Treatise Concerning Things Indifferent* (n.p., 1663), pp. 14, 18.

of human reason and not in the Spirit of God. "Though all the winds of doctrine were let loose . . . whoever knew truth put to the worse." [15] Truth as the Friends experienced it, however, condemned the puritan's intellectualism and awakened his conscience.

The sacredness of conscience was naturally a basic argument for toleration, used by Friends as well as by other groups. They felt it an offense against God if the true conscientiousness and tenderness of any man was crushed. Persecution is evil because "the Lordship over conscience . . . is God's alone." [16] Friends knew that some men had not reached fullness of Light; they also knew that men's self-will might masquerade as conscience. But coercion even in the name of truth destroyed real obedience to the Light; it could never produce faith. It might produce hypocrites who outwardly conformed without facing the evil within them, or it might lead sensitive men to "make Shipwrack of Conscience" and lose what faith they had.[17] Though conscience was necessary as being man's means of responding to the Light, only the Light itself was good; conscience was not an end in itself. Early Friends always felt that persecution was wrong not because it hindered but because it exalted human freedom. All seventeenth-century churches believed that conscience had to be rightly taught and led: the Catholics depended on the apostolic hierarchy for guidance, the puritans on the Bible, the Anglicans on right reason, and the Friends on the Spirit. Quakers assumed that every man's conscience would respond to the Spirit and lead him to Quakerism. Their pleas for conscience never undercut their claim of absolute authority for their own leadings by the Spirit.

The Friends drew their most numerous arguments for toleration directly from the Bible. They used as fully as Cromwell's Baptists the classic passages: the advice of Gallio and Gamaliel, the parable of wheat and tares, the fate of the Old Testament persecutors from Cain and Pharaoh to Nebuchadnezzar. Though ap-

15. John Milton, "Areopagitica," in *Prose Works,* 2 (London, G. Bell, 1914), 96. Cf. Waldo Beach, "The Meaning and Authority of Conscience in Protestant Thought of Seventeenth Century England" (Yale University, 1944), p. 115.

16. Edward Burrough, *The Case of Free Liberty of Conscience in the Exercise of Faith and Religion* (London, 1661), p. 5.

17. Penington, *Works, 1,* 476; Fox, *To the Protector and Parliament,* p. 28; Nayler, *Works,* pp. 184–85; Josiah Coale's broadside *To the King and Both Houses of Parliament* (Kingston-on-Thames, 1664).

propriate against puritans, their choice of biblical texts also reflected Quaker emphases on the relation of carnal and spiritual weapons, the humble nature of the early church, and the coming of Christ to save rather than destroy.[18] Their texts show furthermore that the Friends, like early Israel, considered persecution the rejection of their God.

In action as well as in words, Friends showed no doubt that they were led by the Spirit, and inevitably in the right. Although they have added only a little to the range of doctrines about toleration, their contributions to the actual achievement of toleration have been great, especially in early Massachusetts, in England under Charles II, and later in Pennsylvania. But one particular contribution ought to be discussed before going on to this history: Friends' own actions sharply posed a number of issues that showed the inadequacy of certain common ideas of toleration. This also clarified for Friends and their opponents the significance of their most basic answer, the Testimony against violence.

Conflicts over religious liberty arise in five general areas: freedom of belief, freedom of worship, freedom to cause offense, freedom to interfere, and freedom to upset public order. These issues turn up constantly, and their limits are still not surely defined with regard to many ideologies, such as Marxist communism.

No one in England was executed after 1612 for religious belief as such, and few doctrines were matters of law. Systematic doctrinal persecution really implies that the salvation of the heretic and of anyone he may persuade can be prevented by false doctrine alone. It also assumes that persecution can silence false teachings and perhaps even re-educate the offender.[19] Protestants, unlike Catholics and Marxists, have rarely attributed such power to ideas and have assumed that, insofar as belief represents allegiance, it cannot be changed by force. Yet differences of belief may be insoluble and serious, as when each partner in an interfaith marriage genuinely believes the other may go to hell unless converted. Early Friends were often completely cut off from families and friends merely because of their ideas about the Light.

Freedom of worship was allowed under the Commonwealth

---

18. Other favorites included I John 3:12; Jude 11; Acts 5:38–39; Matt. 5:45.
19. Cf. Roland H. Bainton, *The Travail of Religious Liberty* (Philadelphia, Westminster Press, 1951), p. 17.

except to Catholics and Anglicans. After the Restoration of Charles II, the Conventicle Acts forbade any worship other than that from the Anglican Prayer Book. The Quakers and puritans fought this to the death, but after 1689, nonconformist worship was allowed. Calvinists proscribed idolatry for the sake of God's glory, and worship is often restricted only by those who are sure that false worship leads to a heretic's damnation and may also seduce innocent souls. But the Restoration Parliament believed that the form of worship was not important for salvation and felt free to demand uniformity for the sake of national unity. Quakers never agreed that worship was unimportant: "We meet together . . . because the Lord of Life requireth it of us . . . and in our Meetings waiting upon the Lord, we have the presence of the living God of Life with us. . . . Judge how we can . . . do that which Man requireth of us, contrary to the Truth . . . How can we deny the Lord who hath . . . redeemed our Souls from death?" [20]

Freedom for actions that cause offense is a subtler issue than freedom of worship. The puritan Parliament passed a fairly mild Blasphemy Act aimed at the Ranters, who called themselves God and claimed that all their impulses were morally right. Americans today rarely feel the shock that immorality and blasphemy brought to a puritan, although polygamy, ritual sacrifices, and oriental fertility cults sometimes produce this intense horror even now. In Spain Protestant churches have been closed on the claim that seeing them offends the Catholic majority. This is a matter of conscience versus conscience.[21] Americans often assume that freedom of action and belief need stop only with injury to others or oneself, but psychological injury can be worse than physical, as in racial segregation; nor can belief and action be separated. When John Clarke was banished from Massachusetts in 1652 for illegal worship in public, he was told: "the Court sentenced you, not for matter of judgment and conscience, but for matter of fact and practice," and Clarke replied, "man is void of judgment and conscience with respect unto God, that hath not a fact and practice suitable thereunto." [22]

Friends were led by the Spirit into many actions that offended

20. Camm and Audland, *Works*, pp. 214–17, 220, 230–32.
21. Cf. Miner Searle Bates, *Religious Liberty, an Inquiry* (New York, Harper, 1945), pp. 14 ff.
22. John Clarke, *Ill Newes from New-England*, p. 21, quoted in Hertz, "Bible Commonwealth," p. 157.

their neighbors. The most obvious were "going naked for a sign" and the refusal of hat honor and greeting. Preaching by women or preaching in the open marketplace was merely a nuisance and could be met with a charge of vagabondage, which the absence of Friends from their jobs made plausible; but the claim that Nayler announced and acted upon—namely, that Christ dwelt in him— seemed to be blasphemy. The claim of perfectionism by many other Friends was equally offensive. Neither Nayler nor theologians like Baxter clearly understood their differences; so much the less did ordinary Christians. There was no theoretical answer to the Quaker offense. After the Nayler trial in 1656 Friends acted more soberly: while still believing themselves to be led by the Spirit, they examined far more warily their leadings to go naked for a sign. In the same years the average Englishman became more familiar with Quakers and his conscience less easily upset by them.

Freedom to interfere is much less accepted today than freedom of worship, speech, or action. Quakers went into parish churches and independent congregations to challenge or denounce the ministers, not just occasionally but on principle and whenever possible. A statute passed under Mary Tudor allowed lay preaching during church services once the minister had finished, but the Quaker attacks seemed to puritans to violate their own freedom of worship. Cromwell, struggling for toleration against all sides, issued an injunction:

> [The] free and uninterrupted passage of the Gospel running through the midst of us . . . without any interruption from the powers God hath set over this Commonwealth, [is] a mercy that is the price of much blood, and till late years denied to this nation. [But] take care that on no pretence whatsoever such freedom . . . should be extended by any, beyond . . . the royal law of love . . . to the disturbance or disquiet of any of their brethren in the same free exercise of their faith and worship, [as has happened] by divers men lately risen up under the names of Quakers, Ranters, and others. . . . If in contempt hereof any persons shall presume to offend as aforesaid, we shall esteem them disturbers of the civil peace, and shall expect . . . officers . . . of justice to proceed against them.[23]

23. *FPT,* pp. 350–51.

But interfering with false worship may seem to be commanded by conscience itself. Friends cited Amos' sermon interrupting worship at Bethel, and Christ's cleansing of the Temple. As Elijah learned from the "still, small voice," to stop idolatry may be a prophetic call from God. So also among Friends: "Some are moved to reprove a Hireling teacher . . . It is a matter of conscience to the servants of the Lord to do so, and they cannot leave it undone, least they should transgress the law of God in their own consciences." [24] To interfere with public peace may be a public duty if men's lives are in danger. Friends certainly had no sympathy for the peace that was merely restfulness in sin; even Cromwell's troopers did not hesitate to break up Catholic worship and other illegal gatherings. Where consciences collide, there is no abstract answer through a golden rule of equal rights, for equality applies only where natural law and men's equal humanity are involved, and not to revealed truth or religious duty.

The issue of public order is the toughest of all. In one form this may be regarded as a sharper form of the freedom to interfere and to upset the public peace. In Massachusetts, Friends challenged the right of the colony to a way of life ruled by orthodox Puritanism and excluding Quaker ideas and worship. Yet the puritans had come to America at great sacrifice, to set up a biblical commonwealth for the glory of God. Purely in obedience to their consciences, they extended to the state the principle of the church covenant, restricting their voting rights to loyal church members and the right of residence to those who would accept their pattern. They gave all Anabaptists, Familists, and Antinomians the freedom to stay away. Those within the Commonwealth who disagreed with its ideals were sent to Rhode Island, and not always gently, but the survival of the godly experiment was at stake. Two Friends, Mary Fisher and Ann Austin, landed in Boston not to settle but to preach and warn. The New England puritans had read many comments about Quakers in tracts by their English brethren, and concluded that they had come for religious and political revolution and might be in league with the pope or the devil. The Boston magistrates took care to send the first two teams of Quakers back by sea directly to England, and to pass a law fining shipmasters who brought any more. The next year eleven

24. Burrough, *Message for Instruction*, pp. 13–14. Cf. Nayler, *Works*, p. 41.

Quakers landed in their own ship, the "Woodhouse," having steered by "neither latitude nor longitude" but by the Lord's guidance. From that time onward, Friends entered by way of Rhode Island and Plymouth, which soon developed local Meetings and brought the danger nearer. The growing series of Quaker intrusions in 1657 and 1658 was not stopped even by a harsh law of banishment and whipping or the cropping of offenders' ears. Elizabeth Hooton in 1662 reported being whipped through three or more towns, ten triple lashes in each town, and at least four times on one visit to New England, for as soon as the constable released her on the edge of the colony, she would double back to Boston again and make a new protest.[25] In desperation the Massachusetts General Court passed a law permitting a death sentence upon Quakers who returned after banishment. Quakers from London, Yorkshire, Rhode Island, and Barbados converged upon Boston "to try their law." Governor Endicott presided in 1659 at the trial of William Robinson and Marmaduke Stephenson, both making their first major journey as Quaker ministers and both arrested after banishment, along with Mary Dyer of Rhode Island:

> John Indicott began to speak unto us as a man out of the dust, whose life is departing from him, so faintly did he utter his words unto us, to this effect, that they had made several Laws and tryed and endeavoured by several wayes to keep us from among them, and neither whipping, nor imprisoning, nor cutting off ears, nor banishing upon pain of death would keep us from amongst them, and he said also He or they desired not the death of any of us; yet, notwithstanding, his following words were: "Give ear & hearken now to your Sentence of Death." [26]

25. Emily Manners, *Elizabeth Hooton* (London, 1914), pp. 39–45, quoting Swarth. 3/27.

26. Marmaduke Stephenson and William Robinson, *A Call from Death to Life* (London, 1660), p. 24. This pamphlet, partly written in prison by men awaiting execution, is less well known than the inclusive martyrology written later by George Bishop, *New England Judged, Not by Man's but by the Spirit of the Lord* (London, 1661). Bishop's book, together with Burrough's earlier verbal report to Charles II, was influential in securing "the King's missive" which restrained later persecution in Massachusetts. Cf. Mary Agnes Best, *Rebel Saints* (New York, 1925), p. 290; G. P. Gooch and H. J. Laski, *English Democratic Ideas in the 17th Century* (2d ed. Cambridge, Cambridge University Press, 1927), p. 236; Rufus M. Jones, *The Quakers in the American Colonies* (London, Macmillan, 1923), chap. 4.

Robinson and Stephenson were hanged and Mary Dyer pardoned but finally hanged after she came back to Boston yet again. William Leddra of Barbados was executed early in 1661. All of these Friends were offered pardon even after their return to Massachusetts, if they would promise never to come again, but it lay upon their consciences to conquer the law excluding "God's people" from the colony. No easy answer could prevent this collision of conscientious beliefs. Public opinion in Massachusetts, at first united against Quakerism, was divided over the death sentence, and finally turned against the puritan laws. Quakers were reluctantly given freedom, but the price was the loss of unity in Massachusetts and of confidence in its ideals.

The anti-Quaker laws in New England were created for the occasion and condemned by many besides Quakers, but Friends challenged the social authority of all law. Most discussions of toleration, civil rights, and freedom assume that society has certain axiomatic rights and claims. Early Quakers conceded nothing to majority agreement, social contract, or the divine right of rulers; the only basis for law that they recognized was God's righteousness. They thus confused their opponents, since they refused to be restrained and yet accepted the puritan belief that a godly ruler must be zealous in the restraint of vice and vanity, and may even use force, since "outward evils or violence, or other like visible crimes . . . forbid not external punishments." [27] Friends were naturally bitter when preachers were arrested while drunkards and adulterers were ignored. At the same time they claimed that righteousness could only be recognized by God's guidance and not by any human or rational means. Now, every Christian must ultimately place God's command above the state's authority and may conscientiously object to his nation's laws, and in puritan Massachusetts or totalitarian states he may seem a hero to do so. Yet Friends made their stand less justifiable because they denied to anyone outside the Christian viewpoint, which meant all non-Quakers, any authority to judge good or bad men and to make or unmake laws.

The Spirit's role in judging motives seemed a simple thing to Friends: "To all such as have the spirit of the Father . . .

27. Burrough, *Antichrist's Government,* p. 27.

this is an easy thing to discerne, and such as cannot discerne
. . . in these matters . . . hath not the Spirit of God . . .
neither . . . is fit to judge the people." [28] The same principle applied to making laws. A lawmaker needed God's Spirit to guide
all decisions, for "that which invents a Law or an Act which doth
oppresse, . . . it is made by that which has transgressed the pure in
his owne particular. . . . Therefore take heed all ye Law Mak-
ers." [29] This stated clearly why bad men make bad laws but seemed
to imply that only Quakers could make good ones. Such an approach strongly reinforced the puritan and Quaker demand for
the rule of Saints and the remaking of the laws in England. The
problem was the basis for new law. Most legal reforms base civil
law on natural law or on common international customs (as by
Roman theory), or else on the pragmatic needs of society (as by
Justice Holmes), but thereby the authority of God in lawmaking
is denied. Puritans tried to find a divine undergirding for social
order, even if it meant radical rebellion against existing society.
They found the Bible laws, and to some extent pointed to God's
pattern in natural Creation. Friends proposed to base laws purely
on the commands of the Spirit, and this was no foundation for
most men. In Massachusetts the basis of lawmaking itself was really
at stake, and no clear answer was found.

The authority of laws over individuals is an issue distinct from
the right to make laws. Approaches to civil law through natural
law assume the legal equality of all men, within certain fixed
limits. Moreover, most Christian law theory, whether Roman
Catholic or Lutheran, assumes that, as sinful human beings, we
all need laws and policemen to restrain our thoughtless selfish-
ness, however fully grace has reached our hearts. But Quaker and
puritan ideas emphasized man's thorough conversion to saintly
conduct. Even Paul and Luther had said that Christian love will
fulfill the law by causing many actions that achieve its purposes:
thus, wherever love is present, Christians have no need to be com-
pelled by laws. Friends and radical puritans extended this "Christian liberty" to all areas of a Christian's life: "If thou art such an
one that canst do nothing against the Truth, but for the Truth, then

28. Burrough, *Message for Instruction*, p. 19.
29. Fox, *To the Protector and Parliament*, pp. 6–7.

mayest thou safely be left to thy Freedom, but if thou pleadest thy freedom against . . . good and wholesome and requisit things, thy Freedom is Nought, Dark, Perverse, out of Truth." [30]

Friends believed that the law was not made for righteous men like themselves: "the law is not to be laid upon them." [31] They exasperated puritan judges, who could not believe that any law which convicted Quakers was ipso facto unjust. Thus, for instance, a law against men who maliciously, or with evil purpose disturbed public preachers obviously could not apply to Quakers, whose intents were good.[32] To the men of seventeenth-century England the Quaker theocracy was virtual anarchy, outwardly the same as Ranterism. Pagitt's *Heresiography* listed the rejection of all laws and magistrates as a basic doctrine of Quakerism. Though this was unfair, Friends were entirely subject to the Spirit and ultimately to nothing else. Joseph Nicholson was cross-questioned by Endicott in Boston: "hee asked mee what I came into th're country for. I tould him I was moved of the lord to com . . . Hee asked mee . . . what would I follow when I had my liberty. I tould him labor with my hands [at] the things that were honest as formerly I had done, if the Lord called mee therto: he sayd, could I not tell. I tould him I could not tell to day what the lord might call mee to to morrow." [33] Nicholson was banished. In a similar situation at Appleby, Howgill writes that he was told: "I must enter in bond, or noe liberty, so then I tould them iff I should doe soe I wear trecherious to God & my owne conscience & they would loke upon me as an hipocritt." [34] There could be no guarantee of what a Quaker would do next, since he set no limit short of the world rule by Quaker Saints.

Such an impasse may develop whenever men are totally committed to an ideal their opponents do not share, and no abstract theory can overcome it. If both protagonists in such a clash—Moslem, Jesuit, Marxist, Anabaptist, Protestant fundamentalist—concretely understand each other's actual ideals, they may be able

30. William Penn, *Works* (2 vols. London, 1726), 2, 693. Cf. Kühn, *Toleranz und Offenbarung*, p. 261.

31. Burrough, *Message for Instruction*, p. 3.

32. Fox, *To the Protector and Parliament*, pp. 11, 20.

33. Swarth. 4/107 (*EQL* 520), Joseph Nicholson to M. Fell, Boston, April 3, 1660.

34. ARBarc./92, Howgill to Fox, March 23, 1663/64. This letter is also important for the relation of Friends to the Kaber Rigg plot. Cf. *JFHS*, *44* (1952), 44; Swarth 3/36 (*EQL* 5), Aldam to Fox, York prison, 1652.

to foresee each other's actions and to respect each other's integrity. Where ideals are irrevocably antagonistic, however, it is hard to achieve enough mutual respect to remove the fear and hatred aroused by conflict. The Friends' great contribution to statecraft was to realize that their own Peace Testimony was not simply a response to actual war but an answer to the deadlock of consciences. Love for an enemy is itself an innate part of Christian commitment, they said unsentimentally. It was part of their basic faith, not an external political doctrine. Friends saw that they could point to their attitude toward violence and "carnal" weapons as part of their commitment to love. Their opponents could know and trust that Friends, on principle, would never use violence against them or cause them physical harm. Their answer to the deadlock did not require surrender of their claim to absolute authority for the Light within their conscience, and yet it gave non-Friends a solid basis for tolerating them.[35]

Good intentions toward their enemies were not necessarily obvious to outsiders, but the Quakers' rejection of violence was another story. Though historically Friends first came to understand and expound their Peace Testimony in reaction to the Restoration of Charles II, it already had a visible tradition behind it. A number of Friends had left the armed services as soon as they were convinced Quakers. Thomas Lurting, a gun officer with a record of bravery aboard his ship, found as he prepared a bombardment that his conscience would not let him kill and so reported to his commander.[36] Peter Hardcastle was one of the Quakers in the army who concluded that it was not lawful to use weapons in any war. Indirect reports from captains and officers suggest many other similar cases.[37] Others were offended at being discharged, not for being Quakers but for disobedience to their officers.[38] Yet some Friends had remained in Cromwell's army, with no hesitation about defending the nation against its enemies.[39]

35. See also Roland H. Bainton, *Christian Attitudes towards Peace and War* (London, 1961), chap. 10.

36. Cf. Margaret Hirst, *Quakers in Peace and War* (London, 1923).

37. P[eter] H[ardcastle], *The Quakers Plea* (London, 1661); cf. *ESP*, pp. 14, 27.

38. Colonel Ingoldsby, quoted in *JFHS*, 7 (1910), 56. Cf. Braithwaite, *Beginnings*, p. 219; Burrough, *Good Counsel and Advice Rejected* (London, 1659), p. 15; Fox, *Journal*, Nickalls, p. 329.

39. Anon., *To the Generals, Captains, Officers and Souldiers of the Present Army*, quoted in Cole, "Quakers and Politics," p. 56.

One Quaker actually re-enlisted in 1659, and a puritan colonel that year offered Francis Gawler a commission, accepted his brother John as his own lieutenant colonel (until Fox disapproved), and was a "loveinge man to friends." [40] But in spite of Burrough, Bishop, and the Bristol Quaker militiamen, and before the crisis of 1659 was past, Fox and the leading Friends had restated a clear Quaker testimony against fighting: "Taking up arms outwardly . . . is not our Principle and out of the Covenant and Life & Peace with God." [41] The basis of this stand was religious; only after 1670, for reasons shown later, did Penn and Robert Barclay use humanitarian arguments against war's injury to the innocent and its economic wastefulness. At that later period Barclay, in the spirit of a modern "vocational pacifist," began to make exceptions for non-Quakers: Those who "have not come to the pure dispensation of the gospel . . . while they are in that condition, we shall not say that war undertaken upon a just occasion is altogether unlawful to them." [42] Before Barclay, the Friends simply regarded war, like persecution, as the devil's way of tricking men into attacking evil in the wrong place and in the wrong way.

When Charles II and the restored Cavaliers suspected Friends of threatening revolt, the Quakers could fortunately insist that they had never basically violated their peaceful principles. Some Friends admitted their former Cromwellian soldiering, but others asked: "have we not always been a *quiet peaceable harmless people?*" [43] They had now, however, to go further and restate their relationship to the laws of the nation. They maintained the Spirit's authority above all laws, and yet showed how their peace testimony brought them into a positive relationship even to evil laws:

> For Conscience sake to God, we are bound . . . to yield obedience . . . in all matters actively or passively: that is to say, in all just and good laws of the land, we must be obedient by doing . . . but . . . if anything be commanded of us by the present Authority, which is not according to equity, justice, and a good conscience towards God . . . we must in

40. SMS 4/219 (*EQL* 511), Francis Gawler to Fox, Cardiff, January 26, 1959/60. On John Hodgson's re-enlistment see Alan Cole in *JFHS, 46* (1954), 48–52.

41. Fox's broadside *Our Covenant with God.*

42. Wragge, *Barclay,* p. 37.

43. Thomas Ellwood, *A Seasonable Disswasive from Persecution* (London, 1683), p. 8.

such cases obey God only, and deny active obedience . . .
and patiently suffer what is inflicted upon us for such our disobedience.[44]

Such nonviolent resistance was different in principle from the
nonresistance preached by Anglicans or Lutherans, which was
based on God's ordaining of the king and the state. No such claim
of a non-Quaker society was acknowledged by the Friends: certain
laws they could not obey, nor could they avoid the conflict and
threatened penalties that resulted. Yet they could claim that even
in disobedience they preserved a form of loyalty to the nation:
"he who submits to the *punishment* doth . . . really fullfil the
Law." [45] Quakers could also trust that their disobedience would
ultimately be for the good of the country—and so in the end it
proved. During the intense persecutions after 1661, Quaker non-
violence won the respect of England and was eventually the largest factor in bringing the nation to a policy of toleration. Cromwell's ten-year rule had not convinced most Englishmen that a
united nation was possible without a unified church; they "never
knew a toleration which did not require an army to keep all
quiet." [46] Since the costly persecutions of the 1660s, however,
England has always trusted its nonconformists. The principle of
"loyal opposition"—which has been a greater English contribution to world history than Parliaments or muddling through crisis
by compromise—was a puritan and, above all, a Quaker contribution.

The Lamb's War was not given up by the doctrine of nonviolent and loyal resistance, for Quaker policy was active, not
passive. Friends continued to preach and win converts, at least
until all their leaders were in prison. Even when they seemed in
danger of being wiped out, a Friend could confidently say, "I do
not expect deliverance by a carnal Sword, and yet I know deliverance shall come, with or without the help of men . . . that
so it may plainly be made manifest, that we are a people saved by
our God." [47] Though the later years of persecution were to change

44. Burrough, *Works,* pp. 778 ff. Cf. Whitehead, *Two Seeds,* pp. 28–29.
45. Henry Stubbs, *A Light Shines out of Darkness* (London, 1659), p. 118.
46. William Cobbett, *Cobbett's Parliamentary History of England, 4* (London, 1808), 413.
47. G. Fox the Younger, *Noble Salutation,* pp. 19–20.

Quaker attitudes, they suffered for decades without losing confidence in the world-wide victory of the Lamb: "the Lord will carry on his own word by his owne power." [48] Edward Burrough, in prison and at the point of death, wrote: "Friends, Doubt not of these things, for verily the time is at hand, my Spirit shall see it . . . if in this body I may not behold it, that imposing and forcing of conscience by Laws and Ordinances of men . . . shall be abandoned in these Nations and Kingdoms of the World." [49] Most Friends put this in its ultimate perspective, confident of deliverance because "the Truth must flourish and prosper, and the Kingdoms of the World must become the Kingdom of our Lord and of his Christ." [50]

The persecutions of 1660 to 1685 centered on freedom of worship, but they were not a struggle over faith. When the Cavalier Parliament tried to force the whole country back into the Episcopal Church of England, true religion and heresy were not at stake. Unlike the burning of Protestants by Mary Tudor, or the extermination of the Lollards a century before, no death sentences were passed,[51] but the number of victims injured was greater than in any English persecution before or since. Most of the former puritans, whether orthodox or radical, Congregational, Baptist, or Quaker, lost the influence and prestige (and sometimes the property) they had gained. They became merely Dissenters or Nonconformists, and the pattern of social strata in England was set against them and has remained so ever since.

As soon as they were strong enough, the Anglicans passed the Clarendon Code, aimed with precise malice at the main goals of puritan life as well as at their congregations. The Act of Uniformity required that by August 1662 all parish ministers use the Book of Common Prayer weekly and swear to uphold it. All oaths and ordinations under the Commonwealth were also declared to be invalid. Of the 5,100 ministers in the parish churches of England, between 1,750 and 2,685 were evicted or "deprived," for refusing to accept the Act of Uniformity.[52] Others who stayed at-

48. Swarth. 1/161 (*EQL* 140), Alex. Parker to M. Fell, London, 1655.

49. Burrough, *Antichrist's Government*, "Epistle."

50. Coale's broadside *To the King and . . . Parliament*.

51. Twelve Baptists received death sentences under old laws meant against Catholics but were pardoned by Charles II. Many Baptists were, of course, executed for taking part in the fifth Monarchist or Kaber Rigg uprisings.

52. Nightingale (*Ejected of 1662*) cites Calamy's figure of 2,685 and Baxter's of

tempted to evade the act and often were ejected later. In most cases a proportion of the congregation, many of whom had never before been separatists, followed their puritan pastor out of the parish churches of their fathers. Torn between loyalty to the nation and the pastoral needs of their followers, most of the ejected clergy felt a continuing vocation and began to organize worship and group life. Parliament bore down. The Five Mile Act kept puritan clergy from towns and from their former congregations, also barring them from teaching school. The Conventicle Act forbade all religious gatherings of more than four people besides the home family. The Corporation and Test Acts barred nonconformist laymen from all offices in city, county, and national government, the army, the navy, and the universities.

Of these laws, only the Conventicle Act applied directly to Friends, but a special Quaker Act was passed after the Fifth Monarchists' revolt in 1661, and any law requiring an oath could be used to outlaw Quakers. The oath of allegiance could be tied to the devastating penalties of the Act of Praemunire. In later years nonpayment of tithes re-emerged as a major issue, as it had under the Commonwealth, but with much greater fines and distrainments. The storm was severe. In 1658 only 119 Friends had been in prison, and 140 during the crisis of 1659. By 1660 the numbers jumped: amid the antipuritan revelry there were 700 Quakers set free by King Charles at his coronation. The next year 120 were arrested on one day from one Gloucester Friends meeting, and in 1664, 400 were taken in two successive Sundays from the Bull and Mouth in London.

Though Quakers were outnumbered by the puritans, they suffered disproportionately. Of 1,240 dissenters convicted in London in 1664, about 850 were Friends, and they totaled 859 out of 909 imprisoned in the rest of Middlesex, though these were puritan strongholds.[53] The reason was the spirit with which Quakers faced persecution. Though the trials of leading puritans like Richard Baxter, Calamy, and Alleine made as great a stir as did the trial

---

1,800. Nuttall, Braithwaite, and Matthews incline to the lower estimate and Cragg to the higher. Whitley (*British Baptists*) points out that nearly 2,000 other pastors returned to the pre-1640 pattern of silent evasion, and were individually uncovered later. Cf. also Braithwaite, *Second Period*, 2d ed., pp. 649–50; A. G. Matthews, *Calamy Revised* (London, 1934), pp. xii–xiii, xxxviii–xxxix.

53. For these figures see *ESP*, pp. 37–54; *FPT*, p. 352; *JFHS, 44* (1952), 24–25; Braithwaite, *Second Period*, pp. 42–54, 114–15; Whitley, *British Baptists*, p. 99.

of William Penn, most Baptists and Presbyterians met quietly
in woods or private homes. Quakers kept up their Meetings openly,
however, and after they were arrested, their children (who were
exempt from the penalties of the Conventicle Act) kept up the
Meetings in some places. Meetinghouses were torn down, even
around worshiping groups, so Friends transferred their title deeds
to individuals who could legally protect their property. At Colchester, in 1670, the mayor had the meetinghouse boarded and
bricked up twice, and, after twice reopening it, Friends finally
met all winter in the street.[54] The puritans and Anglicans noticed
this Quaker behavior with surprise, and Friends reported proudly:

> The Brunt of the Storm fell most sharply on . . . the Quak-
> ers, not that it seemed to be more particularly levelled at
> them, but that they stood more . . . steady and open. . . .
> Quakers . . . could not dodge and shift to avoid Suffering,
> as others of other Denominations could . . . altering their
> Meetings with respect both to Place and Time. . . . The
> *Quakers* only held up a publick Testimony . . . by keeping
> their Meeting duly and fully at the accustomed Times . . .
> This bold . . . Behavior in the *Quakers* disturbed . . . the
> *Persecutors,* who complained, that the stubborn Quakers
> brake their Strength, and bore off the Blow from those other
> Dissenters whom . . . they principally aimed at.[55]

Quakers made this strong resistance part of their spiritual warfare,
whereas the puritan wished to be part of the nation and its church
so far as his conscience would allow and felt bound to suffer publicly only when, by his shrinking, the truth or the souls of other
men were in danger. Foolhardiness might come from weakness,
said the puritans, and "a man is not bound by the law of his Lord
to put himself into the mouth of his enemy." [56] For Quakers, however, suffering was a weapon in the Lamb's War, and "this is your
day and hour of your Trial wherein the Lord by you shall be
honour'd." [57] Those who were not "willing to bear the Cross cannot bear the Crown, and they that will live Godly in Christ Jesus

54. *FPT,* p. 95.
55. Ellwood, *Life,* pp. 275, 304–05.
56. John Bunyan, *Works,* 2 (Glasgow, 1862), 715, cited in Cragg, *Puritanism in
Persecution,* pp. 66–67.
57. Burnyeat, p. 110.

must suffer Persecution. . . . Do not hearken to that Spirit in you, which would say you may go to the World's Worship, and yet . . . serve God well enough." [58]

Periods of persecution were not always sharply marked, as some men remained prisoners into the years of relative quiet, nor was the pattern uniform in all regions. In parts of Cumberland and in the West Indian colonies there was little persecution. In Ireland, Bishop Jeremy Taylor, the author of *Liberty of Prophesying,* sat on the Council and, with Lord Mountrath and Orrery, three times cleared the prisons of Quakers (a total of 306) in 1660–62. After they offered a pledge that substituted for the oath of allegiance, they were not much molested. In Virginia and Massachusetts, Friends suffered harassment. In England there had been mass arrests of Quakers in 1660 and 1661 by nervous justices fearful of revolts. The arrested men were mainly released by the direct action of the King, following the presentation to him of the Peace Testimony by Fox and by Margaret Fell (who was in London far oftener than at home until she was imprisoned in 1664 for four years in Lancaster Castle).[59] But the steady pressure and mass arrests that began in 1662 lasted for seven years. In 1663 two forlorn bands of puritans tried to rally for revolt at Kaber Rigg and Farnley Wood in northern England, but dispersed without risking a fight. Local royalist justices like Musgrave and Fleming, who had suffered in the Cromwellian wars, tried unsuccessfully to implicate the Quakers. George Fox and many other Friends were arrested on suspicion and jailed in any case. A few, including Howgill, may have known that the plot had been afoot, but none took part.

During these years when hundreds of Friends were more often in prison than out, a majority of the great leaders died there. Burrough was first, his death causing a shock to the preaching band who had hoped to see the coming of God's kingdom together. Howgill survived in the jail on the town bridge of Appleby until 1669, showing a faith and confidence that strengthened his friends. John Camm, like James Nayler, had died after earlier

58. Banks, pp. 165–67. For other Quaker users of the phrase "no cross, no crown," which became the title of Penn's best-known book, see Braithwaite, *Second Period,* 2d ed., pp. 657–58. See also Yearly Meeting Advice of 1675, e.g. in Kendal MS No. 1, p. 202.

59. See Douglas, in *JFHS, 48* (1956), 18–28; ARBarc./92 and 93; M. Fell, p. 1.

imprisonments under Cromwell. Fox, Dewsbury, and Burnyeat barely survived until toleration came in 1688, but Audland, Hubberthorne, Ames, and Caton died early in the struggle. For a few years after 1667, when England had been through the plague, the Fire of London, and the Dutch war, few new Quakers were jailed, and the King essayed toleration; but Parliament forced him to recall it, and renewed the Conventicle Act in 1670. When the King again tried a Declaration of Indulgence in 1672, toleration became a political issue that rose and fell rapidly with parties and powerful ministers, but in 1675, 1682–83, and 1685 over a thousand Friends were again in prison.

The penalties under the Clarendon Code were fines and imprisonments multiplied according to repetitions of the offense. The renewed Conventicle Act gave large rewards to informers, creating a group of greedy and unscrupulous professional ferrets who lived by informing on puritan neighbors. Most sentences were set by local justices of the peace (though county courts and assizes also took part), and there was much variation in rigor between towns and justices, some of whom punished as little as the government would allow, while by others "the rules of evidence were treated in the most cavalier fashion." [60] After a third conviction for attending a conventicle, the legal penalty was transportation to a penal colony overseas, but this "last offense" was seldom charged against Friends. Of about sixty cases actually transported, mainly from London, nearly half died of the plague during the nightmare weeks when the *Black Eagle* was moored below London, and perhaps only eighteen, on three other ships, actually reached the colonies.[61] Fines, on the other hand, were increasingly common and were intended to bankrupt: one man was fined £840 in four months. Thomas Camm was distrained 33 times for tithes. In 1683 there were exchequer suits for £33,300 pending against Quakers in Suffolk alone; and the total of fines levied against puritans and Quakers was estimated as between two and fourteen million pounds. Where cash was not available, property was seized for a sheriff's sale if any neighbor was heartless enough

60. Cragg, *Puritanism in Persecution*, p. 53. Cf. Braithwaite, *Second Period*, chaps. 2–4.

61. Cf. ARBarc./78, Howgill to M. Fell, Appleby, 1665; also Braithwaite, *Second Period*, pp. 43–46, 50–51, 655.

to buy it or, if not, to enforce the principle of the law. Livestock, working tools, cooking utensils, beds, a coat off a man's back, and all things portable were taken.[62]

Prison sentences were also frequent: John Crook was imprisoned six times in eight years in the 1660s, and few Leading Friends were out for long. Where prison conditions were best, customs of the day allowed tools, books, daily meals, and frequent visitors from outside the prison; wives and families might stay for months with the prisoner, if he had his own cell; and jailers allowed puritans and Quakers to leave prison briefly (or in a few cases for months on end) on their own parole.[63] But prisons were usually cold and wet. At Norwich one affidavit stated that "in one room, called the Hole, which is the place wherein ffelons are usually imprisoned, which is a room [16 feet by 37] 12 steps into [the] ground, and in the house of office belonging to the said room, there are 16 bedds & a hammock . . . In which bedds do constantly 29 persons lay every night." From another statement: "9 persons, calld Quakrs, being prisoners in the prison in Norwich, were put into a Dungeon belonging to the said Prison, being 27 steps down in the ground. In which place there is but one small light, which descendeth through 2 iron grates, just by the ground, nigh which grates the ground is constantly annoyed with Excrements & filth." [64] Jailers had unchecked authority, and prisoners who refused their high charges for bedding or meals were assigned to dungeons with little of either. Epidemics were inescapable: 3 Quakers died in Northampton jail in one day, and Dewsbury's granddaughter died beside him at Warwick. When the plague or smallpox broke out, prisoners were sent home as their only hope for life. The overcrowding cut down sleep, work, and worship: 81 were in one room at Ilchester, 50 women in four beds at Bristol, and 797 Quakers consigned to Newgate prison in five weeks during 1664. Sentences were often indeterminate, or release was conditional upon paying fines which a conscientious Quaker indefinitely refused to pay. Fox, Howgill, Aldam, and several others spent more than five years in such conditions.

62. Cragg, *Puritanism in Persecution*, pp. 57 n., 88, 102–03, 108, 114. On Thomas Camm see Somervell, *Westmorland Wills.*

63. Dews./29, Mary Smith to Dewsbury, York, December 4, 1662. Cf. Cragg, chap. 2.

64. *FPT*, pp. 181–82.

Under the pressure a few Friends defected: Anthony Pearson himself, William Adamson, and others unnamed. Most of the Meetings in northern England reported Friends migrating in the 1670s and 1680s to southern England or the colonies, and some of these were probably men driven off their farms by fines for tithes.[65] The public maintenance of Quaker worship and ways of life became a key issue in the conflicts within Quakerism opened by Perrot in 1661 and by Wilkinson, and Story in the 1670s after formal Monthly Meetings were set up. These men felt that the Spirit need not lead Quakers to worship at the same time or place, or in groups under permanent leaders. A basic stand had to be thrashed out here, as the absolute authority of the Spirit over each individual was a crucial Quaker belief. But Robert Barclay insisted that the Spirit's self-consistency meant that the Light could work uniformly through a group; organized leadership and group discipline therefore were legitimate:

> I affirm: first that there never will . . . be wanting, in case of controversy, the Spirit of God to give judgment through some [person] or other in the Church of Christ. . . .
>
> Secondly, that God hath ordinarily, in communicating of his will . . . employed such whom he made use of in gathering his church. . . .
>
> Thirdly, that . . . meeting together, and giving a positive judgment . . . will not import tyranny . . . or an inconsistancy with the universal privilege that all Christians have to be led by the Spirit.[66]

Though many Friends would not go so far, the immediate effect of Barclay's book (*The Anarchy of the Ranters*) was to reinforce the disowning of Wilkinson and Story and their followers, and to enhance the authority of Fox and other pioneer Quaker leaders, giving them institutional rather than charismatic authority. The less obvious but more crucial effect was to hold Quakers unwaver-

---

65. Cf. *FPT*, pp. 53, 64–65, 264, 265, 271, 272.

66. Barclay, *Anarchy of the Ranters* (Philadelphia, 1822), p. 80. Penn, on the other hand, tried to persuade the individualists that organization was merely a practical step, not a challenge to the Spirit (the same argument used by Cavalier Anglicans): "purely discipline in government, not in worship, formality in order, not in religion" (*Select Works*, *4*, 439, cited in Hertz, "Bible Commonwealth," p. 283).

ingly together through the period of persecution. For both these reasons, pressure in the 1660s crystallized Quaker organization. During the respite in 1668, and again in 1672 and 1676, Fox worked to set up a framework of local Monthly Meetings, regional or county-wide Quarterly Meetings, and larger General Meetings, each usually divided in turn into Men's and Women's Meetings. A series of meetings for ministers grew into a Yearly Meeting, held regularly in London from 1678. Contact was thus kept with all Friends, records were preserved, and a national stock of funds for relief of all prisoners and dispossessed Quakers was set up. After 1679 this was supervised weekly by a "Meeting for Sufferings" (begun quarterly in 1676) in London. Books for publication were scrutinized and underwritten. After 1668, committees began to fight back against persecution through the English courts. Tracts were sent to Parliament, and families of prisoners were supported. Meetings for worship in prison were as large and as deeply moving as any in normal surroundings. Marriage banns were published in prison and epistles exchanged between prisoners in different jails.[67]

Friends were not content merely to hold their battlelines. Howgill, replying to a scholar's tract, thought it enough "to give him a knocke, and sett the simplicity of treuth above him, & though it convince none, yett if we keep our owne, in this day off opossicion and blasphemy, its well from faynting." [68] Most Friends, however, continued to seek the transformation of the world. Preaching missions continued. Josiah Coale preached to Land's End and back "to sound the trumpet of the Lord"; Friends traveled in Germany and the West Indies; and a solid team including Fox, Burnyeat, and Widder preached throughout the American colonies during a respite from persecution. New members were reported in many English Meetings, though some converts were slow to announce themselves. Even more interesting are accounts of new outbreaks of "the power" and fresh emotional strength in the midst of persecutions, notably in Cumberland villages after 1672 and at Waltham Abbey School in 1679. Though many Friends dropped away under pressure, the evidence of marriage

67. Cf. Yearly Meeting Advices at this time, e.g. in Kendal MS No. 1. See also Braithwaite, *Second Period*, chaps. 9–11.
68. ARBarc./90, Francis Howgill to M. Fell, Appleby, February 18, 1665/66.

records suggests that English Quakerism reached its peak in numbers in the 1670s.[69] Thereafter many Friends began to migrate to "the new countries," New Jersey and Pennsylvania, although Meetings often noted that these emigrants were not running from persecution and wrote careful minutes endorsing their travel and commending them to American Meetings.[70]

The main battle was still against persecution. Englishmen in general were becoming weary of informers and imprisonments. Witnesses became harder to find. Neighbors would "borrow" a Quaker's furniture and tools when the sheriff's men were known to be on their way to distrain them, and return them when the danger was past. Justices winked, and one "at last . . . went to the kinge & told him hee had sent to prison some of us contrary to his Conscience, and hee coulde not doe soe noe more." [71] By 1676 the ideas of the Toleration Act of 1689 were a foregone conclusion, for England had learned to think of itself as a complex society rather than as a unified organism. Alongside the national church, still acting in theory as "the nation on its knees," there were now expected to be a block of Nonconformists living and worshiping differently, but sharing the national ideals of Christian morals and government. No church expected to stand alone, and except for the Catholics, each was basically trusted by the others. For Friends the first stage of victory was won.

But the persecutions were not yet over. The moral victory was won a decade before the balances of political power finally shifted dependably. Anglican fears of Puritanism and everyone's fear of Catholicism combined to keep restrictive laws in force. The number of Friends in prison in 1680–85 averaged almost as high as in 1662–67. These last years before the Toleration Act were thus confusing. The heart and terror had gone out of persecution, but the harassment continued. Rather than seek allies in government to reform the nation, Friends found allies in the nation to modify the government. The meaning of the Lamb's War was no longer clear, and by the time toleration was won, both sides were des-

69. See ARBarc./64, Coale to Fox; *FPT*, pp. 41, 50, 53, 64; Tolles, *Atlantic Culture*, p. 103. For the American trip see Burnyeat; also Fox, *Journal*, Camb., 2, 202–14. The estimate of maximum Quaker enrollment in 1675–80 comes from Cole, "Social Origins," *JFHS*, *48*, 100.

70. See *JFHS*, *35* (1938), 31, for Christopher Taylor's Minute of Emigration.

71. Fox, *Journal*, Camb., 2, 133.

perately weary. Freedom had been gained, but it was merely a truce in the Lamb's War as a whole. Basic changes had occurred in Quaker thinking during the years of endurance, however, and the spiritual warfare that they suspended in 1689 was never renewed.

9

Peaceable Conversation: Changes in Quaker Outlooks after 1662

... THE trying of your faith worketh patience. But let patience have her perfect work, that ye may be perfect and entire, wanting nothing. If any of you lack wisdom, let him ask of God . . . Blessed is the man that endureth temptation: for when he is tried, he shall receive the crown of life . . . Wherefore, my beloved brethren, let every man be swift to hear, slow to speak, slow to wrath . . . Pure religion and undefiled before God and the Father is this, To visit the fatherless and widows in their affliction, and to keep himself unspotted from the world. (James 1:3–5, 12, 19, 27.)

QUAKER attitudes changed gradually and unevenly during the twenty years of persecution. Throughout the 1660s the prophetic note was still dominant. In 1669 Fox still urged Friends to record formally the testimonies that they were moved to give in churches, marketplaces, fairs, and meetings of the Nonconformists,[1] and as late as 1672 Robert Barclay went naked for a sign through the chilly streets of Aberdeen. A careful study of the records of Bristol shows that prophetic visions and warnings of doom were transmitted to Bristol city or to the King himself throughout the 1660s and 1690s and at intervals between. Earthquakes were mistakenly prophesied, but several Friends felt they had foretold the Great Fire of London and the Irish wars of 1688–90. By 1700 it was clear that weighty Friends regarded such prophecy as odd, and those who gave it were counseled with "Charity which thinks noe ill but rather Couers weaknesses." Some Friends continued to

---

1. Kendal MS No. 103, p. 37, from Fox's Epistle of 1669.

record visions and premonitions, however, and as late as 1694 Friends apparently encouraged Thomas Rudd, who went through the streets of Bristol with several friends, saying: "Woe from God. Woe from God. Oh all be warned: Oh to feare god." [2]

Questioning the nature of such leadings had been inevitable since Nayler's extravagant procession in 1656. Perhaps a turning point came with a pamphlet of 1660 in which such dubious signs were linked with Quaker claims to infallible judgment and to unique powers not given to other sects. This tract, *The Image of Jealousie Sought Out,* is anonymous, but it was published on Giles Calvert's press and possibly he wrote it:

> You who are called Quakers . . . God hath discovered more to you, and wrought more by you, then by any sect since the great Apostacy. . . . Yet know of a surety that he will sift once more; ye have indeed led many in the way, but . . . many sincere souls have stumbled . . . and ye have . . . pleaded for the buffetings of Satan, calling them commands of God, (to wit), going naked, and in sackcloth, and fasting from outward food. . . . Many, being under a sense of their sinfulness, Satan takes . . . and making that appear to be sin to them which is no sin, thereby to make them think hardly of God, and then to appease the wrath that is gone forth, the Divell presents something to be performed, persuading the creatures they shall have peace in the performances thereof.
>
> . . . He that takes upon him to judge mens thoughts by feeling, doth he not set himself in the seat of God, to judge of the secrets in the heart of another. . . . Ye have pusht the weake with side and shoulder . . . by your judgment . . . in excluding all from an entrance into the door of hope but those that bow to your Idoll. . . .
>
> Oh that all that fear the Lord, of every sect and people, would instruct one another in love . . . Thou mayest find the saints companions in tribulation.[3]

2. Letter from J. Blayklinge and others to Richard Snead and others, December 21, 1700, quoted in Russell Mortimer, "Warnings and Prophecies," *JFHS, 44* (1952), 17, 18. See also John William Graham, *Psychical Experiences of Quaker Ministers* (London, 1933).

3. *The Image of Jealousie Sought Out* (London, 1660), pp. 6–9. The second paragraph quoted, though suitable to Fox's condemnation of Nayler's followers

Many Friends learned to pray and worship with Baptist and puritan fellow prisoners in jail, but found that equality of love for other sects was a new idea, which grew only slowly. Fox, however, was no pope; at the same time that he was facing Wilkinson's and Story's attempt to fragment Quakerism, he wrote to the Barbados Meeting in disapproval of a minute by which some of its members proposed to yield their judgment permanently and in all matters to the decision of the Quaker group.[4] He felt that the Spirit was still each man's own guide. The emerging new leaders, nevertheless, were men like George Whitehead and Ellis Hookes, gifted mainly in legal problems and practical administration.

As Friends restrained themselves from foolish attacks upon the outside world, most of them turned their attention inward. The discovery of the power of worship was most rich in the gatherings during the persecution years, which were intervals of pure joy to those who had long since passed through their time of inward judgment. The serenity which has ever since been present in the silent meeting, the security and sweetness, as distinct from struggle and exaltation, grew up in England mainly in this time of outward misfortune: "Those that have seen the sweet lovely precious state of Unity and Concord, that the excellent Power of the Lord God Almighty gathered into . . . in the blessed morning of our day, and the spiritual joy, refreshments and divine Satisfaction that attended . . . in this true and spiritual Unity with the Lord Jesus . . . cannot but . . . greatly dread the turnings aside and going out of it." [5]

Life in the American colonies also presented situations that gradually changed the early Quaker spirit of the Lamb's War. To be sure, the first Quaker invasion, especially in Massachusetts, was as headlong and hard fought as the battle of Friends anywhere. Moreover, the first experience of some colonists won to Quakerism was often like that of Banks and others in England earlier. Humphrey Norton on Long Island reported: "In my distress— when gross darkness covered me—I heard a cry that Light was

---

(such as Calvert's sister), seems to refer to Quaker leaders' judgments against a marriage. At this time Calvert was under court injunction and his press was run by his wife.

4. ARBarc./46 and 49, John Rous to Fox.

5. "Testimony of C. Marshall Concerning the Unity of the Spirit," in Camm and Audland, *Works.*

Fig. 5. The setting of silent worship: Yealand Conyers Meeting House, built 1692 and 1745. On the raised or "facing" bench sat the elders of the Meeting, from whom silent leadership or spoken ministry most often came.

Fig. 6. The moorland home of Quakerism: Cartmel Fell and Height Meeting House, between Swarthmore and Kendal.

broken forth. . . . My desire to live justly and *enjoy God,* set
me to inquire after this new Light. . . . I heard that it did convince of sin; and being believed in, obeyed and followed, led out
of all manner of uncleanness. Then said I in my heart, if so, it
should not want following, for I was weary of my sin, yea I loathed
my life." [6] Most of the converts in that same year of 1657 lived in
Rhode Island and were up to their necks in the struggle against
Massachusetts. But while the basic message of the preachers was
the same, their warfare against the world was not relevant in the
backwoods, for the proud did not live there. The clergy, especially
in New England, were indeed enemies, and authorities in Maryland and Virginia represented hostile attitudes of the English
government. Even the controversies within Quakerism, especially
over Wilkinson and Story, were reflected by splits in America.
Quaker preachers in the colonies, however, mainly won response
not in the cities but in wild country. Where little groups of hearers
gathered in frontier communities, the visitor would encourage
as well as challenge, for the main enemy was the wilderness itself.
Burnyeat's Journal records in 1672:

> I appointed a Meeting at West-River in Maryland for all the
> Friends in the Province . . . for the setling of Things, that
> *Men*-and *Womens-Meetings* might be established in the Prov-
> ince . . .
> And George Fox, Robert Withers, George Pattison and I,
> . . . took Boat and went over to the Eastern-shore . . . and
> on the second-day we began our Journey through the Woods,
> to go over Land to New England. And on the fourth-day we
> came to Saxifrax-River and did swim our Horses . . . and
> got to Delaware to Newcastle, and got Lodging . . .
> And next day we got over the [Delaware] River. . . . We
> could not get an Indian for a Guide. . . . And the next day
> . . . we hired one; and so began our Journey . . . through
> that Country, which now is called New Jersey; and we did
> suppose that we travelled that day near forty Miles. . . . We
> lodged that Night in an Indian Wigwam and lay upon the
> ground, as themselves did: and the next day . . . towards
> the Evening we got to an Indian Town . . . we went up to

6. [Humphrey Norton], *The New England Ensign* (London, 1659), pp. 2–3.

the "King's House", who received us very kindly. . . . But
alas he was poorly provided . . . most of us could neither
get to eat nor drink . . . but it was, because he had it not.
So we lay as well as he, that was, upon the Ground, only a
Matt under us. . . . Next morning early we took Horse
. . . and that night we lodged in the Woods. And so the next
day . . . we got to an English Plantation, called Middle-
Town in East Jersey . . . and so we came down with a Friend
to his House near the Water-side, and he carried us over in
his Boat, and our Horses also, to Long-Island. . . . We took
our Journey to Oyster-Bay . . . and several Friends from
Gravesend and Flushing with us, for the next day their Half-
Years-Meeting did begin.[7]

From Baltimore to Brooklyn they had passed only three English
settlements, but held a Yearly Meeting at each end. In America
the Quaker preachers were doing a work more like that of Fox in
the Westmorland Fells or of a later Methodist circuit-rider in
Kentucky than like the warfare upon the proud gentry and priests
of England.

Some Friends in America soon attained local leadership. John
Archdale wrote from North Carolina in 1686, while persecution
was still dying in England, praising the local commodities of "To-
baccoe, Oyle, Hides & Tallow," and reporting proudly that he
had patched up a quarrel between "the great Hat King of ye
Tuskiroroes" and an Indian of another tribe who had committed
murder. Archdale had prevented war between the Tuscaroras
and a third tribe, and hoped he would "leave the country att peace
with all the Indians & one with another." [8] Ten years later he was
governor of the colony; but when he was later elected to the English Parliament, he was refused his seat, because he could not take
an oath. Friends held the Rhode Island governorship for 36 terms
out of the first 110. But clearly Quakers did not set up a rule of
the Saints over their fellow frontiersmen. While committees of
Quakers had control over East and West Jersey, and later when
Penn laid out his colony across the river, they insisted on tolera-

7. Burnyeat, pp. 43–45. New England was well settled, and travel was physically
easy there. Yet New Jersey had scarcely changed since Thurston and Coale had
gone through it fifteen years earlier.

8. ARBarc./68. Cf. also Drummond, *American Protestantism,* pp. 17–18.

tion for all faiths. Economic necessity drove them to woo non-Friends as settlers.[9]

Friends in England were still fearful when William Penn abetted Shaftesbury in organizing the Whig party on a platform of reform. They naturally condemned him when the Whig plans of 1676–80 backfired, causing the King and the Anglicans to renew persecutions. But in their different ways both Penn and his critics had accepted the fact that Quakerism would not conquer the world. After the Toleration Act of 1689 was passed, there was a new enthusiasm for winning converts in some local Meetings, and, for a few years a renewal of conflict within their own group and a renewal of tract warfare with the puritans, which gradually died away after 1700. The final flourish was a series of verbal debates led by the brilliant ex-Quaker George Keith and a closing barrage of tracts by two other former Friends, John Pennyman and Francis Bugg, whose *Bomb* was less lively than the Anglican Charles Leslie's *Snake in the Grass*.[10] Friends replied in kind to these tracts, but, in relation to the tolerant rulers, their main concern was caution and respectability. Yearly meeting epistles after 1690 are in direct contrast to the petitions of the 1650s:

> Since the Lord's Good Providence has so far Blessed ffriends as to give them favour with the Government, It is desired that ffriends would continue with all Humility to walk worthy of that Mercy, and improve the same by a gentle and peaceable Conversation towards all men.
>
> It is advised that Friends be circumspect, and not make it their business to Discourse of the outward Powers. . . . To our Grief, we have heard . . . some who have not observed a true Bridle to their Tongues, but have been too busy loose & airy in Discourses of that Nature.[11]

Basic theory regarding non-Friends also quietly changed. At first Quakers under persecution merely widened the circle of the Saints

9. See Wilmer Cooper, "The Ethical Implications of Quaker Participation in Politics" (Haverford College, 1948), pp. 15–16. Cf. *JFHS, 31* (1934), 44, and *35* (1938), 101, on Archdale.

10. See Braithwaite, *Second Period*, chap. 17; Charles Leslie, *Snake in the Grass* (London, 1696); also Barbara Bowden's thesis in progress, London University.

11. Yearly Meeting Epistles of 1705 and 1690, as given in Kendal MS No. 1, 141. Cf. Yearly Meeting Epistle for 1689, and Braithwaite, *Second Period*, pp. 160, 179.

to include fellow sufferers; now a new relativism grew up toward
all outsiders. Beginning before 1670, a key change came about in
the concept of conscience. Earlier, Friends had defined conscience
as primarily the agent of the Light, the beachhead for attack and
transformation within each "child of the devil." Though God
must use the human instrument of conscience, the Light and not
the conscience in itself was authoritative. When they first appealed
for freedom of conscience, it was in the name of the Spirit, but
after 1660 it was increasingly tempting to appeal in the name of
conscience itself. The danger of hypocrisy in coerced churchgoing
was one that even the Anglican magistrate could understand. His
own conscience could be reached, if the justice was a sensitive
man, *without* converting him to the Light, for he could be touched
by the sufferings of men with whom he had no intention of agree-
ing. Moreover, wounding of the consciences of persecuted Baptists
or puritans seemed wrong in itself, though Quakers did not fully
accept them as "Children of the Light." The beachhead of conscience had thus become a bridgehead. Quaker leaders urged,
"where any ffriend . . . shall be Prosecuted for the Truth . . .
that such labour . . . with the Prosecutors before or at the beginning of his Prosecution; that so (if possible) the Witness of God
in him may be reached, & he convinced that their Refusal [as
Friends] to comply Proceeds not from Obstinacy or Self-interest,
but from a Godly Care . . . a conscience void of offence towards
God and man." [12]

Such an approach implied that conscientiousness was good in
itself, whether or not it led men to the Quaker Light. William
Penn, for instance, stressed on the one hand that conscience led
to action in worship before God, so that to neglect it out of fear
or favor toward any mortal man would be sinful; but he also
called conscience a "heavenly instinct," and said that those who
persecute it "destroy nature or that privilege which men are
born with." [13] Conscience was regarded no longer as a passive
channel for God's voice but as a divine and active guide. A breach
was thus quietly made between the conscience and the infallible
Spirit, one which deepened the rift already opening in practice
between experiences shared with Friends alone and those which

12. Yearly Meeting Epistle of 1703, in Kendal MS No. 1.
13. William Penn, *The Great Case of Liberty of Conscience* (London, 1670), p. 19.

many non-Friends could share. The old, unchanging testimonies and standards of Quakerism were based on the infallible authority of the Spirit within the Quaker fellowship and tradition, but on the other hand, conscientious appeals to which any sensitive man would respond might bring about new political and social reforms in the unconverted nation. This double standard for Quakers and the outside world was the beginning of the end of the Lamb's War. The breach was not total, for even in the outside world a Friend looked individually to the guidance of the Spirit and did not entirely deny it to non-Quaker Christians. But these areas of shared guidance did not include worship or the unique Quaker ideals. Within the group itself a double standard might ensue: where Friends disagreed, instead of waiting until the Spirit brought everyone into a united Sense of the Meeting, as would have been absolutely inescapable in early Quakerism, they might agree to differ. Over the validity of using affirmations as a legal substitute for oaths, the satisfied and dissatisfied Friends were almost evenly divided, and both parties respected each others' conscientiousness. For twenty years neither disowned the other, until a new Act of Parliament in 1722 found an answer acceptable to all.[14]

As the hope of conquering the world faded, the meaning of Quaker customs and testimonies quietly changed. They had been upheld steadily throughout the persecutions, but were maintained in loyalty to Friends as much as in direct obedience to the Spirit. When persecution ended, they had lost their sharp power for piercing the conscience of the unconverted, for these customs no longer had direct command over a Friend's relationship with non-Quakers. A Friend kept clear of the world's standards but did not expect to change them, and their customs therefore became the badge of peculiarity for a sect. Their costume, originally a workday appeal against proud dress, became a gray or black uniform of a cut quite unique and often quite expensive.[15] *Thee* and *thou* were maintained after the rest of England ceased to say them even to social inferiors, and became a mark not of equality but of uniqueness. Quakers still kept their hats on in London drawing rooms, but their simple speech became as courteous as

14. See Braithwaite, *Second Period*, pp. 182–90; Penn, *Witness*, p. 69.
15. Cf. Tolles, *Meeting-House*, chap. 6.

a gentleman's. They refused oaths but used a form of affirmation equally distinct from everyday speech. These habits, and Quaker pacifism itself, came to be regarded in England as harmless deviations and as perhaps commendable—but of course utopian— ideals. For the individual Friend such distinctions could still be a searching challenge, especially since they cut him off from certain contacts with non-Quaker companions. Many families came later to be divided between "plain Friends" and the "gay Quakers," who ignored some of the customs and risked disownment. The original Quaker Testimonies were no longer expected to offend or convert anyone and were left by the passing of time and the end of conflict as a former shoreline cut by the high tide of the Spirit before it shifted to new beaches.

Those areas of action in which Friends still pioneered were thus mainly ones which had *not* originally distinguished Friends from other groups: education, war, slavery, prison reform, and business ethics. Where they had taken stands in some of these areas from the start, other churches had shared their standards; and certain problems, such as slavery and care for the insane, came into clear focus only after the early years. As in the beginning, new Testimonies were brought forward by the burdened conscience of a few individuals and their sense of God's leading. A Sense of the Meeting was still hoped for, and attempts were made toward united action. But whereas the early standards had normally become infallible and unanimous at the time and holy in retrospect, a Friend was now expected to follow his own concern alone, if need be, in an experimental spirit, or—a more crucial allowance—he might appeal to the consciences of non-Friends if the issue seemed a universal human problem. Slavery, for example, was attacked by William Edmondson in 1675 and by George Keith in 1693 as individuals, and publicly condemned by the Germantown Meeting of Pastorius in 1688, before Friends considered the issue as a group. The next steps were taken within Quaker circles: London Yearly Meeting censured the slave trade in 1727. John Woolman and Anthony Benezet persuaded Philadelphia Yearly Meeting in 1758 to disown Quaker slave owners. In the seventy preceding years the consciences of many Friends must have been privately touched before collective action was taken. Further work for the national abolition of slave trading and slave owning in England and America, however, was carried on largely by individuals such as J. J. Gurney and Whittier, and these men worked almost entirely with non-Friends in the setting up of antislavery societies and the pressure for legislation.[16] Even on issues to which all Quakers became committed, there was a clear distinction between the purity of conduct within the Society of Friends and the more piecemeal steps of equally earnest Quakers outside the fellowship.

This was Quaker "reformism," which was not as negative in its reactions to theocratic dreams as were most persecuted sects. The Friends still felt responsibility for government and law-making and still wanted as rulers saintly men who would be guided by conscience and, in some cases, open to the Spirit. But they were regularly warned by their Yearly Meetings—by those in England and North Carolina, as late as 1854—to avoid even a local political office, for it might threaten to compromise their Testimonies. Quakers since 1689 have gone about the world doing good by small degrees. From the beginning "Friends [had] been known for frequenting the official courts or waiting rooms of government officials." [17] No longer do they attempt to convert ministers of state, however, and the Quaker has become a "limited prophet." [18] Socially, Friends have quietly undertaken a series of impressive reforms: John Bellers suggested turning poorhouses into trade-school cooperatives, building a working model; John Howard and Elizabeth Fry visited the prisons; Tuke reshaped mental hospitals. Each of these developed new ideas and practices, but their disciples have been non-Quakers.[19] The conceptions of the world, of human nature, and of society that such reforms assume are in marked contrast to those of the Lamb's War.

From the viewpoint of Quaker reformism, the world was no longer a hostile field to be conquered but a neutral arena. Indi-

16. Tolles, *Atlantic Culture*, pp. 51–54. Cf. Rufus M. Jones, *The Later Periods of Quakerism* (2 vols. London, Macmillan, 1921), *1*, 23–26; John Woolman, *Journal* (Philadelphia, 1900).

17. Cooper, "Quaker Participation," pp. 77–78.

18. Cf. Kühn, *Toleranz*, chap. 4.

19. Work for prisons and slaves soon passed mainly out of Quaker hands in England, and more gradually in America. John Bellers has recently been unjustifiably hailed by Marxists as a protosocialist, but his type of vocational training in community settings has been taken as a national responsibility in many countries. See John Bellers, *Writings*, ed. A. Ruth Fry (London, 1935).

viduals were no longer simply divided into Children of Light and
Darkness, for the relativism of the conscientious allowed for all
shades of good and evil. Men and nations who ignored the full
truth of Quakerism could be improved in specific points. Friends
did not give up their claims of absolute authority for the Spirit
within them, however, but limited the areas to which the Light
applied; in business and human contacts Quakers responded to
other men as equals.

To guide areas beyond the Quaker tradition where conscience
might rule, Friends began, in addition, to appeal to reason and
nature. Such a revolution in Quaker thought was largely led by
William Penn, the optimist, Whig, and scholarly gentleman. Until
his frustrating experiences in Pennsylvania, Penn kept the love
for radical social reform and rebellion against injustice that had
first won him to Quakerism. In 1670 he became a popular champion by his trial at the Old Bailey. He was acquitted of the charge
that he had caused a riot by speaking at a Quaker meeting in
Grace-Church Street. His case was a victory for the freedom of
juries but seemed to the conservative judges and alderman to
justify the renewal of the Conventicle Act in the same summer of
strife. Penn was already writing tracts for toleration which praised
conscientiousness in general. Against the irreligious Cabal then
controlling the King's cabinet, he used a skillful ad hominem
argument: for "men thus liable to change, and no ways certain of
their own belief, to be the most infallible to . . . enact any religion or prohibit persons from the exercise of theirs, sounds harsh
in the ears of all modest and unbiased men." [20] Arguments from
religious uncertainty, however, had seldom before been used by
a Quaker and belonged to the repertory of the skeptics and hu-
manists.

Penn also appealed to reason, since "the understanding can
never be convinced nor properly submit but by such arguments
as are rational, persuasive, and suitable to its own nature." [21] The
conclusion from both reason and conscience was the same: force
may make a hypocrite, but faith grounded upon knowledge and

20. Penn, *Great Case of Liberty*, preface. On the Penn-Mead trial see Penn,
Witness, pp. 87 ff., from "The People's Ancient and Just Liberties."
21. Penn, *Great Case of Liberty*, p. 22.

consent is what makes a Christian. Yet he approached faith by a line no early Friend would have used. In the 1650s this was Milton's argument, not Fox's. Most Friends and puritans, like Luther and Calvin, would have expected sinful men to rationalize and misuse reason. Penn's innocently open faith in reason was closer to the Cambridge Platonists or Penn's fellow members of the Royal Society. In particular, "reason, like the sun, is common to all," said Penn, "and 'tis for want of examining all by the same light and measure that we are not all of the same mind." [22]

His attitude to nature was similar. Through persecution, "all natural affection is destroyed . . . for nature, being one in all, such as ruin those who are equally entitled with themselves to nature . . . bring the state of nature to the state of war." [23] Penn's confidence in natural affection would have surprised early Friends. For George Fox nature was "the Creation," to be used joyfully in the service of the Spirit, but human nature was corrupt. Fox and Penn both used the same biblical passages supporting toleration, but Penn added a deistic flavor: "We see the God of Nature hath taught us softer Doctrine in his great Book of the world; his Sun shines and his Rain falls upon all." [24] He appealed to natural rights in many political tracts; he was after all an Englishman, and Parliament's case against both Charles I and Charles II was based on natural rights wherever historical precedents were in doubt. But Penn was unusual among Quakers in shifting so easily back and forth between God, conscience, reason, nature, and private interest: "Interest is the choice men naturally make. Nothing, humanly speaking, fixes a man like his interests, and whatever be the morality of any party . . . I am sure of them by the side of Interests." [25] He was not merely worldy-wise; he presented the economic inconveniences of persecution and warfare in his *Essay towards the Present and Future Peace of Europe,* a written plea for toleration to the rulers of England and to the European powers who were fighting for and against Louis XIV in Holland. His identification of religion with natural rights ex-

22. Penn, *Witness,* p. 191, from *More Fruits of Solitude.*
23. Ibid., p. 74, from *Great Case of Liberty.*
24. Penn, *Works,* 2, 746. Cf. Kühn, *Toleranz und Offenbarung,* p. 267.
25. Penn, as quoted in Philip S. Belasco, *Authority in Church and State* (London, George Allen and Unwin, 1928), p. 306.

tended to private property: "I am sure 'twas to enjoy Property
with Conscience that [Protestantism] was promoted, nor is there
any better Definition of Protestancy, than protesting against Spoiling Property for Conscience." [26] Only the ruthless fines of the
Second Conventicle Act could have brought a Quaker to such a
financial view of faith. Fox had once thundered against confusion
of the Spirit with self-love; that he did not restrain Penn may show
his own confusion of thought and Penn's also.

As political allies for achieving toleration, Penn accepted first
the Whigs and, after their defeat, the Catholic James II, whom
almost no one else would trust. The rural Friends of northwestern
England were fiercely critical of Penn's political enthusiasm and
preferred isolation, as in 1659, but they were themselves willing
to trust the King. Nevertheless, the bloodless revolution that
brought William of Orange to the throne in 1688 produced freedom in a different way. The Whigs had won after all.

In Pennsylvania, William Penn applied the same blend of principles: Quaker standards on war, oaths, and marriage; reformist
ethics in laws about prisons, workhouses, and inns; and the theory
of natural rights stated in his basic *Frame of Government*. Theo-
cratically, he set up the colony not simply as a refuge from persecution but as a "Holy Experiment" in statecraft. Like the Puritans, he saw the role of government as creative law-making, not
as restraint. But he canvassed the Rhineland for colonists, and
allowed all property owners to vote. When conflicts occurred in
early Pennsylvania, they were seldom over religion; mainly, they
arose between the paternalism of Penn and his agents, and the
independent spirit of the poorer farmers. Penn had himself restricted his own powers and those of the legislature in the name
of constitutional rights, but his supporting argument, in the spirit
of Calvin, pointed out the need for restraint of all men by the
law, since all were sinful.[27]

The focus in which all Penn's principles cohered was morality,
and not the Spirit. His confusion of thought partly arose from
equating all forces that worked toward morality. Even political
freedom in Pennsylvania was limited to men "within the bounds

26. Penn, quoted in Perry, *Puritanism and Democracy*, p. 297.
27. Penn, *Witness*, pp. 107–09, from his *Frame of Government*.

of morality, and neither frantic nor mischievous." [28] The careful planning by which Penn's colony, almost from its start in 1681, overshadowed the equally idealistic but haphazard New Jersey settlements was vindicated. By 1700 there were about 40,000 Quakers in America in contrast to only 50,000 in England, and more than half of them were in Pennsylvania. But morality for most of them had become more vital than radical obedience to the Spirit. By respectability and hard work, integrity and concern for practical needs of neighbors, they maintained the affection and cooperation of all men in their colony long after they were outnumbered four to one by members of other denominations. Yet men like John Woolman, who kept the original openness of heart, were much submerged by weighty Friends who built solidly, ate solidly, and liked clothes and furniture "of the best sort, but plain." [29] The Lamb's War had been intensely moral, yet in the new period the expectation of new leadings and new moral conquest was largely gone.

The compromise of reformism itself would not always work. In 1757, while still holding a majority in the Pennsylvania Assembly, the Quakers had kept the colony at peace with the Indians for seventy-five years, despite periodic injustices and misunderstandings. The German pacifists shared the Quaker ideals, but even with their help Friends were in the minority. Pressure from England had driven the legislators to allow certain disguised military taxes and to allow the militant Scots-Irish and others in the colony to form a volunteer militia. When war broke out against the French and Indians, these Scots-Irish were most numerous in the exposed frontier settlements, and Pennsylvania was also pressed to join by the other colonies and England. The Quaker majority in the Assembly could have overruled their fellow citizens in the name of what they felt to be God's will, as Cromwell had done in enforcing toleration upon England, or they could have compromised their principles and declared war. Instead, they resigned or withdrew from the Pennsylvania government entirely. Still feeling their responsibility, they worked by in-

28. Quoted by Edwin Corbyn Beatty, *William Penn as Social Philosopher* (New York, Columbia University Press, 1939), p. 132.
29. See the delightful study in Tolles, *Meeting-House*, chap. 6.

formal commissions to mediate for peace with the Indians. In America, as in England, Friends ended up in the role of a responsible minority, keeping their own lives pure and influencing the national life in marginal ways.[30]

The American Quakers were mainly homesteaders while those in England increasingly rose in commerce: some had unwillingly left their farms rather than battle endlessly against tithes; others were born townsmen and prospered in trade. By the end of the eighteenth century, Friends had come to dominate English banking, iron and brass foundries, and clock-making, and were strong in the manufacture of cloth, tin, and drugs. The Darbys of Coalbrookdale gave up cannon-making on pacifist grounds and thus lost pre-eminence in the iron industry but won fame by making the first iron bridge.[31] Honesty and hard work led to prosperity and respectability for them, as the same virtues did later for the Methodists. By 1700 the Barclays, Gurneys, Hanburys, and Lloyds had made the Grace-Church Street Meeting in London the richest merchant group in the city.[32] The resulting changes in Quaker attitudes reinforced the other shifts from the views of early Friends.

Quaker Meetings were still intended to supervise thoroughly the economic as well as the moral life of Friends. The original ideal of a united witness to the world, however, had been reduced by men like George Whitehead to preserving a collective good name. Quaker committees supervised styles and standards in tailoring, furniture design, shoemaking, and other trades. Monthly and Quarterly Meetings watched over apprentices, disowned gamblers and the bankrupt, aided emigrants, and provided help for members who needed work or had been burned out of homes or barns. The Yearly Meeting in London worked through a standing committee, the "Meeting for Sufferings," to help Friends in prison while persecution lasted and thereafter to supervise books, travel-

---

30. The story of Quaker actions in the Seven Years' War against the French and Indians is vividly told by Isaac Sharpless and A. Gummere in *A Quaker Experiment in Government* (Philadelphia, 1902), chaps. 7 and 8.

31. Cf. I. Grubb, *Quakerism and Industry*; Paul Herman Emden, *Quakers in Commerce* (London, Sampson, Low, 1940); Lloyd, *Quaker Social History*; Arthur Raistrick, *Quakers in Science and Industry* (New York, 1950), especially on the Darbys.

32. Tolles, *Atlantic Culture*, p. 58.

ing ministry, and other national needs. It was easier, however, to watch over the honesty and sobriety of Friends than their attitudes to their own wealth.

Some Friends throughout the eighteenth century continued to put the calls of the ministry above their work and wealth. John Woolman and a few others chose to cut down their businesses in the prime of their lives to give themselves more to religious service. But before the American Revolution brought a general reaction against piety, American Friends had already begun to accept, as the British Friends had earlier, the bourgeois standards that Max Weber attacked as typical of Protestantism: individual initiative, energy, probity, thrift, and avoidance of luxury and debt.[33] The concept of "calling" in relation to one's private business had replaced the united vocation of early Friends—the transformation of the world:

> We have Liberty from God . . . to work or seek for food or Raiment; tho' that ought to be a Work of Indifferency, compar'd to the great Work of Salvation. . . . Our Lord [said] to his Disciples 'Children, have you any Meat?' . . . and he bid them cast their Nets into the Sea. . . . Fishing being their Trade, no doubt they sold them . . . By this it appears that we not only have Liberty to labour in Moderation, but we are told that it is our Duty so to do.[34]

Toward wealth the old prophetic protest was sometimes heard, and Bellers and Penn tried to set up practical institutions to apply their conviction that "a *comfortable* living to the industrious labourer is the rich man's debt, not his charity." [35] But Penn never questioned slavery or the right of a master to arrange and veto his servants' marriages. Even Robert Barclay went back to the Elizabethan ideal of the social hierarchy to set the standards of wealth:

> The servant is not the same way educated as the master; nor the tenant as the landlord; nor the rich as the poor. . . . He

33. Max Weber, in *The Protestant Ethic and the Spirit of Capitalism* (London, 1930), tends to read the eighteenth–century outlooks back into the seventeenth and has been well corrected by R. H. Tawney in *Religion and Capitalism* and by Winthrop Hudson in "Puritanism and the Spirit of Capitalism," *Church History, 18* (1949), 3–17.

34. Thomas Chalkeley, *A Journal*, quoted in Tolles, *Atlantic Culture*, pp. 61–62

35. John Bellers, *College of Industry*, quoted by Belasco, *Authority*, p. 102

that by reason of his estate and education hath been used to eat flesh and drink wine, and to be clothed with the finest wool, if his estate will bear it . . . he may do it. . . . But if a man, whose estate and education hath accustomed him to both coarser food and raiment, should stretch himself beyond . . . what he were used to . . . no doubt it would be unlawful to him.[36]

Toward the poor the reversal of early Quaker moral concern was much more complete than toward luxury. Penn himself urged the poor to be silent and patient and to trust in the Lord.[37] Some later Friends came to identify wealth with virtue and poverty with laziness. Logan of Pennsylvania, who headed the wealthy and conservative party there, said that the poor "grow factious and turbulent. . . . They are for Inventing extraordinary Measures for their Relief and Ease, when it is certain That nothing can prove Truly Effectual to them, but a change of their own . . . exercise of those wholesome and healing Vertues . . . Sobriety, Industry and Frugality." [38] Respectability came to Friends from the start because of their self-sacrifices for the sake of moral witness; they cultivated it later insofar as it might allay persecution, and, by 1700, men were proud to be known as Quakers. Having set out to transform the world, Friends ended the eighteenth century as a "somewhat eccentric but respectable body of people." [39]

The formal name of the Society of Friends arose only when Quakers accepted existence as a permanent minority. Inwardly and outwardly, they no longer expected warfare and conquest but rather constant pruning and improvement. The first generation of Quakers had needed to fight the inner Adam and the world as well. The second generation faced daily outward danger, and inherited self-sacrifice with little choice. The third generation inherited the Quaker life without a struggle. The formal recognition of birthright membership in 1737 simply standardized the existing custom of drawing up lists of those for whom the Meet-

36. Barclay, *Apology* (1678), pp. 369–70. This was the attitude of conservative puritans like Perkins under Elizabeth. See "Discourse of Conscience," in *Works, 1.*
37. Penn, "Journal of His Travels in Holland and Germany," quoted in Beatty, *Penn,* p. 194.
38. Logan, *Charge Delivered from the Bench,* quoted in Tolles, *Meeting-House,* p. 105.
39. Emden, *Quakers in Commerce,* p. 10.

ing made itself responsible; it assumed that the children of Quakers would live by the Testimonies from infancy onward and would obey the inward Spirit without rebellion. A personal struggle was still in fact often needed before young Quakers could accept this life and obedience, as many journals show, but each man passed through this time of conflict quietly, in private, and in his own way. The collective inward wrestling with sin was past.

Eighteenth-century England reacted with bitter skepticism to enthusiasm and fanaticism—any claim, that is, to direct divine authority for individuals, or efforts to make religion interfere in all of life. Friends were by this time as aware as anyone else of the intermixture of human ideas and irrational impulses in some of their old spontaneity. They worked to keep the purity and infallibility of the Spirit by the watchful limiting of the Spirit's scope. Except by a few Friends, leadings were expected only in worship and in special concerns of the Meeting's own life. Friends waited in their meetings until they were sure that the impulse to speak came genuinely from the Spirit, even if this meant sitting in silence for months on end. This period of Quietism produced a rare combination of sensitivity and action in Woolman and Job Scott but mainly devotional literature from other Friends.

The cold climate of deism and rationalism kept all religious groups on the defensive in the eighteenth century, no longer against each other but against public skepticism and optimistic humanism. Various responses were tried out. The deists themselves tried to set up a reduced religion on a secure basis of pure reason. The Calvinists produced a highly refined theology: they attempted to maintain their old doctrines intact but with science and reason as helps. In daily life, however, they often accepted the new outlooks, giving up theocracy and the hope of radical conversion. The Anglicans at their best preserved personal devotion, as did William Law, but most churchmen were content to maintain tradition and ritual with little vitality. The Quakers consistently refused a diluted or rationalized religion. They maintained the purity, authority, and power of the Spirit by keeping it within a protective shell, where like a stream in winter it flowed, hidden and quiet but clear. When emotion and warmth returned to Christianity in the Wesleyan revivals, Friends were dubious. Later they accepted the gentler evangelicalism of men like Charles

Simeon early in the nineteenth century, and Friends like Joseph John Gurney found emotional and intellectual renewal; others lost some of their purity of spirit as the price of the new enthusiasm.

In 1827–28 American Quakers split permanently into "orthodox" (the evangelical) and the "Hicksites" who stressed the quietness of waiting upon the Spirit.[40] The cleavage has continued to pull American Meetings in opposite directions, toward the old tradition of the silent meeting and toward the new life of evangelical Christianity. The social roles have changed, and except in a few Conservative Meetings, the pastorless worship and the Testimonies no longer belong to close-knit farming communities. Where these are caught up by new Meetings in colleges or cities, liberal thought has changed the religious mood. The evangelicals, on the contrary, arose where contact with non-Quaker Christians was closest, among city merchants and in new towns of the American Middle West. But in the twentieth century Quaker evangelicalism has clashed with urban modernism, and it keeps its main strength in the congregations of little prairie and corn-belt towns. British Friends have kept unity both in spirit and in organization, but face terrible problems of aimlessness.

The diminishing power and outreach of Quakers since the early years have caused fears of further decline, but deliberately to revive the attitude of the Lamb's War may not be possible. Modern Quakers who show a radical, world-changing spirit are sometimes confused or shallow in their vision of the evil they are fighting. Their own fierce, inner fight may not yet be won and so is projected crookedly upon the world. Some recognize more clearly the world's enormous evils, but cannot show a victory over them, for their conscientiousness is still tight and negative. Both types of men were found among early Friends, but the heart of Quakerism was the freedom of those confidently dependent on the Spirit; only men who have known such power can confidently lead the Lamb's War. In our day such empowered men are seldom radical in their insight, and often stay steadily in a quiet home and vocation. Early Quakerism will be reborn in our time only when personal understanding of the depth of evil (with a precision drawn from psy-

40. See Bliss Forbush, *Elias Hicks* (New York, 1956).

chology and theology) can be combined with the free power of the Spirit of God to overcome it.

The conception of leadings by the Spirit needs much rethinking in our day. It is still dominant in prayer groups and pietistic circles in almost every church in America and many in England. "Moral Rearmament" is a vivid example. It has come under fierce fire from neo-orthodox and Barthian theologians, as it did from Luther and Calvin, who have seen it as a product of man's self-righteousness, self-delusion, and unwillingness to live as a simple, forgiven, ignorant, sinning human being. Many modern psychologists also challenge trust in divine guidance; they see compulsive drives simply as inward urges which men fear to examine, and they are suspicious of the need for dependence on infallible answers and guidance from beyond oneself.

The believer in guidance or leadings must hear these warnings. Familiar human impulses can more and more clearly be recognized behind some leadings, and perhaps the experience is never as completely purified of self-made urges and limits as the early Friends believed. But the validity of intuitive discovery and the flash of insight has been demonstrated in art, poetry, music, and even the exact sciences; there the breadth and precision of the gradually assembled raw materials is great, and the sudden and unforeseen results in the form of a poem, a symphony, or an equation will stand the full rigor of testing appropriate to the field. The process of creative intuition is as valid as that of reason, often leading to a similar end product.[41] It is also potentially as valid in prophetic inspiration or personal religion. Friends may hope for God to work within as well as beyond such a process. Moreover, the basic attitude that sets the stage for leadings involves an expectancy which theologians and psychotherapists are also seeking. The demand for moment-by-moment existential self-surrender, confession, and obedience seems to recur constantly in neo-orthodox theology despite all theoretical arguments against it. Likewise, the ability to know and accept (though not, in all cases, to follow) one's spontaneous response to each person and situation is a way of life which is one goal of psychotherapy. Some Christians

41. See Henri Poincaré, *Science et méthode* (Paris, 1908), pp. 50–52; Brewster Ghiselin, *The Creative Method* (New York, 1955).

who act daily as they are led seem to achieve the same spirit of faith—though at times naïvely and not without danger—as that which is the aim of their critics. Such responsible trust is part of the meaning of salvation.

It seems necessary here to underline the contrast between early Quakerism and the usual idea of a sect. A typical sect,[42] such as the Mennonites, is noted for withdrawing from society and its corruptions, from the sins of war, commerce, magistracy, and oaths, and from worldly living in luxury and indulgence, whether in dress or literature, or in tobacco, liquor, tea, and coffee. Such a sect also disavows churches which accept the unconverted, and sometimes rejects all Christian groups except its own. It is likely to live out in detail, often with power, an ethical code such as the Sermon on the Mount, but its ethics are legalistic. It expects to be a small minority, often persecuted. Its new members will be committed adults: children of members are brought up within the fellowship but rarely baptized until they make their own commitment.

All these attitudes appeared in some degree among early Friends, especially after persecution had become severe. But Friends did not withdraw from the world except to attack and transform it. Their attitude to the state, to industry, and to social legislation aimed at control by the Saints and by the Spirit, and failing that by men's successively purified consciences. This was different from the sects' attitude and closer to Puritanism. Friends, moreover, did not seek holiness by rule-keeping despite the Meeting's rules. Sin was measured not by specific deeds or thoughts but by self-will, by impulses of disobedience to the Light within. The Quaker ethics sought out new needs and problems, and provided power as well as righteousness. Also, Quakers never thought of themselves as a "gathered Church" based on individual commitment to a church covenant. The Spirit moved and drew men together, but there was no limit to whom it might reach.

Just as Friends were not simply a sect, neither were they basically mystics or a mere blend of mysticism and sectarianism. Neither outlook could have given rise to the Lamb's War. To call early

42. The standard discussion of the "Sect-Type" and "Church-Type" in Christianity is by Ernst Troeltsch, *Die Soziallehren der christlichen Kirchen und Gruppen* (Gesammelte Schriften, *1*, Tübingen, 1923).

Quakerism a prophetic outlook or to speak of early Quakers as spiritual reformers is more sound but not always clear in meaning.[43] The heart of early Quakerism was its religious experience, which included both inward knowledge of the Spirit or Light and a knowledge of their inner selves; upon these was based their idea of the world. Theirs was above all an experience of power. Though its first effects were bitter inward struggles, the ending was joy, and its results were to change the Quaker's life and, through him, the world.

The closest parallels to early Quakerism may be in movements of "Awakening" such as the campaigns of the early Methodist fellowship, the American Great Awakening, the later frontier awakenings, and, in more complex and distorted ways, those of the Adventists, Shakers, and several modern pentecostal groups. The early and explosive stages of many sectarian movements such as the Anabaptists had more in common with this type of experience than is sometimes shown. Such movements start from accepted Christian ethical standards and from the Bible, often from Calvinist theology as well, but they seek personal commitment and conversion. They attack an unconverted ministry [44] and reject the established churches or live at odds with them. Their field is the world. They expect to change all of life for their members, and often to reach all men. They are usually mass movements that spread by challenge, faith, and enthusiasm rather than by their teachings. When the first great period of intense experience has passed, they leave behind smaller groups of dedicated Christians whose lives are permanently changed; such relics are somewhat like sects, but they continue to emphasize conversion and the Spirit and to maintain missions. There is a strong temptation, rarely resisted for long, to try to repeat the awakening experience within their own group. Thus comes revivalism.

But the inward experience of the early Friends went beyond most such movements of awakening. The bitter self-judgment of sin—often accompanied by violent emotions, physical upheavals, and fiery preaching—are common to many groups. Quakers, how-

43. Whereas Troeltsch classified Quakers as blending sectarian and mystical outlooks, Rufus Jones calls them spiritual reformers, and Kühn (*Toleranz und Offenbarung*, chap. 1) calls them "prophetic." Whether the "awakening" type of outlook will stand testing as an independent category needs discussion.

44. See on Gilbert Tennant, Gaustad, *The Great Awakening*, pp. 30–39.

ever, opened themselves to a much more deep, careful, and intense
self-discovery than is usual in groups that present Christ's atonement too easily. The sense of the Spirit's leading, following conversion, also develops in many movements, but among Quakers
there arose a continuing guidance and growth that allowed spontaneous reaction to new problems. The social background of the
Quaker pioneers made them much more radical in their challenge
to the customs of society than groups following Wesley or Edwards
could be. Their inward radicalism reinforced their puritan social
attitudes toward the rule of Saints and toward national responsibility, which left them always unsatisfied with individual conversion. The Lamb's War aimed at opening all of life to the continuing and transforming power of the Spirit of God.

REGIONAL BACKGROUNDS OF QUAKERS AND PURITANS

	A Early Puritan Ministers	B Later Orthodox Puritans	C Independents before 1645	D Baptists & Separatists before 1645	E Leading Quakers to 1660	F Quaker Writers, etc. 1647–90
Kent, Sussex, Surrey	17	9	5	10	7	5
Middlesex and London	43	36	17	32	33	25
Essex, Norfolk, Suffolk	33	42	11	13	5	12
Cambridge and Ely	20	15	0	2	3	0
Hertfordshire, Bedfordshire, Huntingdonshire, Northamptonshire	7	12	2	12	5	3
Buckinghamshire, Berkshire, Oxford	12	10	7	9	10	8
Hampshire, Wiltshire	8	5	1	2	1	3
Somerset, Dorset	7	4	2	2	14	7
Devonshire, Cornwall	1	6	5	2	4	3
Gloucestershire and Bristol	5	7	0	5	21	5
Worcestershire, Herefordshire, Shropshire, Warwickshire	10	12	4	6	3	4
Wales, Isle of Man	2	0	5	6	5	6
Staffordshire, Cheshire, Derbyshire, Leicestershire, Rutland	13	9	4	3	5	3
Nottingham, Lincoln	2	6	7	6	3	4
South Lancashire	11	11	1	4	7	1
Yorkshire	5	1	1	2	52	41
Westmorland, Cumberland, Furness, North Lancashire	4	2	0	2	80	38
Northumberland and Durham	4	2	1	1	6	3

Note: Figures on early and later orthodox puritans and Independents are based on birthplaces or major pastorates of prominent writers and leaders. These figures are far from complete, though proportional to local puritan influence. Figures for Baptists and separatists are unsure because of inadequate surviving records. Quaker figures are based on residence or childhood home.

Bibliographical Note

THE QUAKER LIBRARIAN Joseph Smith wrote a 2400-page *Descriptive Catalogue of Friends Books* (London, 1867), which lists over 18,000 titles and is still the only exhaustive Quaker bibliography. The few titles he missed, and also those omitted from his much less complete *Bibliotheca Anti-Quakeriana* (London, 1873) can be found among the much wider listing of the *Short-Title Catalogue of Books Printed in England, Ireland, Wales, and British America, 1641–1700,* compiled by Donald G. Wing of Yale (New York, Index Society, 1945–51). This huge catalogue is based solely on the collections of the major libraries in each country. Such a work cannot present evidence for its assumptions regarding the authorship of various anonymous works, but very little else is missing.

The first Quaker tracts appeared in 1652 from Aldam, Farnworth, and others, and throughout the 1650s those writings which Friends put into print were mainly of the same character: vigorous, argumentative pamphlets of four to twenty pages, answering the attacks from the pulpits or presses of the puritan pastors. James Nayler, Edward Burrough, and Francis Howgill were the masters of this rhetoric among Friends. Personal epistles to Meetings or groups of Meetings were used early by Fox, Dewsbury, and others, and were often reproduced in print from about 1656 onward. These have perhaps been overemphasized in modern efforts to paint the picture of early Quakerism. Though some were copied by hand into the minute books of many local Meetings, others were perhaps little known until they were published posthumously in their writer's works. Collective epistles produced by General and Yearly Meetings appeared in 1657–59 and became important after 1670. Owen C. Watkins' thesis, "Spiritual Autobiography from 1649 to 1660" (University of London, 1952), has shown that in the 1650s many puritan religious diaries were reshaped as published pamphlets. Friends produced some dozen of these autobiographical tracts, but the best-known Quaker journals were written in the 1670s and '80s and mainly printed posthumously; despite the influence of subsequent reflection, they fortunately do not basically contradict the accounts of religious experiences published in the earliest years. Thomas Ellwood's *Life* and the *Journals* of Fox, William Edmondson, and, later, John Woolman became standard reading in Quaker circles and beyond, but the journals of John Banks, John Burnyeat, Stephen Crisp, and John Whitehead are almost as rewarding to a modern reader.

Printed editions of collected works were less closely bound by biblical models, but in Quaker circles they usually included messages of testimony to the character and achievements of their late author. Though Fox's *Great Mistery* (1659) and George Bishop's *New England Judged* (1661) were collections of tract material made by the authors themselves, the first memorial volume was the *Collection of the . . . Writings of . . . George Fox the Younger* (1662), the doughty old Cromwellian soldier-politician. Unlicensed printing had now become illegal, and hence printers of this time often remained anonymous. But quiet spaces in the great persecution allowed similar volumes to present the works of the martyrs Richard Hubberthorne (1663), Edward Burrough (1672), Francis Howgill (1676), and young Parnell (1675). Most of these collected works and journals of Friends, however, did not come out until the less dangerous years after 1689, climaxed by Penn's *Works* in 1726. Though rewarding to the reader and much more accessible than the original pamphlets, the collected works usually did not present all the writings attributable to their authors, either from ignorance or from the desire to gloss over excesses and conflicts in early Quakerism. Even Fox's *Journal* was retouched by its editor, Thomas Ellwood. However, manuscripts of Fox's writings remain, not only for the main sections of the *Journal* but for many epistles and other documents. Fox regarded his movement as a re-enactment of primitive Christianity, and especially after 1673 preserved papers of all kinds with future historians of the faith in mind.

The biggest group of manuscripts from early Friends are the letters written to Swarthmore Hall by traveling preachers all over the world. Fox instituted this reporting process, probably at Swannington late in 1654, and edited and arranged the letters during visits to Swarthmore in the 1660s; his own letters are significantly rare. These Swarthmore Manuscripts, to which were added manuscript minutes and epistles, were kept at Devonshire House in London and are now in the Friends House Library there. Copies are available on microfilm at Earlham, Harvard, Haverford, Swarthmore, etc., and Geoffrey Nuttall has made these immediately useful to scholars by a superb chronological catalogue of the letters written before 1660, with exhaustive indexes and cross references to all historical sources concerning the personalities and events

mentioned.[1] Another important collection of early letters, edited in
the nineteenth century by A. R. Barclay, has appeared in successive
issues of the *Journal of the Friends Historical Society* since 1930, and
in fact it is doubtful if any important early Quaker documents exist
which have not been quoted or reported either in that British journal
or in the American *Bulletin of the Friends Historical Association*.[2] Minutes and records from early times are still retained by local Meetings
such as Kendal and Philadelphia, but even for these there has been a
consistent effort to assemble the original manuscripts in the vaults of
Friends House Library or the libraries at the American Quaker colleges.

Two collections of data by the early Friends themselves are also in
print: the first, a survey of all local persecutions of Quakers between
1650 and 1689, was assembled by the "Meeting for Sufferings" for presentation to the government and was published in London in 1753 as
Joseph Besse's *Collection of the Sufferings of the . . . Quakers*. The
Yearly Meeting of 1676 also asked Meetings in the English counties to
report their own historical origins and early leadership. The resulting
documents, with only a few counties unrepresented, were finally edited
and printed by Norman Penney in 1907 as *The First Publishers of
Truth*. The same scholar, on whose work all late Quaker writers have
depended, after research in the British Public Records Office, published *Extracts from State Papers Relating to Friends, 1654–1672*. The
time has perhaps now come for a new publication of anti-Quaker material, including sermons and tracts. Good popular anthologies from
the works of Barclay, Burrough, Howgill, Nayler, Penn, and Penington
have lately appeared in England or from Pendle Hill near Philadelphia, but there is need for a modern edition of major works by Burrough, Fox, Nayler, Penn, etc., that would be shorter, more readable,
and more scholarly than the twelve-volume Friends Library of 1837.

Just before his sudden death in 1905, J. W. Rowntree won the enthusiasm of the Friends for writing a careful history of Quakerism in
both England and America based on the manuscripts edited by Norman
Penney and others. The five-volume series, completed by W. C. Braithwaite and Rufus Jones, was prefaced by Jones' *Spiritual Reformers in
the 16th and 17th Centuries* (London, 1914). Braithwaite's *Beginnings*
and *Second Period of Quakerism* (London, 1912 and 1919) have recently
been reissued, with new notes by Henry Cadbury (Cambridge, 1955 and
1961). More recent one-volume histories of Quakerism by Elbert Rus-

1. Nuttall also complements the remarkably thorough biographical notes and
cross references on the main figures in Fox, *Journal*, Camb., by life sketches and
index keys to all figures mentioned in the Swarthmore letters.
2. Now known as *Quaker History*.

sell, Charles Woodman, Elfrida Vipont, John Sykes, Henry Van Etten, and Howard Brinton are careful and readable, though they do not basically alter the picture. Individual biographies, such as Arthur Roberts on Fox, Isabel Ross on Margaret Fell, and William I. Hull, C. E. Vulliamy, and Edward Beatty on Penn, have added new dimensions and details. The main new insights on the meaning of early Quakerism as a whole, however, have come from sources of other types.

In the great flood of literature that has remade the modern understanding of the main stream of English Puritanism, Marshall Knappen's *Tudor Puritanism* and the two works of William Haller will perhaps remain unchallenged as introductions for the student. For the separatists and Baptists, no comparable work exists except the early documentary studies of Champlin Burrage and the survey of *The Inner Life of the Religious Societies of the Commonwealth* by the second Robert Barclay of 1876. For the years before 1640, their story tends to be subsumed under general studies of puritan movements or specialized viewpoints like W. K. Jordan's *Development of Religious Toleration in England* (1932–40) and the various books on Reformation mysticism by Rufus Jones. The Baptists and Congregationalists claimed their pioneers for their own, but even such excellent histories as C. G. Atkins and Fagley's *History of Congregationalism* and A. C. Underwood's *History of the English Baptists* (1947) tend to forget that under the Commonwealth none of these groups was in the modern sense a denomination. Theologically, some of the more useful insights have come from German scholars such as Michael Freund (*Die Idee der Toleranz in England der Grossen Revolution,* Halle, 1927), Johannes Kühn (*Toleranz und Offenbarung,* Leipzig, 1923), and especially Theodor Sippell (*Werdendes Quäkertum,* Stuttgart, 1937). The first fruits of the better understanding of radical Puritanism as a whole include Geoffrey Nuttall's little books on *Visible Saints* and *The Holy Spirit in Puritan Faith and Experience.* The others still mainly remain in the form of theses and of articles in *Church History* by Gerald Brauer, James F. Maclear, Winthrop Hudson, and others.

In the important fields of economics and ethics, completely new perspectives have become firmly established since the first probings of Max Weber and the socialist David Petegorsky. Though this field is still dominated for English history as a whole by the work of Richard H. Tawney, there is more value for students of Quakerism in the specific studies of George H. Sabine on Winstanley, W. Schenk on Walwyn and others, and Helen White on *Social Criticism in Popular Religious Literature of the Sixteenth Century* (New York, 1944). Louise Fargo Brown's *The Political Activities of the Baptists and Fifth Monarchy*

Men (Washington, D.C., 1912) presents especially well the crisis of 1659, which has been more carefully studied in relation to Quakerism in articles by James Maclear and Alan Cole, modifying the somewhat idealistic conception of Quaker pacifism in Margaret Hirst's *Quakers in Peace and War* (1925). The economic outlooks and practices of Friends have been studied frequently since Isabel Grubb's *Quakerism and Industry before 1800* (1930), notably by Arthur Raistrick (*Quakers in Science and Industry,* 1950) and with regard to Pennsylvania, by Frederick B. Tolles (*Meeting-House and Counting House,* 1948). The social attitudes of early Quakerism are perhaps still best set forth in Auguste Jorns' *Studien über die Sozialpolitik der Quäker* (1912), misleadingly translated as *Quakers as Pioneers in Social Work* (1931). Arnold Lloyd's *Quaker Social History, 1660–1738* (1950) is mainly helpful on the growth of Meeting organization. Russell Mortimer's thesis, "A Guide to the Administrative Records of the Society of Friends in Bristol, 1669–1869" (University of London, 1937), is a more sophisticated case study of the same issues. Other useful theses are Owen Watkins' "Spiritual Autobiography from 1649 to 1660" (London, 1952), Ralph P. Bohn's "The Controversy between Puritans and Quakers to 1660" (Edinburgh, 1955), Alan Cole's "The Quakers and Politics, 1652–1660" (Cambridge, 1955), as well as Wilmer Cooper's "Ethical Implications of Quaker . . . Politics" (Haverford, 1948), Rachel Hadley King's at Yale, published as *George Fox and the Light Within* (Philadelphia, 1940), and T. Canby Jones' "George Fox's Teaching on Redemption and Salvation" (Yale, 1955). To these could be added the theses of Judith Welles, Karl H. Hertz, and John A. Newton on the puritans.

Index